P9-DVO-980

CALGARY PUBLIC LIBRARY

APR   2012

LATIN
LESSONS

LATIN
LESSONS

How South America Stopped Listening to the United States and Started Prospering

Hal Weitzman

John Wiley & Sons, Inc.

Copyright © 2012 by Hal Weitzman. All rights reserved

Published by John Wiley & Sons, Inc., Hoboken, New Jersey
Published simultaneously in Canada

No part of this publication may be reproduced, stored in a retrieval system, or transmitted in any form or by any means, electronic, mechanical, photocopying, recording, scanning, or otherwise, except as permitted under Section 107 or 108 of the 1976 United States Copyright Act, without either the prior written permission of the Publisher, or authorization through payment of the appropriate per-copy fee to the Copyright Clearance Center, 222 Rosewood Drive, Danvers, MA 01923, (978) 750-8400, fax (978) 646-8600, or on the web at www.copyright.com. Requests to the Publisher for permission should be addressed to the Permissions Department, John Wiley & Sons, Inc., 111 River Street, Hoboken, NJ 07030, (201) 748-6011, fax (201) 748-6008, or online at http://www.wiley.com/go/permissions.

Limit of Liability/Disclaimer of Warranty: While the publisher and the author have used their best efforts in preparing this book, they make no representations or warranties with respect to the accuracy or completeness of the contents of this book and specifically disclaim any implied warranties of merchantability or fitness for a particular purpose. No warranty may be created or extended by sales representatives or written sales materials. The advice and strategies contained herein may not be suitable for your situation. You should consult with a professional where appropriate. Neither the publisher nor the author shall be liable for any loss of profit or any other commercial damages, including but not limited to special, incidental, consequential, or other damages.

For general information about our other products and services, please contact our Customer Care Department within the United States at (800) 762-2974, outside the United States at (317) 572-3993 or fax (317) 572-4002.

Wiley also publishes its books in a variety of electronic formats and by print-on-demand. Some content that appears in standard print versions of this book may not be available in other formats. For more information about Wiley products, visit us at www.wiley.com.

Library of Congress Cataloging-in-Publication Data:

Weitzman, Hal, date.
    Latin lessons : How South America stopped listening to the United States and started prospering / Hal Weitzman.
        p.   cm.
    Includes bibliographical references and index.
    ISBN 978-0-470-48191-2 (hardback); ISBN 978-1-118-14011-6 (ebk.);
    ISBN 978-1-118-14012-3 (ebk.); ISBN 978-1-118-14013-0 (ebk.)
        1. Latin America—Foreign relations—United States.   2. United States—Foreign relations—Latin America.   3. Latin America—Foreign economic relations—United States.   4. United States—Foreign economic relations—Latin America.
    I. Title.
    F1418.W323   2012
    327.8073—dc23

                                                                                2011042286

Printed in the United States of America
10 9 8 7 6 5 4 3 2 1

For Lorna

CONTENTS

PREFACE

In December 2009, I took a trip from Chicago, where I was the correspondent for the *Financial Times*, back to Peru, my previous posting for the newspaper. It was not the best of days for the Windy City. The financial crisis had hit hard. The unemployment rate in Chicago exceeded the national average. The city had a $14.5 billion hole in its pension funds and a $650 million budget deficit. On my way to the airport, I drove past apartment complexes half-built and abandoned, haunting reminders of the construction boom that had started to bring buyers back downtown from the suburbs. The Chicago Spire, an ambitious project to build the tallest residential building in the world, on the shore of Lake Michigan, was nothing more than a deserted hole in the ground, having collapsed amid debt, lawsuits, and acrimonious squabbles between the developers. To add insult to injury, two months earlier Chicago had lost its bid to host the 2016 Olympics, which the city had trumpeted as a way to bring investment and development to blighted areas of its south side. Much to the dismay of the assembled crowds watching the voting on giant screens in Daley Plaza, Chicago was eliminated in the first round of voting.

Lima could not have been more different. In many ways it was the same city I had left a couple of years earlier—dirty, chaotic, and sprawling—but where Chicago was struggling, the Peruvian capital was more vibrant than ever. The country had quickly brushed off the global economic downturn, and its economy was growing at a brisk clip. The signs of this activity were everywhere—in the furious shopping, enthusiastic eating, the better quality of cars on the streets, and, most obviously, in the swarms of workers putting up residential buildings at a blistering pace.

I should not have been surprised. The contrast between Lima and Chicago pointed to a much bigger geopolitical trend: Latin America was on the way up and the United States was in relative decline, at least in economic terms. This was nothing like the Great Depression that followed the 1929 Wall Street crash, which had a devastating effect on Latin America. Back then, exports slumped, countries defaulted on their debts, and there was a surge in civil agitation by radical groups; a rash of military coups and attempted coups swept across the region, and a wave of populist nationalism was unleashed. Now Latin America had emerged relatively unscathed from the financial crisis prompted by the collapse of Lehman Brothers, the Wall Street investment bank, in September 2008.

In 2010, the economies of Latin America would grow at an average rate of 6 percent—twice as fast as the United States. Paraguay grew at 10 percent, Uruguay and Peru at 9 percent, while the economies of Brazil and Argentina expanded at a rate of 8 percent. Unemployment across the region fell to about 7.6 percent, while joblessness in the United States hovered near 10 percent. The previous year, the Dow Jones Industrial Average gained 19 percent—a welcome advance considering the losses endured in the prior two years—but positively snail-like next to the 104 percent advance in Argentina's stock exchange, 101 percent growth in the Peruvian bolsa, and 83 percent growth in Brazil. The International Monetary Fund, which had so often in the past warned Latin America that the end was nigh, even started to fret publicly that the region might be growing a little too fast for comfort. The biggest corporate takeover of 2010 was the $28 billion purchase of Carso Global Telecom, a Mexican telecom company, by América Móvil, an even bigger Mexican telecom company. Money managers in Argentina and Peru ran the year's best-performing emerging markets funds.

While Peru was a remarkable story, the headline-stealing star of Latin America was Brazil. It had been the last country to enter the Great Recession that began in 2008 and the first to leave it. It was poised to overtake France and the United Kingdom to become the world's fifth biggest economy. It was the world's biggest producer of iron ore, and the top global exporter of beef, chicken, orange juice, sugar, coffee, and tobacco. Its companies were transforming themselves into global titans. Vale, headquartered in Rio, was the world's second biggest mining company. Gerdau, based in Porto Alegre, was the leading producer of long steel—used in construction and infrastructure—in the Americas, with operations across Latin America as well as in the United States, Canada, India, and Spain. Embraer of São José dos Campos was the world's third biggest aircraft maker. BM&FBovespa of São Paulo had become the second biggest financial exchange in the world. In September 2010, Petrobras, the state oil company, conducted the biggest stock sale in financial history, raising $67 billion from eager investors. Eike Batista, a mining and oil baron once married to a *Playboy* cover girl, was by 2010 the eighth richest person in the world, with a net worth of $27 billion, according to *Forbes*. Batista predicted that he would soon be the world's wealthiest man, an ambition that would see him replacing another Latin American—Carlos Slim, the Mexican telephone tycoon.

Back in the United States, not only was economic growth sluggish, but the world was also growing increasingly concerned about the country's debt burden. The national debt was nearly $14 trillion—close to the US gross domestic product. The United States showed little stomach for tackling the problem. In 2010, after a bipartisan commission recommended slashing the federal budget, President Barack Obama instead agreed to an $858 billion deal with Republicans to extend the tax cuts put in place under his predecessor, George W. Bush. The following year, the federal government flirted with default because of a political stand-off over how to raise the country's debt limit. The United States was looking like a country devoid of a long-term plan, putting off the inevitable as long as possible, engaging in the same sort of unsustainable fiscal irresponsibility of which it had long accused other countries—especially those in Latin America.

With the economies of South America growing so fast, you might have thought the United States would be looking to catch a little of the action, to shackle the stuttering engine of its economic growth to the supercharged developing countries of the south. US corporations had long cottoned on to what was happening. Latin America accounted for one-quarter of US exports. While North America continued to grow anemically, the United States' leading companies funneled investment into countries such as Brazil, where demand was growing much faster. The US government was much slower on the uptake.

For decades, Washington had been lecturing to Latin America how to behave. It had told the region to cut the size of government, to set business free, to lower taxes and burdensome regulation, to open itself up to foreign trade.

In the aftermath of the 2008 recession, not only did the wisdom of that advice look questionable, but the United States was increasingly doing just what it had cautioned Latin American countries not to do. The lack of federal oversight was being blamed for having enabled the financial crisis. George W. Bush, a tax-cutting Republican president, had overseen a vast increase in the national debt. Whereas his predecessor, Bill Clinton, had declared back in 1996 that "the era of big government is over," the financial crisis and subsequent economic downturn had forced the federal government to throw itself back into the US economy, injecting hundreds of billions of dollars into Wall Street, Detroit, and the national mortgage market. Barack Obama set a decidedly protectionist tone by inserting a "buy American" clause into his $787 billion stimulus package of 2009.

Meanwhile, the biggest Latin American countries were paying off their debts and expanding their ties with the world's fastest-growing and most exciting market—China. Instead of schooling its southern neighbors, it was starting to look as if the United States might actually have something to learn from them.

As Latin America's economic might grew, the region was considering what its future role might be in the new geopolitical order. Brazil was starting to flex its muscles on the international stage, showing diplomatic as well as economic ambition. Other South American countries were also extending their international reach. Might that present an opportunity for the United States to engage in some strategic alliance building, to find a new international role as part of a hemispheric coalition that could collectively formulate a vision for the whole of the Americas and a vision of North America's and Latin America's joint role in the world?

1

How the South Was Lost

In 1868, Queen Victoria abolished Bolivia.

At the time, the South American country was ruled by General Mariano Melgarejo, a repressive and incompetent military dictator with a billowing, ZZ Top–like beard. Melgarejo was a moron of outstanding proportions. According to legend, he was once given a gift by a Brazilian minister—a white horse so fine that to show his appreciation the autocrat pulled out a map of Bolivia, traced the horse's hoof, and gave away the land to the right of the line to Brazil. When Germany invaded France during the Franco-Prussian War of 1870–1871, Melgarejo ordered one of his top generals to send most of his army to help defend Paris. Since his boss clearly had no idea where the French capital was, the general tried to explain gingerly that Paris was rather distant, and there was something of an ocean along the way. Melgarejo was furious. "Don't be stupid!" he cried. "We'll take a shortcut through the brush!"

The incident that brought Bolivia to Queen Victoria's attention came when Melgarejo invited a British minister to attend a reception in honor of the president's new mistress. Ever the proper gentleman, the diplomat refused point-blank. Melgarejo flew into a rage. He ordered the man seized, tied to a donkey facing the beast's rear end, and paraded three times around the main square of La Paz. When the poor envoy returned home and the queen was informed of what had occurred, she demanded to know where on earth Bolivia was, so as to ready a military response to this humiliation. A map was duly brought, and Victoria was tactfully shown that La Paz was more than four hundred miles from the Pacific coast—too far inland from the guns of a British man-of-war that might have persuaded Melgarejo into an apology. So the queen devised an ingenious solution. She took a pen, crossed out the offending country, and declared, "Bolivia no longer exists."

At times, the United States has seemed equally unconcerned and ignorant about Latin America. "Latin America doesn't matter," Richard Nixon advised a young Donald Rumsfeld in 1971, in a private conversation between the president and his foreign policy aide that was captured on the notorious White House tapes. "Long as we've been in it, people don't give one damn about Latin America." Talking to reporters aboard Air Force One on a return from a tour of the region in 1982, Ronald Reagan remarked, "You'd be surprised. They're all individual countries." But these anecdotes belie the United States' long involvement with Latin America—both as a business opportunity and a region to which it frequently sent troops to defend US interests and ideological values.

Since the early nineteenth century, Washington has regarded the region as its "backyard," a natural sphere of influence. It is not quite accurate to say that the United States has lacked interest in its southern neighbors. Instead, Washington has tended to lack interest in what its southern neighbors thought or felt. US companies have long been active in Latin America, taking advantage of its proximity to American consumers and domestic industry. During the Cold War, the marines were periodically sent to oust left-leaning presidents and replace them with more business-friendly regimes, while the CIA propped up right-wing dictators and trained anticommunist guerrillas. In the same year that Nixon steered Rumsfeld away from seeking a Washington job connected to the region, the Republican president declared a "war on drugs"—an issue that has provided a central plank of US policy toward Latin America ever since. Anti-Americanism has long simmered in Latin America. At the same time, for nearly two hundred years there has been little doubt as to the identity of the most important superpower active in the region.

Having begun, possibly, to doubt its own shrewd solutions for fixing the Southern Hemisphere's problems, Washington in its approach to the region has perpetuated a hodgepodge of remnants from previous initiatives that collectively form an incoherent, unsatisfying, and unproductive muddle. The forty-year-old war on drugs has not stemmed the flow of narcotics into the United States, while drug violence claims the lives of thousands in Mexico and threatens to spill over the border. In spite of repeated pledges from successive US presidents, there has been no reform of the immigration policy or plan to deal with the undocumented workers and their families already living in the United States. The fifty-year-old embargo on Cuba has not only failed to weaken the Castro regime but actually strengthened communism by enabling the legend of the island as a plucky David standing up to a bullying Goliath. The US trade agenda is in shambles, with no prospect for a hemisphere-wide agreement. In 2011, the White House pressured a hitherto unwilling Congress into ratifying a trade agreement with Colombia, but the United States' strongest ally in South America had been waiting for five years since the deal was first struck to enjoy its benefits. It was an odd way to reward friendship and fidelity.

Most notably, the United States has been unable to find a way to deal with the emergence in the past five years of strident left-wing nationalism, a movement that holds the reins of power in three of South America's most important oil- and gas-producing countries. Its protagonists—Hugo Chávez of Venezuela, Evo Morales of Bolivia, and Rafael Correa of Ecuador—are virulently anti-American, blaming the United States for a host of problems and nationalizing industries that were earlier privatized on Washington's urging. Their views may not be widely shared, but they have often punched above their weight, filling an ideological vacuum with a potent populist message of national economic sovereignty and improving the lot of the poor. Their influence has undoubtedly dimmed in the past few years, but more moderate leaders in the region have often seemed unwilling or unable to stand up to them and to articulate an alternative. The radicals have also been successful in promoting the idea that South America should have its own distinct foreign policy. They have courted America's enemies, strengthening relations with countries such as Iran and building ties with rivals such as Russia.

These new leaders have often been seen as retrograde socialist dead-enders trying to revitalize a failed ideology, a hopeless task in the face of the innumerable successes of global capitalism. However, that misses an important change in the dynamic between north and south. The choice these radical leaders have seen themselves making has been between the free marketeers' understanding of globalization, which in practice has often meant putting your economy in the hands of international financiers, and economic nationalism—using your resources to drive the international financiers out of your economy. It's perhaps less a rejection of American-style capitalism per se than a rejection of American capitalists, and to Latin Americans with a deep sense of history, it's been a long time coming.

America's declining influence can't be blamed only on distant history, either. In the early days of George W. Bush's presidency, the United States made more tentative efforts to "reset" the relationship between Washington and the region. But the terrorist attacks of 9/11 changed all that. Unlike elsewhere, Bush's error in handling Latin America was largely one of omission rather than commission. Following 9/11, his administration closed its back door, tightening the US-Mexico border, and handed the keys to a bunch of Washington archconservatives while it focused its attention elsewhere. These caretakers tightened the Cuban embargo by further restricting Americans' ability to visit the island, lumped Colombia's war against the FARC guerrillas together with the global "war on terror," and supported coups in Venezuela and Haiti—classic Cold War policies that were barely updated to reflect the fact that the Soviet Union had not existed for more than a decade. They did a pretty terrible job in terms of the stewardship of US interests and influence. When Argentina's economy imploded in 2001, they did nothing. The following year, when Gonzalo Sánchez de Lozada, the Bolivian president who was one of Washington's closest allies in the region, made an urgent appeal for aid, he was ignored. Even friends of the US could not depend on Washington when it really mattered. An area the United States once considered its backyard gradually filled with weeds—problems Washington seemed uninterested, unwilling, and unable to tackle. In his second term, Bush appointed a different team that began to take a more constructive approach and engage a little more with Latin America, but the region remained at the bottom of a long list of foreign policy priorities. The Obama administration has spoken repeatedly about developing more of a partnership with its southern neighbors, but US policies have yet to match that soaring rhetoric.

In the eyes of several observers, Latin America became "the forgotten continent" or "the lost continent." Obviously this view depended on where you were sitting. In fact, one could argue that the United States was itself increasingly lost—an unwilling superpower unsure of its role in the world and how to use its influence.

America's Industrial Decline

In the twenty-first century, the tectonic plates of economic power around the world began to shift, and America's attention seemed to be focused in the wrong direction. Of course, terrorists had to be confronted and 9/11 could not go unanswered. But although the narrative of the violent struggle between globalization and fire-breathing Islamism was undoubtedly gripping, an even larger narrative was unfolding: the developing world was industrializing at a ferocious pace. The impressive and sustained economic growth in Latin America was part of this phenomenon, but at its forefront were the so-called BRIC countries—Brazil, Russia, India, and China. In the grand sweep of history, this was the true "long game"—a development the United States could ill afford to ignore.

Brazil was the star of Latin America, and India's growth was extraordinary, but the rise of China was the most remarkable and the most transformative. The country was engaged in the most rapid industrialization in history. By the end of the nineteenth century, Britain had been the world's greatest superpower. By the end of the twentieth, the United States had taken its place. Well before the end of the twenty-first, China seemed destined to become the planet's most powerful country. In some ways, that may still seem laughable or at least far off, but that's because the definition of "most powerful" may be changing as well.

In 2010, China overtook Japan to become the world's second biggest economy and was on course to overtake the United States by 2030. The US director of intelligence predicted that it would become a global military power by 2025. In 1999, the biggest banks in the world were Citigroup, Bank of America, and HSBC. A decade later, they were the Industrial and Commercial Bank of China, the China Construction Bank, and the Bank of China.

Since the late nineteenth century, the United States has become accustomed to being the world's leading manufacturing nation. But in 2010 it lost its crown to China. That year, the People's Republic accounted for 19.8 percent of world manufacturing output with a value of $2 trillion, ahead of the United States with 19.4 percent worth some $1.95 trillion, according to research by IHS Global Insight, an American economics consultancy, which examined data from the US Bureau of Economic Analysis and the National Bureau of Statistics of China.

Those figures are far from incontrovertible. Critics pointed out that focusing on the current dollar value of manufactured output is misleading, since it fails to take into account changes in prices and exchange rates, and that IHS should instead have looked at the physical quantity or volume of manufacturing, which would still show the United States at number one. Even measured in dollar terms, it is quite possible that the United States could retake the top spot in future years. Moreover, the United States is vastly more productive than China: while about 11.5 million American workers were responsible for their country's manufacturing output, it took some 100 million Chinese workers to produce more or less the same in dollar terms.

Nevertheless, the IHS report pointed to an important trend. Even if it was wrong, and the United States remains the world's top manufacturer, few would bet that it will be able to do so in the long term. In some sense, the emergence of low-cost manufacturing countries such as China represents the "rise of the rest"—the fact that the United States now has to compete much more aggressively with other emerging economic superpowers than it has done for the past century. But this has come at a time when the US industrial base has long been in a state of decline. In 1965, manufacturing accounted for 53 percent of the US economy. By 1988, it had shrunk to 39 percent. By 2004, it dipped below 10 percent. The number of workers employed in US manufacturing has followed a similar trend. In the 1970s, one-quarter of American workers had manufacturing jobs. By 2005, that figure was below 10 percent. Currently, only about 7 percent of the US workforce is employed in the manufacturing sector. The recession of 2008 hit the sector hard, as industrial companies either went out of business altogether or rapidly shed jobs in order to survive. More than 2 million US manufacturing jobs were lost. With the shift to low-cost countries, greater automation in

North American factories, and the secular erosion in the United States' industrial base, most will probably never come back.

By contrast, manufacturing now accounts for one-third of China's economy. That is by far the biggest in the world, and it continues to grow fast. While the US manufacturing sector grew at 1.8 percent a year between 2008 and 2010, Chinese manufacturing grew by more than 20 percent a year. So if the United States did not lose the top spot among the world's manufacturers in 2010, as IHS suggested, it seems likely to do so soon.

As it moved away from industry, the US economy became increasingly focused on services. The service sector has long been the biggest share of the US private economy, but that dominance has been increasing. In 1980, for example, it accounted for two-thirds of the economy. By 2010, it was conservatively estimated to be 77 percent. By the end of the twentieth century, the finance and real estate sectors alone overtook manufacturing's role in the economy, and by 2006 they were twice as big as manufacturing, measured as a proportion of US gross domestic product. That powerfully demonstrated how the trading floors of Wall Street, rather than the factory floors of the Midwest, had come to dominate America's economy. And it was on Wall Street that the 2008 recession began in earnest, with the collapse of the Lehman Brothers investment bank.

The new foundation of American wealth, it seemed, was not as secure as many had assumed. America's financial sector had demanded complete freedom to do as it wished, to regulate itself and to operate seemingly independently of the kind of checks the state is normally expected to perform. When times were good, hardly anyone questioned what Wall Street was doing. In part, the big banks avoided regulation through skillful lobbying that helped craft legislation that essentially left them to get on with making money without interference from the federal government. In part, they avoided it by creating a highly complex, risky, and system-wide financial derivatives market that few could understand—including many of those invested in it.

This unfettered free-market capitalism ultimately proved little more sustainable than the multibillion-dollar Ponzi scheme operated by Bernie Madoff, the New York financier whose house of cards collapsed in the final days of 2008.

The 2008 recession was not to blame for America's relative decline, but it helped accelerate a trend that had been going on for some time. The international view of the United States' economic might had changed. Faith had waned in the US dollar, weighed down by the country's debt burden and the 2008–2009 economic downturn. Wen Jiabao, the prime minister of China—one of the United States' leading lenders—fretted publicly about the dollar collapsing. Some speculated that the Chinese renminbi or a basket of international currencies could eventually replace it as the world's monetary reserve. During a 2009 visit, Tim Geithner, the US treasury secretary, assured students at Peking University that China's official holdings of Treasury bonds were safe. The audience laughed in response.

Riding the Commodity Boom

In the early 1990s, the United States had emerged as the world's sole surviving superpower. Its might continued to grow for the rest of the decade. But in the wake of 9/11 the United States appeared to have made the classic imperial mistake—overreaching and stretching its resources too thinly. Some worried that its decline was too hasty. In 2006, Wang Yiwei, a professor at Fudan University in Shanghai, caused waves with an article titled "How We Can Prevent the US from Declining Too Quickly." But the financial crisis only accelerated the US's relative decline and China's relative ascent. Even Barack Obama, whose 2008 presidential campaign theme was hope, struck a somber note in his inauguration speech, referring to "a sapping of confidence across our land; a nagging fear that America's decline is inevitable, that the next generation must lower its sights."

The loss of blue-collar American jobs to low-cost emerging economies was a powerful demonstration of one of the negative effects of the rise of China. To be sure, American shoppers, like consumers around the world, were treated to a range of imported goods at unbelievably cheap prices, but that was usually forgotten amid the outrage at how US companies were exporting jobs abroad.

While the US economy was struggling to cope with China's rise, for much of Latin America it meant a bonanza. Countries such as China and India were industrializing at breathtaking speed, building infrastructure and rapidly developing a modern economy, meaning their demand for raw materials was growing at a ferocious pace. The sheer quantity of energy, metals, and food required for this break-neck growth had a potent effect on prices, and that was good news for Latin America, which had long been a key global supplier of basic commodities. The prices for the commodities that Latin America produces started to rise in earnest around 2001–2002, and continued to do so until the 2008 recession, which dragged them down. As economic recovery started tentatively to take hold following the downturn, commodity prices began to rise once more. Crude oil prices had risen from less than $18 a barrel in 2001 to $115 a decade later. Over the same period, gold went from about $256 an ounce to about $1,450; silver rose from about $4 per ounce to more than $37; and copper went up from about $1,350 a ton to more than $9,500. Frozen concentrated orange juice futures increased from $55 a pound in 2004 to $180 in early 2011. Coffee futures went from trading at $41.50 a pound in 2001 to $270 a pound by early 2011. Commodity prices moderated some-what in 2011, but their overall price trajectory was clearly still upward.

Commodity markets had always gone through cycles of boom and bust, but an increasingly large number of analysts began to argue that because of the needs of industrializing countries, raw materials were in a "supercycle," in which prices would be permanently higher than historical norms.

As commodity prices rose, Latin American countries found them-selves the recipients of a welcome windfall. Commodity exports were worth $148 billion to the region in 2000, according to the United Nation's Commodity Trade Statistics Database. By 2008, the value of Latin American exports of oil, metals such as gold, silver, and copper, and crops such as soy and wheat had surged to a total of $512 billion. As a proportion of all exports, commodities grew in importance from 39 percent of the total in 2000 to 54 percent in 2008. Latin American commodity-producing countries came to depend on raw materials for an average of 24 percent of their fiscal revenues, compared to 9 percent for commodity-producing developed countries, according to the World Bank.

This was not completely good news. Some feared the region was falling victim to the "Dutch disease"—a phenomenon in which countries that enjoy windfalls from natural resources also see their currencies strengthen, which can make their manufacturing sectors less competitive. That was an even more acute threat since, like their peers in North America, Latin American manufacturers were struggling to compete with Asian factory production. This wasn't just about a battle for export markets in the developed world. It was also about a battle for the growing Latin American market itself. China was not only buying a lot from Latin America, it was also selling a lot of goods to Latin Americans, a phenomenon that became an increasing concern for companies in the region that found themselves in competition with Chinese exporters on their home turf. Countries in the region were becoming overly dependent on commodities, and in turn their economies were likely to wax and wane with the fortunes of notoriously fickle commodity markets.

On the other hand, it was hard to argue that the sudden influx of cash into an impoverished region was not welcome. To be sure, it enabled populist, unsustainable spending sprees in some countries, but it also allowed Latin American countries to pay off some of their debts, which had so often been a financial and political straitjacket. Across the region's seven biggest economies—Argentina, Brazil, Chile, Colombia, Mexico, Peru, and Venezuela—total public debt as a proportion of gross domestic product plunged from 60 percent in 2002 to 32 percent in 2008. Previous commodity price booms, such as the oil spike of the 1970s, had also brought short-term wealth to Latin America, but with many arguing in favor of the supercycle, it seemed the region might be able to look forward to permanently higher prices for its most important exports, at least for the foreseeable future. In markets, nothing is really permanent.

The Unrequited States of America

With all this in mind, it's hard to imagine a more purposeless exercise than designing a new plan for US influence in Latin America. Recent economic and political changes have rendered most of the premises for exerting influence questionable at best. Any reasons that Latin American countries might have had to listen to the United States have melted away.

During the Cold War, Latin America emerged as a critical proxy battleground between Washington and Moscow. The United States had consistently funneled support to governments and guerrillas fighting against what were perceived as left-leaning factions that might tilt toward the Soviet Union and strengthen the communist toehold in the region that Castro and his comrades had established in Cuba in 1959. This was an ideological struggle for US dominance in its own backyard, an effort to make Latin America look more like the United States, ideologically speaking.

Following the Cold War, Washington embarked on another campaign for influence in Latin America. Although a wave of democracy had crashed across the region, Latin America's economies were still relatively closed. Through the International Monetary Fund and the World Bank, the United States wanted to persuade the region to open for business. It promoted the Washington Consensus, a package of economic reforms that aimed to lower barriers to trade and reduce the role of the state in the economy. In most cases, the United States and the multilateral agencies did not impose these reforms on unwilling governments so much as offer strong encouragement to Latin American governments that were already liberalizing their economies in response to indebtedness, economic turbulence, and hyperinflation. Nevertheless, the United States was an enthusiastic patron of such efforts. Just as in the Cold War, the United States had sought to remake Latin America in its own image politically, so in the Washington Consensus the United States tried to make the region resemble North America economically.

But while the Washington Consensus was supposed to bring economic development and fiscal stability, in reality it failed to secure growth or to tackle the fundamental problems of poverty and inequality that dogged Latin America. Indeed, only when commodity prices began to rise in the first few years of the new millennium did the region really begin to feel that it was progressing economically. Free marketeers argued that they had been proved right, since the region was only benefiting because it had adopted Washington's idea of lowering barriers to trade. But the impression was that Latin America's development had less to do with becoming more like the United States and more to do with the emergence of modern China as a global economic superpower.

The Washington Consensus was also aimed at opening up Latin America to business opportunities for US companies. It worked.

The lowering of tariff barriers helped trade between the United States and Latin America to rise steadily. It was augmented by the 1994 North American Free Trade Agreement, which included Mexico, the 2005 Central American Free Trade Agreement between the United States and Costa Rica, El Salvador, Guatemala, Honduras, Nicaragua, and the Dominican Republic, as well as bilateral trade agreements with Chile in 2004 and Peru in 2009. In 1990, trade between the United States and Latin America amounted to $118 billion. By 2000, it had grown to $380 billion, and by 2008 to $665 billion.

But behind these figures lurks an interesting trend. In 1990, less than 14 percent of US exports, worth about $54 billion, went to Latin America, according to the US International Trade Commission. By 2000, the region received 22 percent of US exports, with a value of $171 billion. By 2010, Latin America accounted for 24 percent of US exports, worth $302 billion. In other words, not only did the value of US exports to the region grow but so did US dependence on Latin American markets and consumers. That trend seemed likely to continue: in 2011, on his first official visit to the region, President Obama expressed his hope that the United States could double exports to the region within three years. The trade flows in the opposite direction, however, tell a quite different story. To be sure, from 1990 to 2000 the United States gained in importance as a destination market for Latin American countries. The United States sucked in 47 percent of Latin American exports, worth $64 billion, in 1990. By 2000, that had risen to 56 percent, or $209 billion. But in the following decade, the United States diminished as a destination for exports from the region. By 2009, it had fallen to 39 percent of exports, worth $285 billion. Admittedly, that low figure reflected the effects of the 2008 recession, but even so, Latin American exports to the United States only bounced back to 42 percent of the total in 2010, or $361 billion, according to the Inter-American Development Bank. Latin America was diversifying its markets away from the United States. While the region's trade with North America fell, China's share of its exports boomed from a paltry 0.8 percent in 1990 to 10 percent in 2008. The longer-term trend is clear: while Latin America becomes an increasingly more important trade partner for the United States with every passing year, the United States is becoming less and less important to Latin America.

Trade played a critical role in extending US influence. What the United States had previously won with force, it became committed to winning with commerce. But while Washington's trade efforts were mostly aimed at the northern part of Latin America—Mexico and the Central American states—most of South America lacked any permanent trade deal with the United States. So Brazilian ethanol, for example, was still subject to a 54-cent-per-gallon tariff when entering the United States, and Brazil's cotton exports were hindered by US subsidies, which had been ruled illegal in the World Trade Organization in a case brought by Brasília.

This was important because it was exactly in South America that the commodity boom had been most pronounced. Growth was fastest in South America, while Central America had been more affected by the 2008 recession, partly due to its closer ties with the United States. It had also been adversely hit by the commodity boom, since Central American countries did not possess big reserves of natural resources. But the United States had no special trading agreement with the very region to which it should have most wanted to shackle its slow-moving economy. Efforts at establishing a Free Trade Area of the Americas had died under George W. Bush's presidency. The idea was widely considered in South America to have been yet another example of an "imperialist" United States trying to foist its will on an unwilling region. It was a clear demonstration of how the United States' diminishing political influence in the region had serious economic implications.

Evo's Sweater

Every revolution has its symbol. The United States had the Boston Tea Party; France had Marianne, wearing a red cap and with her exposed right breast pointing the common people to victory in Delacroix's famous depiction. Bolivia had Evo Morales's red-white-and-blue-striped sweater.

The pullover seemed to emerge just after Morales, the country's first indigenous head of state since the Spanish conquest, was elected president in December 2005. Suddenly wherever you saw him he was wearing it. He wore it to meet the presidents of China, Chile, and South Africa. He wore it to meet the US undersecretary of state. He even wore it to meet the king of Spain.

Morales was apparently unaware that the sweater would prove to be the most talked-about aspect of his world tour, between his election and his inauguration, in January 2006.

The Spanish thought he was being disrespectful. "Is there no one who might lend Mr. Morales a dark suit?" asked a columnist at *ABC*, a conservative Spanish newspaper. "Sweaters like that are given as charity by teachers and then thrown back in their faces by the poor." The more left-leaning *El País* said the pullover had "apparently been bought in a bargain basement."

The garment was the subject of great interest. Was there one sweater or several? Would he wear it to his inauguration? Was it made of Bolivian alpaca wool, as the Morales camp insisted, or was it, as some mischievous reporters suggested, in fact acrylic? Did the president plan to wear the pullover so many times, or had he merely packed badly?

One week into his trip, Morales could no longer ignore the controversy. "I am not accustomed to protocol," he said apologetically to a Chinese official.

But by now the pullover had taken on a life of its own, more talked about than the president himself throughout his world tour. Britain's *Guardian* newspaper said the signature fashion item had "a strong whiff of Christmas jumper [sweater] about it" and offered a helpful guide to its readers of how to re-create the presidential look with items from chain retailers H&M and Gap.

The most outraged seemed to be *Reforma*, the Mexican newspaper, which condemned the sweater as a "garment of discord." *Reforma* also noted, "For the Bolivians, this is a fine sweater of alpaca, which is a Bolivian export. For the Spanish press, it's an offense to its good customs."

In an odd geographical juxtaposition, Marcela Sanchez at the *Washington Post* noted, "As the expression goes, Morales is not in Kansas anymore," and lamented that "his appearance proved to be a distraction from the substance of his message."

But what Sanchez had apparently missed was that the sweater *was* the message. It reeked of ordinariness, of earthy humility, of a kind of willful ignorance of diplomatic convention. While that was inappropriate for the Spanish elite, it was exactly Morales's appeal back home.

Most Bolivians thought the sweater was entirely smart enough for their head of state. Morales actually sparked a mini-craze back home. A company in La Paz immediately rushed to produce a lookalike acrylic version of the sweater, plastering the new president on their advertising and branding it "Evo fashion." Another Bolivian clothing company used the Internet to sell alpaca versions of the pullover to customers from scores of countries. Local newspapers ran "cut out and keep" models of Morales, complete with the sweater and other outfits. A Bolivian version of Barbie was brought out dressed in the sweater.

In fact, the sweater—and the slacks and leather jacket that often accompanied it—was Morales's attempt to smarten up. On the campaign trail he had normally worn black Wrangler jeans, a short-sleeved shirt, and running shoes. The only time he had ever been caught wearing a tie was in 1977, when he had dressed up for a school photo.

But the sweater, the black jeans, the running shoes—this *was* protocol. It was the protocol of the people who elected Morales, and it was his way of telling them he was different from other leaders, that he was of them and would represent them and would not change once he won power. The striped sweater was as significant, powerful, and meaningful to them as a hammer and sickle, the stars and stripes, or the tricolor of the French republic.

Morales and his sweater represented another big change that has come to Latin America. His victory was an important watershed in indigenous politics in Bolivia and beyond. He showed ordinary Bolivians that the mechanisms of governing the state could belong to them. Whereas the power struggle in many Latin American capitals had come to be mainly between a ruling elite and the interests of the United States and multilateral lenders, elections had become more about the ruling elite and the poor and indigenous. Morales was just one leader pledging to use the power of the state to permanently reverse the centuries of marginalization of indigenous people from government. In much of the Andes, the indigenous have become a significant political force. While they are neither a single group nor a united voting bloc, they make up a large segment of the population—a segment that has historically been barred from power, regardless of whether the regime has been colonial, military, or democratic.

It is this change in the dynamics of who wields political power and what they want from it that makes the rise of economic nationalism in Latin America a new permanent feature of international politics, not a passing fad that the United States can simply ride out. The Washington Consensus had a great deal to do with this change, since it essentially recommended ignoring the short-term needs of the many, giving foreign investors more control over national resources, and opening up the economy to foreign trade. Populist, indigenous, and indigenous-friendly politicians, at their most basic level, have tended to recommend meeting the short-term needs of the many at the expense of foreign investors, while caring less about the value of exports than what the state's share will be. It's no surprise, then, that some of these new administrations have withdrawn money from state oil companies faster than Americans could pull cash from their home equity during the boom.

America's Addiction

When most Americans hear about the United States being dependent on foreign oil, they think of the Middle East. In fact, the most important source of US oil imports is Latin America.

In 2010, the nation's top source of foreign petroleum—which includes refined products such as gasoline as well as crude oil—was Canada, according to the US Energy Information Administration (EIA). But when you look at the list of the rest of the United States' top fifteen suppliers, Latin America dominated. The second biggest source of US petroleum imports was Mexico, the fifth was Venezuela, the tenth was Colombia, the eleventh Brazil, and the fourteenth Ecuador. Latin America as a region accounted for 3.1 million barrels of petroleum imports a day in 2010, compared to 2.5 million barrels a day from Canada and 2.2 million barrels a day from all the top Arab producers combined—Saudi Arabia, Algeria, Iraq, and Kuwait. So the United States is not simply dependent on foreign oil—more specifically, it is dependent on Latin American oil.

US dependence on foreign oil is not likely to end anytime soon. To be sure, the United States has its Strategic Petroleum Reserve, which at 727 million barrels is the largest stockpile of government-owned crude oil in the world. But Latin America has 210 billion barrels of proven oil reserves, some 16 percent of the world's total, according to the 2010 edition of an annual report compiled by BP, the British energy giant. By contrast, US reserves stand at 28.4 billion. US oil production has been in decline since the mid-1980s, while oil consumption has been steadily rising, although it fell sharply in the 2008 recession. The gap has been filled by an increasing volume of petroleum imports, which now account for 51 percent of US oil consumption. The EIA projects that that will diminish to 45 percent by 2035, as US crude oil production increases in the Gulf of Mexico and the biofuels industry expands. Even so, the United States' dependence on petroleum imports—and on Latin America—is likely to persist for many decades to come.

In fact, the United States could find itself even more dependent on Latin America than ever for petroleum imports in the years to come. The Arab Spring uprisings that swept the Middle East and North Africa in 2011 demonstrated that that region, widely ruled by dictators, could easily become unstable, potentially threatening oil supplies from countries such as Saudi Arabia, Algeria, and Kuwait. The other big Arab oil producer that supplied US imports, Iraq, had been destabilized by the United States itself. Similarly, big African suppliers such as Nigeria and Angola were not necessarily dependable long-term partners. Russia, another top supplier, was run by an autocratic regime that had repeatedly demonstrated its willingness to devote its energy policy to political ends. Apart from Canada—which could not alone supply all the US's needs—Latin America, a democratic continent, looked like the best bet for secure foreign supplies.

On his 2011 visit to Brazil, undertaken as the United States and NATO attacked the Gadhafi regime in Libya and oil prices hovered at $116 a barrel, Barack Obama recognized not only the relative stability of the region but that the United States was likely to become more dependent on Latin American oil exports in the future. "When you're ready to start selling, we want to be one of your best customers," the president said, referring to the massive oil reserves—up to 100 billion barrels' worth—discovered deep underwater beneath a layer of salt off the coast of Brazil in 2006. "At a time when we've been reminded how easily instability in other parts of the world can affect the price of oil, the United States could not be happier with the potential for a new, stable source of energy."

Enter the Dragon

By the first few years of the twenty-first century, 70 percent of China's foreign investment outside Asia was directed at Latin America. China bought stakes in the oil industries of Venezuela, Argentina, Ecuador, Peru, Colombia, and Cuba, and in mines in Brazil and Peru. Direct investment overseas by Chinese companies increased from $5.5 billion in 2004 to $56.5 billion in 2009, with Chinese officials predicting it would reach $100 billion by 2013.

Across Latin America as a whole, the United States remained the biggest trading partner, with trade of more than $500 billion a year—four times that of China. But commerce with China grew at an annual rate of more than 30 percent a year, and in some countries the United States' role was usurped. In 2009, China overtook the United States as Brazil's principal trading partner and the following year became its top foreign investor. Chile—which in 2005 became the first non-Asian country with which Beijing signed a trade agreement—had seen China become its top trade partner a few years earlier. In 2009, Beijing signed a trade deal with Peru, for whom China also seemed set to become its top trading partner. In 2009, China joined the Inter-American Development Bank (IDB), the region's main multilateral lender, contributing $350 million to the institution's funds. The following year, the Chinese Export-Import Bank and the IDB agreed to set aside $200 million over two years to finance trade between China and Latin America.

These deals were mainly done as part of a broad global plan to secure supplies of raw material to feed China's industrialization. China was primarily interested in securing the flow of products such as oil, copper, iron, and soybeans. In part, it created a demand that Latin America was fulfilling. At the same time, however, China was setting up a race for global resources between itself, the United States, and other rising powers, primarily India and Russia. Beijing also saw the benefit of establishing good relations with countries that were peeved with the United States: it could prove useful in future should China need diplomatic muscle, such as in countering efforts by Taiwan to win greater international recognition. This became evident in 2007, when China signed a deal with Costa Rica in which it bought $150 million of government debt in return for the Central American country cutting diplomatic ties with Taiwan and establishing relations with the People's Republic of China. It was the clearest sign that Beijing intended to use its $2.4 trillion of foreign reserves—the world's largest such fund—as a tool of its foreign policy goals.

Not only did Beijing seem genuinely interested in investing in Latin America, but its affection was also unconditional—the Chinese were as happy dealing with communists as with archconservatives. Free-market economies such as Colombia and Chile were courted as much as socialist brothers-in-arms like Cuba and Ecuador. This refusal to play favorites was a welcome change from the record of US involvement with the region. While the Communist Party in Beijing did have official ties with the political parties headed by Hugo Chávez and Evo Morales, China was agnostic about how governments ran their countries. It was primarily interested in being able to continue to grow at a breathtaking pace, and developed trading ties with a range of countries in the region, mimicking a strategy it had developed in Africa to identify and secure access to raw materials.

China wasn't worried about what you did at home; it was concerned with what you could produce. In stark contrast to the US approach, Chinese foreign policy was focused, aggressive, strategic, long-term, and universal. Beijing, a relative novice in terms of truly global international relations, seemed much better able than Washington to pay attention to lots of different parts of the world at the same time. In return for China's affections, South America got what it had never had before: a sustained period of economic growth, as demand from Asia seemed to permanently drive up prices for the very commodities the region had been producing for decades. Almost every country in the region benefited directly or indirectly: Latin America's economy expanded on average by 5.5 percent a year from mid-2003 to mid-2008. Whereas the Washington Consensus had led (in the short term, at least) to political instability and uncertain economic growth and had failed to rid the region of the scourge of poverty, Chinese demand presented a benign rising tide that came with no political interference or unpalatable policy demands.

Developing good ties with China not only made sense in a world in which Beijing's power was on the rise while Washington's was in relative decline. It also enabled Latin American countries to diversify their foreign commercial relations. For Hugo Chávez and those of a like mind, the new friendship with China was a stick with which to beat Washington. The Venezuelan leader had long threatened to cut off oil supplies to the United States, for example. China's rampant thirst for oil made that threat more credible. Chávez outlined an ambitious plan to triple oil exports to China by 2012, which would mean diverting the flow from the United States. The idea was constrained, however, by the fact that it took an oil tanker one month to reach China from South America—compared to about a week for a US trip—and by the lack of refinery capacity for the heavy oil produced by Venezuela. Nevertheless, it underlined that Latin America was becoming more interested in selling to the rest of the world than in expanding trade with the United States.

Breaking Away

It wasn't only China that was making inroads into Latin America. Jindal, an Indian steel company, entered into a joint agreement with the Bolivian state mining company to exploit El Mutún, the world's largest iron ore deposit, located in the southern part of the country. Russian oil firms struck deals with Venezuela to operate oil concessions and invested in Bolivia's gas industry. Russia's increasing involvement pointed to another worrying factor in the rising influence of other foreign powers in the region. While China and India came primarily with a trade agenda, Russia enjoyed the idea of burrowing into its old enemy's backyard. Moscow conducted joint military exercises with Caracas. Russia sold Chávez $4 billion worth of aircraft, helicopters, and tanks and built a machine-gun factory in Venezuela. In 2010, Russia announced it would help Venezuela construct its first nuclear power station. Even more worryingly for Washington, Iran was also expanding its ties with Latin America.

Mahmoud Ahmadinejad, its volatile leader known for his pursuit of a nuclear capability, toured the region, pledged investments, and was received with warm welcomes. He and Chávez declared a strategic alliance. In 2010, the German newspaper *Die Welt* reported that Caracas had struck a deal with Tehran allowing Iran to establish a missile base in Venezuela. Iran also strengthened ties with more moderate Brazil, which offered to help negotiate with Tehran in its own initiative to resolve the nuclear issue.

Not everyone was so delighted by China's increasing commercial clout in the region. Shougang, a Chinese-owned iron ore mine in southern Peru, was periodically shut down by strikes as workers there demanded better wages, the right to collective bargaining, and improved working conditions. The Chinese appeared baffled by such demands, unused as they were to assertive trade unions. Peru fined Shougang Group several times for abuses of labor law and breaches of its initial investment contract.

Brazil and Argentina grumbled that they wanted to export more than just minerals and food to China. Although Chinese demand had lifted prices for raw materials to higher levels across the board, it also made Latin American countries more dependent than ever on exporting basic products such as oil, metals, minerals, and grains. Soybeans and iron ore accounted for two-thirds of Brazil's exports to China, for example. Some observers warned that China was "colonizing" Latin America (and for that matter, Africa). Not only did this trend keep Latin American countries from diversifying their economies, but it also made them subject to the whims of Beijing. This was highlighted in 2010, when China halted imports of Argentine soybean oil in response to a range of antidumping investigations in Argentina.

Latin American countries also balked at the flood of cheap Chinese imports. Average wages in China were up to two-fifths lower than those in Latin America, prompting worries for the future of the region's labor-intensive manufacturing industries. Nearly all of Brazil's shoemaking and toy-making industries were wiped out in the face of Chinese competition. Latin American countries tabled more antidumping actions against China at the World Trade Organization than did the United States.

The expansion of Chinese, Russian, and Iranian influence and the corresponding diminishing of the United States' presence did not completely pass America by. As a presidential candidate, Barack Obama observed China's rising involvement in Latin America. "The conspicuousness of their presence is only matched by our absence," Obama said. Unusually, that put him in agreement with foreign policy hawks in Washington, who argued that Russian and Chinese "meddling" in Latin America stood in the way of the United States regaining its influence in the region. The US military had been watching the trend for some time. In 2006, its Pacific Command conducted a war game in which China, Venezuela, and Iran united in a military showdown with the United States. In 2008, the US National Intelligence Council produced *Global Trends 2025*, an analysis forecasting that the rise of China and India meant conflicts in the future could be fought over control of natural resources. Policymakers seemed more worried about Iran's role. Hillary Clinton, the US secretary of state, told foreign service officers at a May 1, 2009, meeting at the State Department that Tehran was making "disturbing" inroads into the region, while Robert Gates, the US defense secretary, had spoken out against Iran's "frankly subversive activity" in Latin America. "I'm more concerned about Iranian meddling in the region than I am the Russians," Gates told the Senate armed services committee on January 27, 2009.

Iran's improving relations with Latin America were certainly reason enough for Washington to pay attention to what was going on in the region. It tickled a particularly sensitive nerve at the State Department. But China's involvement was also troubling. Its commercial presence meant that the United States' traditional dominance in the region was being gradually undermined. In a world where Washington should have been preparing for a global role in a multipolar system, it could ill afford to let its influence in Latin America slip away.

This wasn't just a passive process, in which Latin America played the role of a child in the middle of a custody battle and Washington a distracted parent. The region wasn't merely the victim of a commercial battle between two global superpowers. Instead, Latin America was shaping its future, forging its own distinct responses to a world being rapidly altered by globalization. At home, it was developing a distinct range of policies and often thumbing its nose at Washington along the way. Internationally, it was seeking different kinds of alliances, bonds that could enable it, for perhaps the first time in its modern history, to chart a course away from America's influence.

2

Earthquake in the Andes

What do you wear to a revolution?

On May 1, 2006, Evo Morales, the president of Bolivia, looked in his wardrobe for an ensemble fit for a nationalization—something casual, yet with an air of determination about it. He opted for a tan-colored jacket and a white hardhat. Both items bore the diamond-shaped logo of YPFB, Bolivia's state energy company that had been privatized in the mid-1990s.

Morales looks a bit like a Lego man. His body is square, his face is wide and round, and atop it resides a thatch of thick, wiry hair that he keeps in a center-parted mop. The hair sits apparently unchangeable and immovable, like a jet black helmet that has been clicked firmly into place.

Like many South American presidents, he enjoys dressing up—traditional Andean poncho and woolly hat one day, presidential sash and contemporary jacket the next, workmanlike short-sleeved shirt and jeans the day after, and so on—the outfits matching the mood of whatever event he is attending.

Morales called an early-morning cabinet gathering around a large carved wooden table in one of the meeting rooms of Bolivia's equivalent of the White House, the so-called Palacio Quemado (the headquarters of the executive branch had been nicknamed the "Burnt Palace" ever since a mob set it on fire during an uprising in 1860).

It was a short meeting. Morales told his ministers that he planned to fly to the heart of the country's natural gas–producing region and announce that he was nationalizing Bolivia's gas reserves, the second largest in South America. He circulated a decree to that effect and each minister signed it in turn. Then they applauded him, before closing the meeting with a rendition of the national anthem.

When they had finished, Morales smiled. "The plane is waiting for us," he told them. They drove to the airport, boarded a Hercules transporter, and flew from La Paz—the seat of government that nestles in the mountains of Bolivia's northwestern high Andes—some 350 miles southeast to the lush lowlands of Tarija, the country's southernmost province, near the border with Argentina and Paraguay. Their destination was San Alberto, one of his country's biggest natural gas fields, in the region of Caraparí.

For a shambolic administration, the operation had been planned with military precision. The day before, under the pretense of an inspection and training exercise, large numbers of engineers employed by the state had undertaken reconnaissance visits through the country's main gas fields. Their mission had been to work out what emergency action to take should the foreign companies that ran the facilities respond to the nationalization by trying to cut off gas supplies.

The subterfuge paid off. Petrobras, the Brazilian state energy company, had been operating San Alberto for a decade, sending natural gas down a two-thousand-mile pipeline to feed São Paulo, Brazil's biggest city. It apparently had little idea that Bolivia was about to upset the status quo: as Morales approached the plant, the senior staff greeted him and asked which part of the installation he wanted to visit.

The answer soon became clear: surrounded by his ministers and a swarm of government officials, similarly clad in hardhats, and accompanied by a small troop of uniformed soldiers, he marched briskly into the facility, strolled up to a podium, and announced matter-of-factly that he was taking back control of the country's natural gas industry. The event may have seemed well organized, but someone had forgotten the microphone, so the president instead spoke through a handheld loudspeaker. Talk about megaphone diplomacy—this was megaphone insurgency.

On a continent where a good political speech (and many a bad one) can last for several hours, this was no sermon. There was little detailed criticism of the companies that had been running the industry since it had been privatized a decade earlier, no lengthy history lesson recounting how for centuries Bolivians' wealth had been stolen from under their noses by foreigners, no haranguing ideological diatribe against international capitalism.

"The time has come, the awaited day, a historic day in which Bolivia retakes absolute control of our natural resources. From this moment, from this date, all the hydrocarbons in Bolivian territory are nationalized," said Morales, to applause from the handful of supporters in tow. "The looting by the foreign companies has ended.

"We want to ask the armed forces that, starting now, they occupy all the energy fields in Bolivia along with battalions of engineers," he continued, before adding his own name to the decree his ministers had signed that morning. "The state recovers ownership, possession, and total and absolute control of these resources," it stated.

The soldiers had taken up strategic positions all over the plant, and some officials had unveiled an enormous banner over one of the facility's steel towers: in huge red letters painted on a white background, it said: NATIONALIZED—and then in smaller blue type: PROPERTY OF THE BOLIVIAN PEOPLE.

Bolivia is not used to being newsworthy, but now it had the attention of the world. Even the *Financial Times*, a paragon of sobriety, splashed the nationalization on its front page.

For one thing, no one had seen images of soldiers marching in to occupy a facility operated by a foreign company for at least thirty years. Not that the troops were actually taking over the gas fields. Sure, they dutifully marched in and stood impressively armed and apparently vigilant (at least for the first few days, while the international TV crews were still interested in filming them) at San Alberto and fifty-five other natural gas facilities around Bolivia, but the gas fields continued to operate as before. No company was being expelled, no property confiscated—at least not yet.

Rather, the foreign multinationals were given 180 days to renegotiate their operating contracts so that YPFB, the reinvigorated state energy company, had at least a 50 percent stake. Until they did so, the very biggest fields, including San Alberto, would have to pay out 82 percent of their profits to the state. In addition, the nationalization decree gave YPFB a controlling stake in two local oil companies and the refining arm of Petrobras's subsidiary in Bolivia.

Despite the hullabaloo, this was just the new government implementing a law that had been passed by Bolivia's Congress before Morales was even elected. A year earlier, the legislature (controlled at the time by Morales's right-of-center political opponents) had voted to increase taxes on foreign energy companies to 50 percent. But under pressure from the multinationals, the president of the day had buckled and resigned rather than implement the law, creating the vacuum that had allowed Morales to gain power.

Many of Morales's critics pointed out that the troops were not seizing the gas fields, just hanging around in them, exposing this as nothing more than gesture politics, a sop to those Bolivians (and there were lots and lots of them) who wanted to see the foreign multinational energy giants kicked out of the country, good and hard. The government's supporters countered that, like the engineers who had secretly planned to seize operations if the companies should try to cut off the gas, the soldiers were there to ensure that the pipelines continued operating as normal.

There was some merit to both sides. Of course, the troops were there to reassure the Bolivians that, yes, they really had taken control of the gas. At the same time, their presence sent a message to the multinational corporations that if they failed to take the government seriously, next time the troops might actually be sent in to seize assets and expel the energy companies.

Apart from the soldiers, Morales also had picked a good day to get some headlines. May 1—International Workers' Day—is a holiday in many countries (including Bolivia), making it a slow news day, the sort of day in which an unglamorous South American state might find it easier to bag its fifteen minutes of worldwide fame.

America Paralyzed

To those who had been paying attention, the nationalization itself was not entirely unexpected: Morales had promised it as a central plank of his electoral platform. In fact, his two main opponents in the election had also pledged to nationalize the gas industry. Having said that, Morales's administration had faltered on the issue several times, and in the weeks leading up to May all the indications were that his government would advance with more caution.

The international response to the event underlined how most outsiders had failed to grasp the significance of Morales's election. In the United States, for example, it was widely seen as a display of socialist showmanship in an economically backward country, an unruly business in an unruly part of the world, and a brief hiccup in the inevitable conversion of Latin America to a well-ordered complex economy modeled on that of North America. What was missed was that something important had changed. Evo Morales was sending a message to his people: that we will run our country our way, answerable to no one but ourselves, because we know what's best for us.

From the multinationals' perspective, the new president had demonstrated a large dollop of chutzpah. He had held some talks with the oil companies when first elected, but when those stalled, he decided that they would never change the status quo unless forced to do so. Morales didn't follow his predecessors by sitting down with the international oil companies—which over the previous decade had invested some $3.5 billion in Bolivia—and politely asking them to change the way they had been doing business for the past decade. He didn't write letters or even pick up the telephone.

Instead, the first the foreign investors heard about what was happening was when the new president stomped into the biggest natural gas installation in the country and announced that he was giving the industry six months to get on board or get lost.

Whether they were actually as shocked as they made out, the multinationals were certainly highly alarmed, as were their host governments. Petrobras said the policy was "unfriendly" and made its activities in Bolivia "unviable," while Repsol, the Spanish oil giant that was the other main foreign investor, called the nationalization unfair and said it defied business logic. It most certainly did defy traditional business logic, and that was most certainly the point.

"We'd hoped there would be a process of discussion and consultation before they adopted such measures," Johannes Laitenberger, a European Commission spokesman, said at his daily press briefing the day after the nationalization. The Spanish government expressed its "deep concern." The International Energy Agency warned about Latin American countries "embarking on a dangerous path." Condoleezza Rice, the US secretary of state, criticized "demagoguery" in the region.

Dan Burton, a Republican congressman from Indiana, issued a statement saying the nationalization "heralds a troubling leftist slide towards state control and a hardening of nationalist social and economic policies in Bolivia." As chairman of the US House of Representatives' Western Hemisphere subcommittee, Burton should have been somewhat familiar with the situation—although in 1995 he had famously called on the United States military to "place an aircraft carrier off the coast of Bolivia and crop-dust the coca fields" during congressional hearings on the US-sponsored war on drugs. There was only one slight problem with that plan—being landlocked, Bolivia has no coastline.

The nationalization also provoked the ire of Lou Dobbs, a curmudgeonly American TV talk show host singularly unqualified to comment and yet unabashed in doing so. Told on the May 2, 2006, edition of CNN's *Lou Dobbs Tonight* that the US State Department was merely "keeping their eye" on the situation, he growled sarcastically, "The good old State Department," a traditional Dobbsian conclusion to stories about which he was completely ignorant and had nothing substantial to add.

But on this occasion, Dobbs had a point. The United States—which had once overthrown governments for much less than what Morales had done—was seemingly paralyzed. The nationalization of gas highlighted the fact that the United States lacked any kind of policy for Latin America. Even though the nationalization had been promised time and again, Washington apparently didn't see it coming or have any coherent idea how to react when it did. The US rationale for not addressing the nationalization directly was that there were no significant American assets at stake. Morales's move was not aimed at the United States so much as at international business—and, via Petrobras, the government of Brazil. The biggest oil company in Bolivia, Petrobras had plowed some $1.5 billion into its Andean neighbor's gas industry. The nationalization was also an energy headache for ordinary Brazilians, who depend on Bolivian gas to fuel some 50 percent of their domestic demand and much of the energy needs of São Paulo, their industrial powerhouse and financial center.

Brazil dwarfs Bolivia in size and political clout, and in its ten years in Bolivia, Petrobras had grown to become the largest company operating in the country. What's more, of all the big oil giants in Bolivia, Petrobras had bent over backward to develop good relations with Morales's government, a reflection of the fact that a left-of-center government was in power in Brasília. So why was Morales picking a fight with the company?

"Death to the Yankees!"

Five months earlier, Evo Morales had won the presidency in the most dramatic election in Bolivia's history.

The choice facing the Bolivian people had been, to put it mildly, unenviable: the three main candidates were an inexperienced, angry leftist militant; an intelligent but out-of-touch right-wing former president; and a bearded cement magnate with all the charisma of a spadeful of slurry.

No one expected the initial contest to be decisive. The election had been provoked by what was for Bolivia a typically turbulent turn of events. (The torching of the presidential palace in 1860 wasn't a one-off.) Six months earlier, massive street protests had paralyzed the country and forced the resignation of Carlos Mesa, an affable ex–TV host who had proved to be a weak and ineffective president.

Natural gas was at the heart of his downfall. Mesa was the head of state who had refused to approve tax hikes on foreign investors in the gas sector. When Congress insisted, he could do nothing but resign. Mesa himself had been an accidental president, only taking over when his predecessor was forced to resign in 2003 in not dissimilar circumstances.

As Mesa stood down, he warned that the country was on the verge of civil war. Bolivia boasts the dubious record of having had 192 coups—more than any other country—since the republic was established in 1825. It seemed that South America's poorest country might once again be returning to a familiar state of instability and crisis.

By the time the subsequent elections rolled around, the situation had calmed down. But Bolivia—whose motto is "Unity Is Strength"—was still deeply divided. None of the presidential candidates appeared to possess the requisite gumption to bring a desperately needed measure of stability. Besides, all the polls showed clearly that none of them would win the election outright with more than 50 percent of the votes.

Under the arcane rules of Bolivia's constitution, that meant that the final decision would fall to the country's Congress, which was likely to be dominated by the same discredited, stale political parties that had helped bring the nation to gridlock. These traditional parties were widely hated by the majority of Bolivians—would they then accept a president chosen by them? Whoever triumphed, the whole exercise seemed likely merely to prolong Bolivia's agony. The country awaited the outcome with tension and anxiety.

When it came, the result was a shock. It was entirely unequivocal. For the first time since Bolivia had returned to democracy twenty-three years earlier, it was not the hated Congress but the people who decided who their next president would be. And by a landslide they opted for Evo Morales, a man who described himself as "Washington's nightmare."

That nightmare was drug-fueled. For decades, Bolivia had cooperated with successive US governments in programs aimed at eradicating cultivation of the coca plant, a traditional stimulant used for centuries by Andean people. Unfortunately for them, coca is also the raw material for cocaine that ends up on the streets of America and Europe, and from the late 1980s Washington had pressured Bolivia to eliminate it completely. Opposition to that policy had made the coca issue big in the Andes—big enough to propel Evo Morales, originally a coca farmers' leader, into national politics.

Although he had professed confidence in a decisive victory in the first round, it was clear from Morales's face on election night that the result had surprised even him. Beaming and overwhelmed, he was propelled onto a makeshift stage on the street in Cochabamba, Bolivia's fourth biggest city and his political stronghold.

Morales was surrounded by men from the Andean highlands. Their hard, weather-beaten faces—faces that normally looked like wooden carvings—had broken into ecstatic smiles. They shouted and danced and chanted one phrase over and over in Quechua, the indigenous Andean language: *"Kausachum coca! Huaiñuchum yanquis!"*—"Long live coca! Death to the Yankees!"

Chávez's Parrot

"There's a revolution going on in Bolivia, a revolution that potentially could have consequences as far-reaching as the Cuban revolution of 1959. The things going on in Bolivia could have repercussions in Latin America and elsewhere that you could be dealing with for the rest of your lives." Those were the words of Roger Pardo-Maurer, the Pentagon's deputy assistant secretary for Western Hemisphere affairs, who issued his stark warning five months earlier in a speech to a Washington think tank.

Certainly, the election result did cause some concern within the administration of President George W. Bush—although not in the way many people thought at the time. Morales and the *cocaleros* might have been threatening death to America (which, let's face it, added them to a very long list of Bush-haters around the world), but the new president's coca connection wasn't the top worry of many in Washington.

Rather, what really got the Bush administration frothing at the mouth was Morales's international political connections. The new Bolivian leader was a close ally of Washington's biggest enemy in Latin America— Hugo Chávez, the histrionic left-wing president of Venezuela.

Chávez, a former army officer, had won office in 1998 and immediately embarked on a massive social spending program financed by oil revenues. Within a year of taking office, he had also rewritten the constitution to extend the president's term to six years and allow reelection. On top of that, Chávez had changed the name of the country to the Bolivarian Republic of Venezuela after his hero Simón Bolívar, the nineteenth-century aristocrat from Caracas who led Venezuela, Colombia, Peru, Bolivia, and Ecuador to independence from Spanish colonial rule.

In 2000, Chávez had won reelection and secured the right to rule by decree for the first year of his six-year term. Two years after his victory at the polls, the army top brass mounted an unexpected coup. Their government was the shortest-lived in Venezuela's history: four days later troops loyal to the ousted president staged a successful countercoup. Although Washington denied it, Chávez and his supporters always claimed the United States had orchestrated the rebellion, as it had done so many times before in Latin America. There had been various other, less violent attempts to overthrow the president since then, giving apparent proof to Chávez's maxim that the Americans wanted him out.

Chávez saw himself as a maverick. He embraced other mavericks such as Saddam Hussein, whom he visited in Baghdad in 2000 (becoming the first head of state to do so since the 1991 Gulf War); Robert Mugabe, the murderous Zimbabwean dictator, whom Chávez hosted in Caracas in 2004; and Kim Jong Il, the North Korean autocrat, to whom he sent messages of solidarity.

Chávez was by no means as nasty as his friends. He might well have paled into insignificance next to this rogues' gallery but for his big mouth. The media-savvy Venezuelan leader had made a name for himself internationally by publicly taunting and ridiculing George W. Bush. He was an expert at it. Not even Osama bin Laden could match his vitriol. For years the bombastic Venezuelan president had managed to keep himself in the headlines by calling the US president everything from an "asshole" to an "assassin." His favorite moniker for Bush was "Mr. Danger," an ironic sideswipe at the administration's fretting about Chávez himself. The White House claimed Chávez was a threat to his region. Bush, the Venezuelan leader retorted, was a threat to the entire world.

In a world where the occupant of the White House was widely seen as a warmonger of limited intelligence, the ribald Venezuelan president became a magnet for anti-American sentiment, attracting the support of Hollywood movie stars, musicians, statesmen, and writers around the world. While some critics sought to portray him as a dangerous dictator who had manipulated elections to maintain himself in power, to most people his constant jeering more often gave him the air of a lovable, roguish clown.

It wasn't just the sneering. Chávez's behavior was clownlike too: a quick wit, with a love of drama, wild gesticulation, and dressing up, he was viewed as a sort of more benign Latino version of Idi Amin. Perhaps the most memorable photo of Chávez shows him wearing a characteristic red shirt and beret, with a Venezuelan flag tied like a scarf around his neck. Perched on his hand, which is held aloft, is a green parrot—also wearing a tiny red beret. (Rumors that the parrot is one of Chávez's most trusted advisers could not be verified by this author.)

When Evo Morales won his surprise landslide in Bolivia, the clown got an important new friend. Without Chávez, Morales's victory would have been an oddity. But this alliance was backed by cash—and lots of it. Venezuela sits on the largest reserves of oil outside the Middle East, and by 2005 the price of crude was hitting $78 a barrel—a price that just a few years later would have been considered a welcome respite but at the time was a record high, creating billions of dollars in revenues for Chávez to buy influence in South America and around the world.

With Evo Morales installed in the presidential palace in La Paz, Chávez had something more important than just money: for the first time, one of his acolytes had won power through a democratic election. For months, US officials had been warning that the Venezuelan president was bent on spreading his anti-American, nationalistic left-wing ideas throughout the region. Now there was clear evidence that he was succeeding—and yet Washington still apparently had little idea how to react.

Suddenly the political landscape of South America was transformed. Beforehand, Chávez's closest ally had been Fidel Castro, the Cuban leader. Castro was undoubtedly a legendary figure in Latin America, revered across the political spectrum, but his health was failing and his political contribution clearly belonged to history. Now this duo of the decrepit dictator and the flamboyant joker had been joined by a young, committed, serious leader who enjoyed the overwhelming support of his people.

Castro represented the radical leftism of the past, tainted by its ties to Soviet ideology. Morales represented the Left of the future, that of historically marginalized people seizing power for themselves and wielding it in what they believed were their own best interests. Whereas Castro's had been a top-down socialism of the mind, Morales's was a bottom-up socialism of the street. Chávez sat somewhere in the middle, incorporating elements of both and tying them together with potent anti-Americanism.

It has become an often repeated allegation that Chávez funded Morales's election campaign—the implication being that Bolivia had been bought. Even if that were true, the claim misstates what actually happened, what was behind Morales's unexpected landslide. Unlike many election results in Latin America, no one—not even those who had complained about Chávez's secret campaign funding—even bothered crying foul. It was clear that Bolivia's new leader had won not because he had operated a slick, well-crafted modern political campaign. I saw it firsthand, and it really wasn't. He had won because he had captured the public mood perfectly. To anyone who witnessed it, that much was undeniable.

South America Plays Chicken

When Evo Morales nationalized Bolivia's natural gas industry, it was not hard to see the spirit of Chávez hanging over the scene. For some time the Venezuelan leader had been promising to unite like-minded anti-American governments in a "Bolivarian axis," or an "axis of good," as he called it, a snide sideswipe at Bush's "axis of evil" theme in his 2002 State of the Union address.

Few had taken Chávez seriously, but the Bolivian nationalization demonstrated that this radical strategy was beginning to influence events on the ground. Programmatically, the policy brought Morales closer to Chávez and Castro. It seemed no coincidence that the nationalization came after a weekend in which the three leaders met in Havana, signed a "people's trade accord," and publicly attacked Washington's friends in the region such as Colombia and Peru.

The meeting in Havana marked an important turning point. Chávez was now demonstrating the firmness of his new alliance. But there was more. To be sure, Castro still provided the trio with ideological gravitas and global reach, but his physical, mental, and political power was weakening. The Venezuelan leader, by contrast, was in the ascendant, his influence growing, his disciples challenging for power across the region.

Chávez was also keeping the socialist island of Cuba afloat. Venezuela was providing billions of dollars a year in heavily subsidized oil, loans, and investments. Without it, the country's economy would probably be as infirm as Castro himself. The relationship was certainly one of partners, but not of equals: Cuba had now become a satellite for Venezuelan influence. As the three presidents met for the summit, there could be little doubt that as far as the Bolivarian axis was concerned, Chávez was the *comandante*.

Morales, who had often looked uncomfortable in his new role of president, seemed relaxed and happy to be with his senior partners. "Where before there was one or two, now there are three of us to defend the Latin American people," Morales told reporters at the April summit in Havana. The Bolivian president had publicly postponed a decree on nationalization several times, but he appeared to have made the final decision to go ahead with the plan collectively with his Venezuelan and Cuban counterparts that weekend.

This common agenda was exactly what Washington had feared. For one thing, it gave Chávez an even tighter hold over South America's energy supply. Venezuela has the biggest reserves of oil and natural gas in the region, while Bolivia has the second biggest reserves of natural gas. The "axis of good" was now in control of the main sources of energy in South America. The Bolivian nationalization might have barely affected US companies, but it certainly emphasized the radical Left's belligerence both toward international oil companies and other countries in the region.

Now the Bolivarian axis was picking its first big fight—not with its great enemy, the United States, but with Brazil, South America's biggest and most powerful country, headed by Luiz Inácio Lula da Silva, a former militant trade union activist turned moderate socialist politician. When Lula had first been elected in 2002, there were great expectations that he would emerge as a strong regional leader. As Chávez's influence grew, many continued to hope that the Brazilian president would provide a counterweight to his regional ambitions.

Among them was the Bush administration, which counted Lula among its dwindling group of friends in South America. Also among them was the Brazilian diplomatic corps, whose desire to project Brazil onto the regional stage—and the wider international arena— was well known. At the time, the foreign ministry in Brasília had come under a lot of criticism at home for a costly but unsuccessful campaign to win a permanent seat on the United Nations Security Council.

The Bolivian gas nationalization was seen in Brazil as another defeat for diplomacy and the quest for regional leadership in the face of the challenge posed by Chávez. The opposition accused Lula of having a chaotic foreign policy that had singularly failed to defend Brazilian interests. The criticism struck a nerve, particularly since Lula was facing reelection later in the year.

In one blow, not only had the newest member of the Bolivarian axis blindsided Brasília and humiliated it in front of the world, but it had also polarized South America. On one side, backed by Venezuela and Cuba, stood Bolivia, a country flexing the muscle of its natural energy resources, while on the other were Brazil and Argentina, the "non-Bolivarian" consumers of this energy (and, by extension, Peru and Colombia, which had been targets of abuse at the Havana summit).

A public matchup was inevitable, and four days after the nationalization decree, a summit was duly convened between Chávez, Morales, Lula, and Néstor Kirchner, the Argentine president, in Puerto Iguazú in northern Argentina, near the border with Brazil. (Along with Brazil, Argentina was the other main destination for Bolivian natural gas.)

Here was the opportunity Lula needed to show Chávez that he could not bully, charm, and buy his way into the leadership of South America.

The buildup to the encounter was tantalizing. In Brazil, there was pressure on Lula to act quickly and decisively. In the immediate aftermath of the nationalization, the Brazilian president summoned home his top ministers for an emergency cabinet meeting. Following it, his aides told the media he was about to have a "tough" telephone conversation with Morales to tell him the move was unacceptable. Publicly, however, Lula still remained hesitant and reticent when called upon to criticize the nationalization.

In the days that followed, the Brazilian government (though not Lula himself) said it was "perplexed" by the "hostile" decision. "Such an action could be interpreted as a break in the ongoing understanding between Brazil and the Bolivian government," Silas Rondeau, the Brazilian energy minister, told reporters in Brasília.

The buzz around La Paz by now was that Bolivia's energy policy was being set by Venezuelan advisers to the Morales government, who had taken up floors of rooms at the swanky Ritz Hotel in the upscale neighborhood of Sopocachi.

The Caracas connection was not lost on Lula. He felt comfortable enough to say publicly that he was "uncomfortable" with Venezuela putting representatives of PDVSA, its state oil company, in Bolivia to assist with the nationalization. The Bolivians had rights, he said, but those did not negate Brazil's rights. Brasília deemed the nationalization "an act inherent in a sovereign state," but warned it would act "with firmness and serenity" to protect its interests.

The impression was clear: however Venezuela and Bolivia might see the meeting in Puerto Iguazú, the impression Lula wanted to give the world was that the local troublemakers were being hauled into the principal's office to explain themselves—and presumably get a good dressing-down in the process.

But Chávez was prepared. Rather than travel straight to Argentina, he flew first to La Paz, the Bolivian capital, to pick up his protégé. Meanwhile, in Argentina, Lula and Kirchner were holding meetings before the summit to coordinate their strategy.

Chávez, dramatic as ever, arrived in La Paz declaring, "May God always bless Bolivia!" and congratulating Morales for "the sacred exercise of Bolivian sovereignty" expressed in the nationalization. He also issued a warning to Lula. "Sovereignty cannot be discussed," he told reporters after touching down in the Bolivian capital. "What Bolivia has done cannot be questioned. It's the legitimate fulfillment of a popular mandate."

In Puerto Iguazú, the face-off between the representatives of South America's two main factions—the radicals and the moderates— lasted just three hours. When they emerged for a joint press conference, it was clear who had won. "We respect and welcome the sovereign decision of the Bolivian people," said Kirchner. Not only, amazingly, was Kirchner congratulating Morales on behalf of the other three leaders for a nationalization well done, but he also announced that Bolivia had been invited to join their ambitious project for a $20 billion, 5,600-mile gas pipeline linking up a string of South American countries.

Those who were hoping for tougher words from Lula were speedily disappointed. "We recognize Bolivia's sovereign right over its natural resources," he said meekly. He went on to add that the meeting was a sign to investors of regional dialogue: "I don't believe there's an alliance between Bolivia and Venezuela to confront or fight with Argentina and Brazil."

Finally, a day after Petrobras had announced it was freezing investment in Bolivia because of the nationalization decree, Lula suggested the state-owned company might backtrack. "As a company, it will always invest wherever it sees a chance to obtain a return for its investments," he said.

The leader of a country whose aspiration had long been to establish itself as the undisputed leader of South America had behaved as if, when the time came for it, he did not have the stomach for tough leadership.

The reaction back in Brazil was angry. Lula's critics accused him of weakness and confusion. Arthur Virgilio, the opposition Senate leader, told the chamber that Lula had shown he "is less prepared than Venezuelan President Hugo Chávez, who little by little is undermining Brazil's leadership in South America." Rubens Barbosa, a former Brazilian ambassador to Washington, wrote in a column in *O Estado de São Paulo* on May 9, 2006, that because of Lula's feebleness, "the entire thrust of Brazilian diplomacy for the past 20 years has been damaged."

Chávez knew well he had won this important showdown. The summit had afforded Lula the perfect opportunity to challenge the Venezuelan for the ideological leadership of South America—and he had singularly failed to do so. Where there might have been tense words, clenched fists, and banging of tables, there were smiles, handshakes, and slaps on backs.

It was a typically Latin American outcome. In Europe, political leaders tend to pretend there are no disagreements among them as they prepare to go to the summits. Then they beat one another up in the conference room. In South America, they talk a good fight beforehand and end up bear-hugging.

The episode also carried an important lesson for the United States. Brazil, South America's mightiest country, had failed to stand up to Bolivia, a relatively small and impoverished nation. The event encapsulated how, when it came down to it, countries that did not subscribe to the radical left-wing agenda that Chávez and Morales proposed were simply not willing to confront it—even when there was hard cash at stake.

The Venezuelan president, not normally given to understatement, tried his best not to sound triumphalist. He denied the Bolivian nationalization had caused any tension between South America's leaders. "There are those who want to stoke tension, but we're specialists at smoothing things over," he told reporters at a press conference following the summit. "Sometimes we have internal tension, but that cannot persist when we have great leaders with political vision."

Indeed—but whose vision?

Next Stop: Ecuador

If Bolivia had been an unexpected source of exciting news, Ecuador was even more of a surprise. Apart from the Galápagos Islands, with their remarkable blue-footed boobies (sounds racy, but in fact they're a type of bird), Ecuador is not the sort of country the world tends to think about very much. Slightly smaller in size than Nevada, it's somewhat minuscule compared to its South American neighbors. So is most of its population of 13 million, who are also economically poor, socially divided, and politically fickle.

Normally an election in Ecuador wouldn't have captured much international attention. That's partly because the country's heads of state have something of a habit of leaving office before the end of their elected terms—usually to self-imposed exile abroad via the backdoor of the presidential palace, while an angry mob protests out front.

But in the final months of 2006, Ecuador seemed to be on the verge of adding a new dimension to Chávez's campaign for influence in South America. Rafael Correa—young, tall, handsome, and charismatic—was surging ahead in the opinion polls, and, like Evo Morales, he was an ally of the Venezuelan leader.

Correa had even managed to upstage Chávez with his rhetoric— no mean feat. After the Venezuelan leader appeared at the United Nations and compared George W. Bush to the devil, the Ecuadorean grabbed a headline or two himself by saying that the comparison was unflattering to Satan.

Correa, a former economics professor with a PhD from the University of Illinois, got his first taste of governmental power during a short-lived stint as finance minister in 2005. A political neophyte when he was appointed in May of that year (as part of a new government that took over following the previous president's hasty exit amid mass demonstrations, as per tradition), he was to last only three months in the job.

It was enough to make his mark. Two months in, Correa had turned up in Washington to receive an agreed $100 million loan from the World Bank, which lends out money for development. What the bank apparently hadn't told him was that it was canceling the loan because Correa had restructured a fund that used oil profits to pay off Ecuador's debt, in order to spend more of the money on social programs. The bank said that violated the terms of the loan. The inexperienced, somewhat hotheaded finance minister was left empty-handed in the US capital. He returned home fuming and bent on revenge.

Correa decided he would go elsewhere and gravitated to a wealthy nearby patron who had a gleam in his eye. Sensing an opportunity to extend his reach, Chávez's government started negotiating the terms of a $300 million loan with Ecuador.

It was not to be. Ecuador's new president was stung by the high-profile quarrel with the World Bank—run at the time by Paul Wolfowitz, George W. Bush's former deputy defense secretary and a senior cheerleader for the war on Iraq—and none too pleased to see his finance minister cozying up to Caracas. Correa was duly fired.

I interviewed Correa in August 2005, the day before he was sacked, and asked him if he had considered a presidential bid. He pooh-poohed the idea, but the denial struck me as insincere. After he was booted out of government, opinion polls showed him to be the most popular political figure in the country. (At the time, I noted in the *Financial Times* that Correa might well have his eyes on the presidency. This stellar power of prediction, however, failed to discern that he would leave office within twenty-four hours of our meeting.)

By September 2006, Correa's energetic presidential campaign had propelled him to pole position in public surveys. But when the first round of elections was held, the surprise winner was Álvaro Noboa, a right-wing banana tycoon who was Ecuador's richest man. Correa did come in second, however, which meant there was still a chance he would win the runoff contest a month later.

A Correa victory would be especially bad for Washington's ambitions in South America. Ecuador was host to the only US military base in South America, and Correa was threatening to kick out the Americans when the lease expired in 2009. What's more, Ecuador was the only South American country that had officially adopted the US dollar as its currency after its economy collapsed in the late 1990s. Correa was hinting that he might abandon the greenback, which Washington could only see as a step backward.

In addition, Ecuador was an oil producer, the second biggest exporter of South American crude to the United States (after Venezuela, of course). Having more oil reserves under the control of the Chávez camp was a concern for the White House. Finally, the Bush administration had been at pains to try to cement its long-term trading relationship with Ecuador via a bilateral trade treaty. While previous governments had come close to agreeing the terms, Correa was adamant that he would never kowtow to the economic imperialists in Washington by signing such a deal.

By contrast, Álvaro Noboa said that if he became president he would cut diplomatic ties with Venezuela and Cuba and improve relations with the United States. The problem for Washington was that he was not a smart alternative. The billionaire might have been friends with members of the Kennedy clan as well as Susan Sarandon and Tim Robbins—one of Hollywood's most prominent political-activist couples—but he was both odious and untelegenic.

A corpulent billionaire with a tuft of greasy hair, Noboa seemed to encapsulate all that was wrong with a political class that had grown fat on the misery of others while securing its continued dominance with lies and trickery. His campaign went from town to town like a sham faith-healing circus. In every village, Noboa gave away computers, wheelchairs, and sometimes even cash. He cast himself as a Messiah figure, invoking God's help and clutching a Bible to his considerable bosom.

Noboa was not even a self-made man. Although he operated 110 different businesses, his image as an entrepreneurial superstar was totally artificial, his $1.2 billion personal fortune being due less to empire building than ruthless boardroom maneuvering. Luis, his father, had built up the family's fortune, and although he willed Álvaro only $7.5 million, the son wrested control of the banana business—the jewel of the Noboa empire—by buying out one sister and forcing another off the board.

So, contrary to appearances, the United States actually had a lot at stake in Ecuador, but given the appalling choice with which it was presented, Washington decided to sit on the sidelines and just see what happened. American officials thought the Ecuadorean people were sure to reject Correa, widely viewed by the political elite (from whom many in the State Department developed their views) as a crypto-communist who would open the door to Chávez. Although the United States was officially silent, privately its representatives reassured those who would listen that the election would confirm the Venezuelan leader's lack of influence in the region. Analysts working for investment banks in New York—who were analyzing the situation for the holders of Ecuadorean sovereign bonds—repeated the line, reassuring their clients that their investments were secure, since Noboa was going to win and he would honor Quito's debt commitments.

They got it spectacularly wrong. As the election results started to come in, there was never any doubt as to who had triumphed. Correa won with 57 percent of the vote, securing all but two regions of the country.

"We are starting to recover the homeland," he told his supporters at a victory rally in Quito as the results came in. "Today wasn't the end of anything, rather it began a decisive new phase. Our struggle has never been to send a man to the presidency; it's always been for the homeland."

Records recovered years later from the Colombian FARC guerrillas suggested that Chávez had been funding Correa's election campaign. At the time, Correa was careful to point out that he was a "friend" rather than a "client" of Chávez, but, he said, "it would be wonderful to move closer to a country like Venezuela, which can help us a lot because it has $53 billion in cash reserves as a result of the oil surplus." Apparently he was still angling for a loan from Caracas.

Washington was not reassured. A US State Department spokesman told a press briefing that its relationship with the new government would depend on what policies emerged and "whether or not those policies are consonant with our goals."

The cautious tone was not reflected elsewhere. A month earlier, the US ambassador to Managua had warned Nicaraguans not to reelect Daniel Ortega, the Marxist former president against whom Ronald Reagan's White House had funded a guerrilla war (illegally, as the Iran-Contra scandal proved). Sixteen years after he voluntarily stepped aside following an election, Ortega was back as a presidential candidate and looking likely to become another strong member of the region's emerging anti-American axis.

The voters rejected Washington's advice and reelected Ortega. While the former president was far from being one of the young idealists whom Chávez considered his acolytes in the region, his victory nevertheless gave a boost to Caracas's influence in the region, and the Venezuelan leader—along with Fidel Castro—was among the first to congratulate him on his win.

And then there were five. Just twelve months earlier, Chávez had been a lone voice bolstered only by Cuba, Latin America's perennial odd man out. Now he could look back on a year in which his allies had swept to power in three countries in the region, while serious challengers had threatened to grab two more. He was no longer a lone voice ranting into the wind, but a world figure—applauded at the United Nations, welcomed as a friend on every continent, seen in the region as the new leader of a new international movement. Chávez, dismissed by his critics as a clown, had power, influence, and fabulous wealth.

In fact, this gang of five had very nearly become a gang of seven in 2006. In Peru, another Chávez mini-me had come within a whisker of winning the presidency. Ollanta Humala, a former lieutenant colonel in the Peruvian army, led the opinion polls for much of the election, but ultimately lost by a small margin. A month later in Mexico, Andrés Manuel López Obrador, another candidate of the radical Left (though more a sympathizer than a Chávez ally), narrowly lost his presidential race.

Suddenly Latin America's political landscape looked very interesting. In a world gripped by the struggle between globalization and violent Islamism, the rise of the radical Left in South America offered an intriguing subplot and the biggest story to come out of the region for many years.

In some ways, South America's "new Left" seemed to offer an alternative to the stark choices that the narrative appeared to pose. Whereas the jihadists challenged the post–Cold War order with hate, death, and destruction, the "Bolivarian axis" was the acceptable face of revolution for many on the Left around the world who had been searching for leadership of their cause. Had the likes of Osama bin Laden, Mahmoud Ahmadinejad, or Muqtada al-Sadr, the Iraqi insurgent leader, turned up in London, New York, or Vienna, even the hard Left would have found it difficult to welcome them with open arms. But Chávez and his friends were the fluffy end of the same spectrum, greeted by many as heroes of the global backlash against the relentless march of free-market forces. For some of those who claimed to be equally repelled by both Washington and Al-Qaeda, Caracas offered, it seemed, a middle path.

Continental Shifts

By the latter years of the twenty-first century's first decade, much of South America looked to have gravitated to the magnetic draw of the Left to some degree. While only Bolivia and Ecuador were firmly within the Chávez camp, several other more moderate leaders in the region had strong left-wing credentials.

Although he largely disappointed his early fans around the world, President Lula of Brazil was still seen as an important global figure on the soft Left by the time he won reelection in October 2006 with more than 60 percent of the vote. Lula, a former shoeshine boy and metalworker who lost a finger in a factory accident, had organized massive strikes in the 1970s against car companies such as Ford, Volkswagen, and Mercedes. Few other world leaders could claim his experience on the shop floor of international capitalism. He left office in 2010 still immensely popular and handed power over to his handpicked successor, Dilma Rousseff.

Argentina had elected Néstor Kirchner as president in 2003, when it was still suffering the effects of a deep economic crisis that had hit two years earlier. Kirchner, a fierce critic of international financial organizations, defaulted on the country's debt, eventually paying only about one-third of what Argentina owed. He shifted foreign policy, which had previously followed a strategy of automatic alignment with Washington, to stress ties within the region. Kirchner was also close to Chávez, borrowing more than $6 billion from Venezuela and appearing alongside him and Morales at events in Caracas. In 2007, his wife, Cristina Fernández, took over and charted a similarly haphazard leftist course as her husband.

Chile elected Michelle Bachelet as its first woman president in 2006. A separated single mother of three children and a self-described agnostic, she was a remarkable choice for such a conservative Catholic country. Bachelet had been detained and tortured by the regime of Augusto Pinochet, the tyrant who governed Chile from 1973 to 1990. Although she was head of the Socialist Party, Bachelet was elected as the candidate for the Concertación, an umbrella grouping, and in office she continued the market-friendly policies of her predecessor, with an emphasis on opening Chile up to the global economy. After she left office in 2010, Chile swung right, electing Sebastián Piñera, a conservative businessman.

Tabaré Vázquez, a former oncologist, had taken power in Uruguay in 2005, becoming the country's first left-leaning president. In 2010, he was succeeded by José Mujica, another leftist. Paraguay joined the trend in 2008, electing Fernando Lugo, a former bishop who refused to accept the presidential salary and encouraged other politicians to do likewise. His victory brought to an end the sixty-one-year grip on power of the right-wing Colorado Party, which had been dominated for decades by Alfredo Stroessner, a somewhat clownish military dictator.

Alan García, who had been a darling of the Latin American Left when he was first elected Peru's head of state in 1985, was a lot older, fatter, and more moderate when he won the presidency for the second time in 2006. But his American Popular Revolutionary Alliance—one of South America's oldest left-wing parties—was still seen as left of center, and García himself was viewed as a European-style social democrat. Nevertheless, when in power he seemed more interested in continuing to attract foreign investors than in tackling the country's endemic problems of poverty and inequality.

As a result, in 2011, Ollanta Humala succeeded on his second attempt to become president of Peru, beating Keiko Fujimori, daughter of the jailed former strongman, in a second-round runoff election. This was sweet personal revenge for Humala, who had once led a failed coup against Keiko's father. Humala had shaken off some of the militaristic image that had clung to him during the previous presidential election.

In fact, that caricature had never been accurate. In person, Humala, who was educated at an exclusive private school in Lima and at the Sorbonne in Paris, was soft-spoken, calm, funny, and charming. He was short, trim, and handsome, with a winning smile and an attractive thirty-three-year-old wife who seemed to have the potential to become a Peruvian Evita.

Humala's victory confounded many both in Peru and internationally who simply could not understand why if the country's economy was growing so fast (particularly at a time when economic growth in the developed world was moribund), its population was still seemingly so angry.

The election of Humala exposed the fallacy of equating overall economic growth with contentment. It followed a year in which the Peruvian economy had grown at a clip of 9 percent, almost the fastest pace in the world, five years in which per capita gross income had risen by 82 percent, and a decade in which the poverty rate had been halved to 30 percent. Yet most Peruvians still felt that the boom was passing them by, that politics remained as corrupt and ineffective as ever, and that they were being ignored and overlooked as they had been for generations.

The other reason Humala's win was such a surprise was that many observers had assumed by then that South America's radical Left moment had passed. Although Chávez, Morales, and Correa were still in office, their influence was widely thought to have waned considerably within the region, as they withdrew into the day-to-day difficulties of maintaining themselves in power and combating a growing list of problems at home. When Chávez revealed in 2011 that he was suffering from cancer, it only seemed to underline the idea that his power was on the decline.

The Peruvian election, however, had shown that an angry campaign based on squeezing foreign investors and ramping up social spending was still a surefire vote winner.

Humala had learned the lesson of 2006 and distanced himself somewhat from Chávez. Following the first round of elections, he abandoned a radical campaign platform and underwent an apparent conversion to more moderate policies, guided by Brazilian campaign advisers who were former aides to President Lula. Nevertheless, he still proposed a windfall tax on foreign mining companies and a hike for the regular tax and royalty rates they paid. That was enough to prompt deep concern among international mining companies about the future of their investments in Peru, which sits on the world's second largest copper reserves and produces 16 percent of the world's silver, 12 percent of its zinc, 9 percent of its gold, and 7 percent of its copper.

In spite of his attempts to rebrand himself as a centrist, Humala's instincts were undoubtedly on the radical Left. He may not have been proposing widespread nationalizations like Chávez, but at his inauguration in July 2011, he insisted on being sworn in over a copy of the 1979 constitution, the legal document that had been overturned in 1993 by Fujimori's free-market constitution, which had effectively removed the state from the economy. At least symbolically, Peru's new president was rejecting the Washington Consensus.

Asked whether he was a Chávez or a Lula, Humala replied that he was neither, but a leader of Peru who would carve an independent path. That sounded like rhetoric, but there was something to it. By 2011 Venezuela, which was suffering from sluggish economic growth after two years of recession, high inflation, and a crime wave, did not seem the path to follow. Equally, however, Peru, whose mines were mostly located in rural areas surrounded by poor villages full of angry indigenous people, was no Brazil either.

Humala might no longer have publicly associated himself with Chávez, but the campaign against him depended, as it did in 2006, on painting him as an ardent Chavista bent on turning Peru into a socialist economy. That was not enough of a deterrent for the electorate, undermining those observers who had declared that the wind had gone out of the sails of the radical Left in South America.

A few days after the Peruvian election, as if to confirm that Chávez still retained some clout on the international stage, Venezuela and Iran united at a meeting of OPEC, the club of oil-producing countries, to block a proposal by Saudi Arabia to increase production quotas. "OPEC, led by Iran and Venezuela, has snubbed its nose at the United States and the rest of the Western nations addicted to OPEC oil," Edward Markey, the Democratic US representative from Massachusetts, said in a statement. The move prompted President Barack Obama to tap the United States' Strategic Petroleum Reserve for the first time in three years, a policy coordinated with the other members of the International Energy Agency. With the exception of Colombia and Chile, South America was now in the hands of the Left. Many observers called this a pink tide sweeping the continent. But although the root cause of the shift to the left may have been the same—simply put, the desire for fundamental change—more accurately, there were two kinds of responses that emerged. One group was the market skeptics, best represented by Venezuela, Bolivia, and Ecuador. The other was the market enthusiasts, led by Chile and Colombia.

The market skeptics were united by their use of nationalization as a central tool of economic policy. Nationalization meant a variety of different things, but in essence it signified both higher taxes on foreign investors and greater state involvement in the economy. The market skeptics viewed the state, rather than private industry, as the main driver of economic development.

The market enthusiasts saw nationalization as marching backward and instead developed their economies using public-private partnerships or concessioning—encouraging private companies to operate public services or exploit natural resources and to make a profit doing so. In this way, they tied their development to investment by international companies, not state spending.

In terms of trade, Venezuela, Bolivia, and Ecuador focused on developing ties within South America and on regional integration.

In contrast, the market enthusiasts designed trade policies to grow their economies by expanding their share of global markets.

The market skeptics tended to set short-term goals aimed at shoring up political support rather than strategic long-term planning. Their economic policies were generally bent to the more important aim of political reform or, in the case of Venezuela, buying political influence. Even nationalization—on the face of it, an economic policy—was often more of a political move whose timing was designed with political concerns in mind.

By contrast, Chile, Colombia, and Peru prioritized economic considerations over political reform. In general, they had a longer-term vision of where their economies should be going, which guided their policies far more than the very real need for political reform.

In between the market skeptics and the market enthusiasts were Argentina and Brazil, whose governments veered between the two camps. You could call them market agnostics, or market ditherers, perhaps. Some observers saw South America as split between Chavismo and Lulismo, the left-leaning inheritance of Lula in Brazil, which combined free-market trade policies with strong social spending programs. But in many ways, Brazil was keen to maintain the role of the state in the economy in a way that Colombia, Chile, and pre-Humala Peru were not. Argentina's economic policies also veered between free marketeering and economic nationalism, although in a more chaotic and incoherent way.

South America was left with two distinct groups, each offering its own path of economic development. Beyond rhetoric, there were real differences between them, based on contradictory views of the free market, whether or not they had faith or mistrust in international trade, and their attitudes to state involvement in the economy and investment by international companies.

This was quite a different picture from a decade earlier, when most of Latin America had been friendly territory for Washington and free-market ideas. Back then, the dominant economic idea in Latin America was the Washington Consensus, a package of reforms stressing fiscal discipline, austerity, low taxes, deregulation, and the privatization of state-owned businesses. As the first part of the name suggests, it came from three powerful global organizations based in Washington: the

International Monetary Fund, the World Bank, and the US government. But the consensus was just as much among the political and economic elites of Latin America who introduced the reforms.

Perhaps the best example of how close North and South America had become in their economic thinking came at the Summit of the Americas in Miami in 1994. US president Bill Clinton used the meeting to launch an initiative for a free-trading bloc that "will stretch from Alaska to Argentina." It was not an original idea. At a similar summit in 1967, the leaders of the Americas had pledged to create a Latin American Common Market with the United States' blessing. The proposal had withered before it could bear any fruit.

Clinton's idea fell on much more fertile ground. The military regimes that had dominated Latin America in the 1960s, many of which were hostile to Washington or capricious in their friendship, had been replaced by democracies. The region was in the hands of moderates who were reversing the nationalizations of previous decades, opening up their economies to foreign investors, and operating according to strict fiscal orthodoxy. In the wake of the North American Free Trade Agreement, which the Clinton administration signed in 1993, they saw the advantage of strengthening ties with the massive market offered by the United States, Canada, and Mexico.

And so, proving that there really was a consensus part to the Washington Consensus, every leader in the region enthusiastically agreed to the Clinton plan. The only opposition had come from Fidel Castro's Cuba, which, following the collapse of communism in Eastern Europe, had recently lost its principal patron, leaving it isolated, impoverished, and irrelevant.

Fast-forward again one decade. Not only did the shift to the left in South America kill off the idea of a regional trading bloc, but it also heralded the return of revolutionary ideas that had supposedly long been put to bed: free-market reforms were being reversed; foreign investors were being squeezed, expelled, and chased away; democratic constitutions were being rewritten; fiscal orthodoxy was being replaced by profligacy or, at least, an enlarged role for the public sector in the economy.

Although these ideas were echoed in many countries, the heart of this revolution was Venezuela, Bolivia, and Ecuador. Peru, another

Andean state, looked like it might join them. The Andes, that great geographical fault line that runs like a spine down the west of the continent, had become a political fault line. Like an earthquake, its revolution had aftershocks across Latin America—and it shook the world.

More than fifteen years after communism collapsed in Eastern Europe, parts of South America were openly, proudly, defiantly marching toward socialism. Fidel Castro, who less than a decade earlier was dismissed as anachronistic and inconsequential, was suddenly propelled to the spiritual leadership of a new revolutionary movement. That new movement was best characterized by its commitment to resource nationalism—reversing foreign control over natural resources and revitalizing state companies that had often been left for dead after years of privatizations.

By nationalizing his gas industry, Evo Morales had encapsulated the new anti-orthodoxy. In Venezuela, Chávez was taking control of the oil, cement, and steel sectors. Ecuador expelled an American oil company that was its biggest foreign investor and seized $1 billion of its assets. Free markets were out. Nationalizing industries was in.

Globalization had seemed an unstoppable force. Even Communist China was rapidly opening itself up for business. So why was the party being ambushed? And why was this happening in the Andes, of all places?

3

Atahualpa's Ghost

Just off the main square in Cajamarca, a beautiful city in Peru's high Andes more than five hundred miles north of Lima, is a building that haunts South America.

Standing near the corner of Amalia Puga and Belén, the edifice dates back to the time of the Incas, perhaps the greatest civilization South America has ever known. By the time Spanish adventurers first arrived in the region in 1532, the Incan empire stretched from modern-day Colombia in the north, down through Ecuador, Peru, and Bolivia to what are now Chile and Argentina in the south. But this vast empire soon crumbled with the arrival of the Spanish, whose aggression, superior technology, and European diseases quickly overwhelmed the Incas. The building in Cajamarca in many senses symbolizes the moment at which the European invaders first seized power.

Tens of thousands of visitors make the trek to this spot every year. They do not so much come to see the structure itself, the *cuarto del rescate*, or "ransom room," as it is known. In a country stuffed with fantastically impressive examples of Incan architecture, it is somewhat underwhelming—very plain and topped off with a modern roof. Instead, they are looking for a mark on the inside of one of its walls, about eight feet up. By legend, the mark points to the spot where Atahualpa, the Incan emperor who had been captured by the Spaniards and was being held prisoner in the room, reached up and touched the wall, pledging that if his captors spared his life and freed him, he would have the room filled to that point with gold, plus double that amount of silver. The conquistadores accepted the arrangement, and captors and captive sat back to wait for the treasure to be delivered.

While he was a prisoner, Atahualpa continued to function as emperor and settled in with his guards—even learning to play chess with them. It took time for the Incan emissaries to bring gold back. When the Spaniards complained, a few months after his capture, that the items were not arriving fast enough, Atahualpa sent them to Cuzco with instructions that they should be allowed to strip Coricancha, the sun temple, a building whose sides were covered in slabs of gold to reflect the sun's rays. The envoys pried off the plates using copper crowbars. They hauled back objects that when melted down produced 13,420 pounds of gold and 26,000 pounds of silver— worth some $280 million at today's prices. Atahualpa had fulfilled his part of the bargain. But the Spanish discovered he had sent word to the northern reaches of the Incan empire for troops to attack their base. In something of a panic, the Spanish governor sentenced him to death without a trial. On Saturday, July 26, 1533, the last Incan emperor was led by his guards into the main square at Cajamarca. He had been condemned to burn at the stake, but after agreeing to convert to Christianity, he was afforded what was deemed a kinder fate. The emperor was baptized, then duly strangled by a piece of rope tied around his neck.

Atahualpa's execution stunned his followers. Without their leader, any notion of repelling the invaders melted away. Because he had died a Christian, they were not even permitted to bury him according to their ancient traditions. The Spanish had desecrated their holy places, killed their leader, and destroyed their society.

Historians doubt that the *cuarto del rescate* was actually the room Atahualpa offered to fill with gold. The Spanish were apparently so astounded by Atahualpa's generous offer that they drew up a contract to formalize the deal and hold him to it. In it, they describe a room that is smaller than the one tourists visit today in Cajamarca. No matter, the *cuarto del rescate's* significance is for what it symbolizes rather than for what it actually is. It stands as a memorial to how the indigenous people of South America lost their imperial pretensions, how they were betrayed by a foreign power, how centuries of rule from Europe began, how a bunch of outsiders first came and plundered the region's natural wealth.

The Burden of History

History is critically important in Latin America—particularly in the Andes, where the Incas ruled. It is not so much relegated to the past as accumulated and shouldered as a burden in the present. The brutalities of the past, beginning with the betrayal of Atahualpa, continue to shape how Latin Americans view themselves, one another, and those from beyond the region. The desire for a leader who could thumb his nose at the north as Chávez and his allies have done has been burning for centuries.

Of course, North America and Latin America were both conquered by European powers. Their arrival heralded death and disaster for the indigenous people, who found their societies abruptly "discovered." But Latin America was much more heavily populated than the northern part of the Americas before the arrival of the Europeans, and many more indigenous people survived the conquest there.

In the Andes, from which the Spanish ruled the rest of South America, the conquerors developed a castelike society: a tiny number of large landowners, officials, and priests ruled over a huge number of indigenous peasants, many of whom were forced to work the land or toil in the mines. Society was rigid, unequal, and based on racial divisions.

This legacy lives on. The racist worldview of the Spanish conquerors resonates powerfully today in the Andes, where the grades of distinction between those with a larger share of Spanish blood and those deemed more indigenous continue to have enormous political, social, and economic significance. The same is true of the Spaniards' economic legacy. In many Latin American countries, socioeconomic inequality can be traced back to the concentration of landownership in colonial times.

Yet the legacy of conquest weighs heavily not just with indigenous people. Take Rolfi, a friend of mine who works as a tour guide in Cuzco, the former Incan capital in the Peruvian highlands now known as a jumping-off point for visits to Machu Picchu, the mountaintop fortress that is the country's most visited tourist destination. To look at him, you might not consider Rolfi a "typical" Peruvian. He was born in Peru, but his parents were Italian immigrants, and consequently his skin is paler and his black hair curlier than that of most of his compatriots. Yet Rolfi has absorbed a typical Peruvian mind-set that belies his purely European ancestry. When he explains the history of the Andes, he speaks of the tragedy of the Spanish conquest, of the destruction of traditional Peruvian society, of the "real" Peru still relatively untainted by foreign influence.

South Americans tend to think of themselves as victims of history, its subjects rather than its shapers. They often talk as if their history has been the regular raping of their continent and the abuse of their people. When foreigners have become involved in the region, they have usually, in the locals' perception, been perpetrators—of the plunder of natural resources, of violence and aggression, of the destruction of traditional ways of life.

History has shaped in the Latin American mind-set an especially strong attachment to the concept of national sovereignty. The accusation that something trespasses on national sovereignty is among the most serious that can be leveled at a foreign power. When it comes to the United States, with its long and rich history of unsolicited intervention in the region, the accusation is all the stronger. In one very strong current of South American thinking, the United States has often encapsulated the combination of two themes in the region's history: the pillage of its natural resources, and the use of brute force to achieve its aims. In that sense, the United States represents the sum of the plunder and violence visited on the region in the past five hundred years. South Americans' attitudes to Washington contain residual feelings about all the foreigners who have ever been perceived—accurately or otherwise—to have wronged the region.

Take "dependency theory," an idea that became popular in the 1970s in Latin America and elsewhere. It contended that globalization was essentially a process in which resources flowed from poor countries to rich ones, making the former poorer and the latter richer. The psychological foundation of such an idea, which helped make it so popular in Latin America, could be traced right back to the Spanish conquest. The conquest was a Copernican revolution for South Americans, completely altering their perspective. Incan theology had placed Cuzco—the "bellybutton of the world"—at the center of the average South American's universe. Even without this myth, the Andes were beyond question the location of a large and sophisticated civilization. But as a result of the Spanish conquest, the region was suddenly transformed into a mere frontier of a distant and alien power, a backwater that needed to be civilized and colonized, a source of gold and other raw materials for the faraway centers of power. Ever since, Latin America has been periodically reminded that it is a periphery, a means to a greater end, a perennial victim of history, a continent at the end of the world.

The promise of El Dorado—of a city made of gold—drew adventurers to Latin America. Instead, the first big treasure they found after looting the Incan empire was a silver deposit of unheard-of size at Potosí, in the Andean highlands, fifteen thousand feet above sea level in what is now southern Bolivia but was then Alto Peru. Cerro Rico, the deposit, was discovered by an indigenous llama herder in 1545, a dozen years after Atahualpa was executed. Potosí produced so much silver that the Spanish invaders were said to shoe their horses with it. Charles V, the Holy Roman Emperor, declared Potosí an Imperial City—the "nerve center of the kingdom," one Spanish viceroy called it. The city quickly boomed and became one of the top urban centers in the Spanish empire. By the end of the sixteenth century, Potosí was one of the most buzzing metropolises of the world. Cervantes's *Don Quixote* compared the city's mines with the treasures of Venice, as possessing unimaginable value. The US dollar sign may have originated from Potosí's mint mark—the letters P, T, S, and I superimposed on one another.

The pure silver extracted from the mine in the 240 years from its discovery was worth about $44 billion in today's prices. By the seventeenth century, it accounted for almost all the exports from Spain's new territories. The gold and silver were used to create opulent altars for the cathedrals of Europe. They were used to pay Spain's and the Vatican's debtors. They paid for the wars of the Holy Roman Empire and the Inquisition. Of course, much of the wealth was also retained in the colonies, finding its way into the pockets of the continent's new elite—Spanish landowners and businessmen for whom South America offered opportunities they could only have dreamed of back in Europe. The gold and silver also adorned the new churches the settlers built across the region, much as they had once graced the Incas' temples and shrines.

Most of this wealth was obtained by the blood and sweat of indigenous laborers. Countless thousands of indigenous men were pressed into forced labor in the mines, where they died in droves from the harsh working conditions, from inhaling poisonous mercury fumes in the extraction process, and from the bitter cold. Indigenous mothers killed their own sons to save them from perishing in the mines. When the supply of ready workers ran low, the colonials imported thirty thousand African slaves, whom they used as human mules in the mines when the real animals died.

The harshness of forced labor was one way indigenous people died off. In other cases they were simply massacred. By law, the Spanish invaders had to read the indigenous a disclaimer, warning them that if they did not convert to Catholicism they would be brutalized and enslaved. Of course, to the locals, Spanish was nothing more than gobbledygook and the *Requerimiento*, as it was known, was not translated into their tongue. Most of the indigenous who died off did so quietly and unobserved, through diseases introduced by the Europeans to which they had no immunity. Within fifty years of the Spaniards' arrival in South America, one-third of Latin America's indigenous population had been wiped out.

Beginning in the last decade of the seventeenth century, the Portuguese found what was at the time the richest gold deposit the world had ever seen—as well as diamonds, emeralds, topaz, and aquamarines—in Minas Gerais, in southeastern Brazil. Ouro Preto, the town at the heart of the gold rush, was described at the time as "the Potosí of gold." The Portuguese, who had been given control of Africa in a series of fifteenth-century papal bulls, had better access to slaves and brought millions of Africans in chains to Brazil to work in and around the mines.

Plunder and Profits

The plunder of South America that began with the execution of Atahualpa and the rush to find silver and gold spread to other resources. Extracting metal was the first stage of economic colonialism. It soon turned to agriculture: the colonials turned the enforced servitude of indigenous people and imported slaves to the sugar, cocoa, cotton, coffee, and banana plantations. They plundered the forests and jungles for timber, and tapped rubber in the Brazilian and Peruvian Amazon. The plantations cemented the division of land into *latifundios*—large estates handed over to colonials, whose residents then became indentured servants. Metal was not the only precious natural resource, either. In the nineteenth century, Peru's most valuable export was guano, cormorant excrement that was picked off the rocks along the shore and exported for fertilizer. Peru, Bolivia, and later Chile exported their nitrate deposits, also for use as fertilizer.

In the days before the countries of Latin America gained their independence starting in the 1820s, the profits of such ventures were often spirited back to Europe, where they helped fund the Industrial Revolution and imperial expansions elsewhere. After independence, they went more into the pockets of local landowners and helped to create a tiny but hugely wealthy upper class in the region. Men such as Simón Iturri Patiño—the Bolivian "King of Tin" also known as "the Andean Rockefeller" and by the 1940s one of the wealthiest people in the world—became the aristocrats of their countries, their wealth based on the export of raw materials. But for every Patiño there were many more foreigners who, like the Spanish conquistadores, went to South America to find their fortune—men like Henry Meiggs, who sketched out plans for Fisherman's Wharf in San Francisco before becoming a railroad magnate in mid-nineteenth-century Peru, a foundation upon which he built a vast business empire.

What began with metal and turned to agriculture was later to spread to oil. The discovery of massive reserves in Lake Maracaibo in 1918 placed Venezuela at the heart of a "black gold" rush. In oil, as in other resources by this point, the operations were usually controlled by foreign companies. Venezuela granted concessions to multinationals to come in and exploit the oil fields. These were as often European as North American. The oil industry across the region was dominated by Standard Oil of the United States and Royal Dutch Shell, the Anglo-Dutch oil giant.

Given that most of the proceeds were taken out of the country (or squirreled out by local elites who preferred to keep it in savings accounts in Miami or Geneva), it is little surprise that many Latin Americans see their history as the endless repetition of a cycle of plunder: of silver and gold starting in the sixteenth century, of agricultural production from the seventeenth century, of oil in the twentieth century. That history is not important just because of the injustices of the past but also because more than a few of the region's contemporary problems stem from its colonial legacy.

Every so often the local news in South America will carry an item about some gold relic or altar being stolen from a church in the Andean highlands. It is hardly surprising: the ostentatious display of wealth among continuing poverty is a powerful temptation.

In spite of numerous land reform initiatives, remnants of the *latifundios* still exist. In the Chaco region in southeastern Bolivia, indigenous Guaraní people still endure forced labor in plantations owned by wealthy landowners. On a visit there in 2009, the head of the United Nations' Permanent Forum on Indigenous Issues condemned the "landlessness, forced labor, servitude, and extreme poverty" she had witnessed, while "Captive Communities," a report issued by the Organization of American States in December 2009, said many Guaraní families were living in a state of bondage little different from slavery.

Even the cocaine trade—a decidedly modern phenomenon—has its roots in the colonial past. In Inca times, coca use was carefully controlled and only allowed for those who worked in the mines or used it for ritual purposes. The Spanish realized they could profit from the plant by allowing it to be widely available and taxing the trade. In the early seventeenth century, the leaders of the Roman Catholic Church in Cuzco received most of their incomes from tithes on the coca trade.

It wasn't just the expropriation of profits that turned many Latin Americans against foreign companies investing in their countries. The record of many such companies was appalling: they often operated with callous disregard for the environment, for local customs and practices, even for life itself. When workers for the United Fruit Company, the US banana empire, went on strike in Santa Marta, Colombia, in 1928, hundreds of them were massacred, an incident made worse by the company's attempt to cover up the scale of the slaughter. Chevron, the California-based company that is the world's third biggest oil giant, has been embroiled since the early 1990s in a lawsuit brought by tens of thousands of residents of Lago Agrio, in the Ecuadorean jungle. The locals claim that Texaco, the US oil group that Chevron bought in 2001, dumped billions of gallons of waste in hundreds of pits in the area that damaged their health and polluted large areas of the jungle. Doe Run, one of the world's biggest lead producers—owned by Ira Rennert, a New York billionaire—ran a metals smelting operation in La Oroya, a small town in Peru's central highlands, from 1997 until 2010. The smelter belched out toxic fumes that poisoned the area. Almost all local children were found to have harmful levels of lead in their blood and to suffer from bronchitis and stunted growth. In 2006, the Blacksmith Institute, a US environmental group, deemed the site one of the world's worst polluted places in an annual ranking. Peru finally terminated the company's operating license after it failed to come up with $150 million for environmental cleanup. Across South America there are dozens of similar stories.

Ultimately, the economies of South America remain, as they have been since the early colonial period, producers and exporters of natural resources for the rest of the world. Attempts to industrialize the region have historically failed. The region still depends in large measure on its metals, vast plains, oil, and gas—and therefore on the whims of the markets for those products. South America has seen extraordinary economic growth in recent years as it has been lifted by the rising tide of industrialization in China and India, but its most valuable exports to Asia remain those extracted from its earth. As it was when the conquistadores melted down the treasures of the Incas to send them home to Spain, South America remains at its heart a commodity-producing continent.

America's Backyard

These days, if four dozen young men from San Francisco were to show up in Cabo San Lucas, on the southern tip of Baja California in western Mexico, they would most likely have sunny beaches, sweaty nightclubs, and cold beers on their minds.

In 1853, things were different. When a gaunt twenty-nine-year-old Tennessean named William Walker arrived in the area that November with forty-eight followers after a three-week sea voyage from the Northern California port, he was not in the mood to party. Walker was a "filibuster"—a freebooter officially seeking to establish

English-speaking enclaves in Latin America, although perhaps more accurately a soldier of fortune out for money, land, and adventure in Latin America. As a native of the southern United States, he was a strong supporter of slavery and saw the US conquest of Mexico as both part of America's divine right and a chance to expand the reach of the slave states.

Landing in La Paz, about a hundred miles north of Cabo San Lucas, Walker declared that he was seizing control of the region and proclaimed the "Republic of Lower California," which was intended not only to be independent from Mexico but also a place where slavery would be allowed. After a skirmish with the Mexicans, Walker thought it best to retreat northward to Ensenada, just south along the coast from Tia Juana, as it was then called. There, he proclaimed he was abolishing the short-lived Republic of Lower California and instead establishing the Republic of Sonora, consisting of the two states of Lower California and Sonora—and, naturally, he would be the new country's president.

Sonora did not last long. The venture suffered from a lack of supplies, incompetence, military resistance from the Mexicans, and numerous desertions. By the following May, Walker and a handful of followers retreated back across the border into the United States.

But William Walker was persistent, and the Sonora debacle did not deter him from filibustering. A year after he reentered the United States, Walker and sixty followers set sail for Nicaragua, where a faction based in the town of León had called on him to aid them against their rivals in the country's civil war, a faction based in the city of Granada. This time, things went much better: he led the Leonese to victory on the battlefield and, with his reputation newly burnished, declared himself president of the country. At the time, Nicaragua was of great strategic significance. Since the US Pacific Railroad would not be completed for another fourteen years, the country was the main trade route between the United States' eastern and western coasts: ships from New York would take passengers and cargo up the San Juan River and across Lake Nicaragua, from where they would travel by land to the Pacific coast and on to ports in California. As president, Walker reinstated slavery, declared English an official language, and sought white immigrants from the United States. This did not go down well with his new neighbors: within a few months, Costa Rica, El Salvador, and Guatemala declared war on Walker's regime and defeated him. Walker fled and again returned to the United States. Ever persistent, he returned to Central America a few years later to help British colonists trying to set up an English-speaking government off the coast of Honduras. This time, however, he was handed over to the Hondurans, who executed him.

Walker's adventurism and that of other filibusters did not at first enjoy Washington's official blessing, although US president Franklin Pierce did recognize him as the legitimate ruler of Nicaragua. However, the filibusters were animated by the idea of Latin America as "America's backyard," part of its sphere of influence by birthright. This sentiment dated back at least to James Monroe, the fifth US president, who used his 1823 State of the Union address to warn the interfering European colonial rulers that the United States would be the only great power in the Americas. As France, Spain, Britain, and Russia vied for influence in both North and Latin America, Monroe asserted, "The American continents, by the free and independent condition which they have assumed and maintain, are henceforth not to be considered as subjects for future colonization by any European powers."

That chimed with the mood in nineteenth-century America, in which the idea had arisen of the United States having a "manifest destiny" to expand territorially. Much as the emigration of "Anglo-Saxons" to Texas—initially at the invitation of the Mexican government—led to that territory being annexed in 1845 (provoking war with Mexico), so the notion of a divinely ordained manifest destiny envisioned that wherever US citizens settled in enough numbers would eventually become part of the United States. William Walker had shown that for some, the notion of manifest destiny could also be extended deep into Latin America.

Dirty Business

The Monroe Doctrine, manifest destiny, and the notion of the countries south of the United States as constituting America's backyard were a potent combination that became an article of faith guiding US foreign policy for more than 150 years. In 1904, Teddy Roosevelt expanded

Monroe's policy, claiming that the United States had the right—even the duty—to intervene in its neighbors' domestic affairs if they threatened US investments. Roosevelt told Congress that the responsibility assumed in the Monroe Doctrine could force America, "however reluctantly, in flagrant cases of such wrongdoing or impotence, to the exercise of an international police power." What began, then, as at least in some sense an anti-imperialist code became through the twentieth century the ideological justification behind dozens of US military and covert interventions in Latin America and the Caribbean, from Walker's takeover of Nicaragua to the US Marine Corps' nineteen-year occupation of Haiti and the hapless 1961 Bay of Pigs invasion.

Walker's rule in Nicaragua, for example, came to an end largely because he found himself on the wrong side of a fight with US big business. He had accepted $20,000 from Charles Morgan and C. K. Garrison, two local subordinates of Cornelius Vanderbilt, the US railway and shipping tycoon, who were trying to build a canal through Nicaragua to serve better the transit of gold and people back and forth between California and the eastern seaboard. The deal was that once installed as president, Walker would effectively turn Vanderbilt's assets in the country over to Morgan and Garrison. When Vanderbilt learned of the betrayal, he wrote his former employees a letter that serves as a paragon of brevity and menace. "Gentlemen," he wrote, "you have undertaken to cheat me. I won't sue you, for the law is too slow. I'll ruin you. Yours truly, Cornelius Vanderbilt." The great industrialist was true to his word: he got the United States to withdraw its recognition of Walker's regime and persuaded Honduras, Guatemala, San Salvador, and Costa Rica not to recognize it in the first place. Then Vanderbilt hired the Costa Rican mercenaries who helped overthrow Walker's regime. Vanderbilt's individual clout was undeniable, but the broader message was clear: the United States would only support military ventures in Latin America so far as they were in the interests of US business.

Between 1898 and 1934 there were thirty US military incursions in the Americas. Historians debate the motivations and ideology that lay behind the interventionism, but many in the region recall them simply as adventures to protect US business interests there, from banking to oil to agriculture. In 1898, after defeating Spain, the United States annexed Puerto Rico and Guam and occupied Cuba until 1902. It occupied Cuba again from 1906 to 1909, in 1912, and from 1917 to 1922. US marines occupied the Dominican Republic from 1916 to 1924, Haiti from 1915 to 1934, and Nicaragua from 1912 to 1925 and from 1927 to 1933.

These military occupations were often about business, about extending the reach of US commercial interests, about using military might to secure and protect the smooth running of markets and the pursuit of profits. The brutality of the "banana republic"—especially as applied to United Fruit's enormous plantations—spoke to the intermingling of business and interventionism.

Smedley Butler had seen much of this firsthand. A Quaker originally from West Chester, Pennsylvania, Butler dropped out of high school and signed up to join the Marines at the tender age of sixteen in order to be able to fight in the Spanish-American War. He served thirty-three years in the US military, rising to the rank of major general and becoming the most decorated Marine of his day. He fought in Honduras, Nicaragua, Mexico, Haiti, and elsewhere, earning two Medals of Honor. His distinguished record made Butler's subsequent indictment of US military adventurism in Latin America all the more shocking. He had, he observed in 1935 in an article for *Common Sense* magazine,

> spent 33 years and four months in active military service and during that period I spent most of my time as a high class thug for Big Business, for Wall Street and the bankers. In short, I was a racketeer, a gangster for capitalism. I helped make Mexico and especially Tampico safe for American oil interests in 1914. I helped make Haiti and Cuba a decent place for the National City Bank boys to collect revenues in. I helped in the raping of half a dozen Central American republics for the benefit of Wall Street. I helped purify Nicaragua for the International Banking House of Brown Brothers in 1902–1912. I brought light to the Dominican Republic for the American sugar interests in 1916. I helped make Honduras right for the American fruit companies in 1903. . . . Looking back on it, I might have given Al Capone a few hints. The best he could do was to operate his racket in three districts. I operated on three continents.

By the time Butler was expressing his dissent publicly, US policy toward the region had already changed. As president, Franklin Roosevelt took a quite different stance from his cousin, declaring in 1933 that the United States "from now on is . . . opposed to armed intervention" in the region and proclaiming it "the good neighbor—the neighbor who resolutely respects himself and, because he does so, respects the rights of others." Whether this was inspired by a genuine change of heart or a realization that the Great Depression required a retreat of US ambitions was hard to say. In any case, it did not last long.

In the febrile Cold War atmosphere following the Second World War, the US attitude to the rest of the Americas changed again. Officially at least, the new threat was communism. At the founding of the Organization of American States in 1948, the United States persuaded the members of the new association to pledge to fight communism in the region.

The new policy was first put into effect in 1954, when the United States organized a coup in Guatemala. The country's regime had been deemed by President Dwight Eisenhower a "communist outpost on this continent." It was nothing of the sort. The government of Jacobo Árbenz may have had socialist leanings, but it was also democratic and moderate. But Árbenz had earned Washington's ire because he dared to take back land from United Fruit for use by local landless farmers. Most of the land was left fallow in any case, as was common company practice in order to shore up its near-monopoly position and in case of problems with the crop. Moreover, Árbenz had proposed to compensate the company at market rates. But the company had an important friend high up in the US security establishment: Allen Dulles, the CIA chief at the time, had formerly served as a director on United Fruit's board.

Kennedy, Castro, and Coups

If the United States had seen the specter of communism in Guatemala, it was soon to experience the real deal in Cuba. In 1959, Fidel Castro led the revolution against the violent dictatorship of Fulgencio Batista, a murderous regime the United States had supported. As in

Árbenz's Guatemala, one of Castro's principal misdemeanors as far as Washington was concerned was to nationalize industries that had formerly been in the hands of US businesses. By 1959, US companies owned about 40 percent of Cuba's sugar plantations, the entire cattle industry, 90 percent of the island's mines, 80 percent of its utilities, and the oil sector. Under Castro, the industries were nationalized.

One month before he was elected president, John F. Kennedy denounced this foreign policy failure as one of Washington's own making. "The story of the transformation of Cuba from a friendly ally to a Communist base is—in large measure—the story of a government in Washington which lacked the imagination and compassion to understand the need of the Cuban People, which lacked the leadership and vigor to move forward to meet those needs, and which lacked the foresight and vision to see the inevitable results of its own failures," Kennedy said at a Democratic party dinner in Cincinnati. "The great tragedy today is that we are repeating many of the same mistakes throughout Latin America. The same grievances—the same poverty and discontent and distrust of America which Castro rode to power are smoldering in almost every Latin nation. For we have not only supported a dictatorship in Cuba—we have propped up dictators in Venezuela, Argentina, Colombia, Paraguay and the Dominican Republic. We not only ignored poverty and distress in Cuba—we have failed in the past eight years to relieve poverty and distress throughout the hemisphere."

Kennedy had pointed to the United States' wider interference in the region. Not only had it intervened by sending in the Marines, but it had also given aid to odious regimes and remained inert in the face of their abuses of human rights. In the wake of the Second World War, the United States had established the School of the Americas, a military training institute that became notorious as a university for future dictators. Among its alumni were Leopoldo Galtieri, Argentina's last military ruler; Efraín Ríos Montt, who presided over genocide in Guatemala; Hugo Banzer Suárez, the Bolivian dictator; and Manuel Noriega, the Panamanian strongman and drug kingpin whom the United States would later oust from power.

A few months after Kennedy's Cincinnati speech, he found himself at the head of a government that had been planning a covert operation to overthrow Castro. The disastrous Bay of Pigs invasion four months later not only embarrassed the new president but also drastically strengthened Castro's position at home. It also pushed his regime closer to the Soviet Union—a development that was to herald the Cuban Missile Crisis eighteen months later.

The Bay of Pigs also undermined the most progressive agenda the United States had ever promulgated for Latin America. In March 1961, one month before the doomed invasion, Kennedy had sketched out his idea for an "Alliance for Progress," a ten-year plan to end illiteracy, establish democracy, and reform land and income inequalities across the region. Washington temporarily suspended economic and diplomatic relations with a string of dictatorships—Argentina, the Dominican Republic, Ecuador, Guatemala, Honduras, and Peru—as part of the new policy, but the plan effectively died along with Kennedy.

The United States soon reverted to form. In 1964, the year following Kennedy's assassination, Washington supported a coup against João Goulart, a Brazilian president who had dared to nationalize a local subsidiary of International Telephone & Telegraph, a US conglomerate. The following year, the United States sent twenty-three thousand troops to the Dominican Republic to help overthrow Juan Bosch, a democratically elected moderate who had promised land reform, in favor of Joaquin Balaguer, who won power in a rigged election.

In 1967, a team of US Army Green Berets was dispatched on a mission to assassinate Che Guevara, who had returned from the Congo with the aim of fomenting revolution in the heart of America's backyard—Bolivia. The CIA also sent Félix Rodríguez, a Cuban who had been involved in the Bay of Pigs fiasco, to Bolivia on a parallel mission to hunt down the revolutionary. It was he who led the team that captured Che Guevara in October 1967. Rodríguez interrogated Guevara before he was executed. In subsequent years the CIA agent, a friend of President George H. W. Bush, would proudly display a Rolex watch he took from the dead rebel leader.

And so it went on. In the 1970s, the CIA worked to undermine the government of Salvador Allende in Chile, funneled military aid to a brutal military regime in El Salvador, and backed the brutal genocide of tens of thousands of mainly indigenous people in Guatemala.

In the 1980s, the CIA funded the Contras in their bloody campaign again the Sandinista government in Nicaragua. In 1983, the United States invaded Grenada, an episode condemned even by close allies such as the United Kingdom and Canada. In 1989, it invaded Panama in pursuit of Manuel Noriega, the former School of the Americas student, whom it wanted more for being a drug trafficker than an autocratic dictator.

Given this history, it is little surprise that Latin Americans have sometimes blamed all their ills on US interventionism or their colonial legacy. It also meant that Washington was often blamed for coups and insurrections regardless of whether it was behind them or not. This sense of the United States as Latin America's political punching bag is hard to shake. In 2002, Hugo Chávez was briefly overthrown in a coup that the United States appeared to endorse. To many Latin Americans, it seemed all too familiar.

Although the history of military incursions in Latin America and the Caribbean still rankles in the region, it is poorly remembered in the United States. As in so many historical grievances, it is often easy for one side to forget quickly while resentment simmers on the other. On occasion, such amnesia can produce awkward situations. In 1988, the administration of George H. W. Bush appointed a new US ambassador to El Salvador. His name was William Walker.

The Washington Consensus

In retrospect, calling it the Washington Consensus wasn't the brightest idea.

John Williamson, the British economist who came up with the phrase in 1989, later acknowledged that it was ill-conceived. He had developed his plan in a paper for a conference of Latin American poli-cymakers in the United States, and had intended the phrase to show officials in the State Department that Latin America was on the path to free-market reforms and so worthy of debt relief. But the poor choice of words was to come back to haunt the project.

Given the history of foreign interference in the region and the United States' Cold War interventions, praising Latin Americans for adhering to views formulated in Washington was asking for trouble. It touched the region's rawest nerve: the idea that their independence and sovereignty were not absolute, but dependent on the whims of their northern neighbor. Although in reality Latin American governments in most cases implemented free-market reforms voluntarily in response to overwhelming debt burdens, recession, and rampant inflation, it gave the impression that the agenda for Latin America's economic development was being set in Washington and that the best thing the region's leaders could do was follow US policy prescriptions.

In fact, the Washington Consensus could quite easily have been called the Chicago Consensus instead—not that that would have made it any more palatable south of the border. The free-market programs mainly introduced across Latin America in the 1990s traced their origins back to the economics department at the University of Chicago in the 1970s, where Milton Friedman, the great economist, held sway. It was the "Chicago Boys"—economists trained and influenced by Friedman—who really first brought free-market reform to Latin America. In the 1970s, the military dictatorship of Augusto Pinochet in Chile brought the Chicago Boys to Santiago to shake up the country's ailing economy. They cut tariffs and privatized state-held companies. But significantly, they did not sell off the state copper company, which had been created from mines formerly owned by US companies that had been nationalized by Salvador Allende, the socialist president whom Pinochet had overthrown in 1973.

Other Latin American countries would not follow Chile's lead for another decade. When they did, it was in response to one of the most serious economic crises ever to hit a region that was somewhat prone to serious economic crises. By the early 1980s, countries across Latin America were groaning under a mountain of debt, accumulated in prior decades to pay for industrialization and infrastructure spending. By 1983, Latin America's external debts reached $315 billion, half of its entire gross domestic product. Governments simply could not afford to service their loans. In 1982, Mexico defaulted, and since the general global economy was experiencing a downturn, economic gravity could not be defied elsewhere any longer. Governments across Latin America were in a similar predicament. They tried to limit imports and boost exports in order to pay their debts. They cut public spending and devalued their currencies, prompting inflation and, in some cases, hyperinflation. Between 1982 and 1992, the region suffered what came to be known as its "lost decade." Economic growth stalled. Incomes stagnated. The poor suffered the worst.

The Washington Consensus was born from the ashes of this debt crisis. As Williamson and other economists proposed it, the rest of Latin America needed to follow Chile's lead by implementing a broad range of free-market reforms to stabilize their economies. He called for countries in the region to run small budget deficits, focus their spending on education, health, and infrastructure rather than subsidies, privatize state-owned businesses, open up their economies to foreign trade and investment, and tackle the informal sector.

Williamson was merely codifying what had already been going on in the region for several years. Latin American governments had long been transformed into disciples of the new faith. Sensing the opportunity to reduce their debt burdens, fill state coffers with the proceeds of privatizations, and curry favor with Washington and with international institutions such as the International Monetary Fund and the World Bank, they implemented the reforms with an enthusiasm that on occasion demonstrated the zeal of the newly converted. Governments across the region took dramatic steps to open their economies up to foreign investment.

Free markets did not necessarily have anything to do with free societies. Although in many instances the Washington Consensus reforms were implemented by democratically elected administrations, the original program had been put in place by Pinochet's military regime in Chile, while Alberto Fujimori's militarized pseudodemocracy enthusiastically adopted them in Peru. So Latin Americans did not necessarily come to associate the free market with democracy, since it was evidently possible to open up the economy of an autocratic society—as China was soon to demonstrate so dramatically.

The Andean countries were in many cases at the vanguard of this process. Bolivia and Peru, in particular, were among the early adopters of the Washington Consensus reforms, as was Argentina. Other countries followed them. In response, Nicholas Brady, President George H. W. Bush's treasury secretary, championed the issuing to Latin American states of "Brady bonds" aimed at lowering the interest rates on their existing debts. The Washington Consensus seemed to hold out the prospect of a new chapter in relations between the United States and Latin America. It was in this context that the Clinton administration signed the North American Free Trade Agreement and proposed a free-trade agreement that would stretch "from Alaska to Argentina."

But this wave of optimism would swiftly crash down, adding another false dawn to Latin America's long history of disappointments and leaving a legacy among many in the region of hostility to free-market policies that involved opening up their economies to the whims of international trade and investment.

The End of the Experiment

The most obvious problem was that the Washington Consensus made things better in the way that economists measure, yet worse in ways the public at large can see clearly. A primary effect was that whereas a few stood to benefit from taking over nationalized companies, many others suffered. When state-owned companies were sold into private hands, the new owners invariably shed the workers who had enjoyed steady employment when their employer was owned by the government. While privatized industries could be profitable, the societal effect was usually an increase in joblessness. When multiplied across sectors and across countries, that spelled a big rise in unemployment in the region. In the last decade of the twentieth century, formal unemployment across the region went from 5.8 percent to 10.4 percent, according to the UN Economic Commission for Latin America. To be fair, the same organization recorded a modest fall in poverty rates, from 48 percent in 1990 to 44 percent in 1999, although the region's population grew so fast that there were more Latin Americans living in poverty by 1999—211 million people—than in 1990, when 200 million lived below the poverty line. At the same time, some people were clearly making serious money from opening up the economy. Foreign investors had often done well, as had local businesspeople who had been able to take advantage of the sell-offs of state-owned companies. Probably the best example is Carlos Slim, the Mexican telephone magnate and sometimes the world's richest man (depending on stock valuations

and other variables). Slim made a $60 billion fortune by first taking
over Telmex, the Mexican telecom giant, from government control
in 1990. Understandably, such examples caused resentment, given
that the Washington Consensus had been touted as helping societies in general. This was apparently trickle-down economics without
much trickle.

Governments in the region had largely failed to take adequate account
of the societal costs of their policies. A paper published in the January
31, 2009, edition of the medical journal *Lancet* found that "shock
therapy"—the kind of rapid privatization of state-owned industries that
Latin American governments undertook in the name of the Washington
Consensus—was responsible for the early deaths of a million people
in the former Soviet bloc in the first half of the 1990s. The paper ana-
lyzed the deaths of 3 million working-age men from former communist
countries in Eastern Europe and argued that at least one-third were
victims of the widespread unemployment and social disruption that came
from mass privatization. Of course, the state-owned sector was much
larger in communist countries than in Latin America, but the research
suggested the extent to which economic dislocation can have a devastating effect on societies. In more developed economies, such as Margaret
Thatcher's Britain, free-market policies had created civil strife and social
unrest. Those effects were bound to be more pronounced in less developed economies such as those in Latin America.

Unlike advanced economies, which had gradually developed a complex web of watchdog agencies overseeing different industries, Latin
American governments lacked the know-how and manpower to regulate
privatized companies properly. When it came to the economy, there was
quite simply a lack of supervision. Because economies had been relatively closed up until that point, such oversight had not been deemed
necessary. When it came to implementing the Washington Consensus,
the policy wonks in the US government, the IMF, and the World Bank
apparently failed to realize that if you were going to open up swaths
of the economy, you might want to keep an eye on what was happening within them. Even Williamson, the brains behind the Washington
Consensus, later acknowledged that that was a serious omission from
his original plan for the region.

The consequences were soon felt in the region's banking sector. By
opening their doors to foreign investors to come in and spend money,

Latin American countries had also introduced the possibility that the same doors could swing in the opposite direction. While money initially flowed in, it could just as easily be withdrawn. That phenomenon helped to lead to the "tequila crisis" in Mexico in 1994—when lax banking oversight dented confidence in the Mexican economy and ultimately led to currency devaluation and an international bailout—and then to banking crises in Argentina and Ecuador. A similar lack of regulation and foresight meant that in practice some privatizations merely turned public monopolies into private ones.

Inadequate supervision was not the only hole in Williamson's plan. His outline of the Washington Consensus platform also failed to tackle the region's age-old problems of poverty and inequality. Economists argue over whether the Washington Consensus actually increased poverty and inequality. What is clear is that it made few inroads into cutting them. The region was among the most unequal in the world, where persistent, grinding poverty existed alongside fabulous, opulent displays of wealth. If anything was holding back Latin America's economies, it was this structural imbalance. It hampered the development of a mass consumer economy and a dynamic workforce capable of competing in a globalizing world. It aggravated social tensions and killed ambition. It condemned large sections of the population to perpetual indigence, generation after generation.

In the developed world, the state, through taxes and benefits, makes a significant contribution to combating poverty and inequality. But Latin America simply lacked extensive social programs, and the opening up of economies was not accompanied by policies that might have offset the worst effects and encouraged social mobility. The thinking—against all evidence—was apparently that what was expected to be a rising tide of resulting economic growth would simply lift everyone to a better standard of living.

The problem with this notion was that the Washington Consensus did not result in economic growth—at least not at first. The introduction of the reforms was followed by a further five-year period of economic stagnation across the region from 1998 to 2003. In 2001, in the midst of this sluggish growth across the region, Argentina's economy collapsed, after a recession led to a run on the banks, prompting the government to freeze deposits and causing angry demonstrations. Unsurprisingly, many Latin Americans blamed the Washington Consensus. Free-market economists noted that Argentina's problems were largely confined to that country and of its own making, but it was hardly unreasonable that in the minds of many in the region, the one caused the other. The perceived injury was aggravated by the fact that the United States merely stood and watched while Argentina crumbled.

Growth across Latin America only really picked up in about 2004. The fuel for that was mainly the rise of China, a phenomenon that would transform South America in particular, as the communist country's rapid industrialization created a seemingly unslakable thirst for raw materials, from the metals that were plentiful across the region to the soya grown on the vast plains of Brazil. Supporters of the Washington Consensus—by then a sullied brand—argued that the growth showed the reforms that had been introduced a decade earlier were finally paying off. By that point, however, it was a tough argument to make. In Central America, economic growth after 2004 was more based on manufacturing and assembling products for the US market, but in South America it was largely driven by higher prices for the region's natural resources. Growth seemed not so much due to anything the region had done for itself, but rather the benign effect of China's industrialization and the astonishing increase in the prices of such commodities as oil, copper, gold, silver, lead, and other minerals such as molybdenum that had hitherto been known only to mining geeks and periodic table enthusiasts. To argue that the Washington Consensus had finally proved its worth was to contend that countries in the region would have been less able to benefit from the rise in commodity prices had they not introduced free-market reforms, or that if China and other emerging world economies had not industrialized, a more open South America would nevertheless have broken into a virtuous cycle of economic growth. The strength of such arguments was far from self-evident.

The Washington Consensus had one very important effect in South America: it spurred widespread support for the nationalizing tendencies of Hugo Chávez, Evo Morales, and Rafael Correa, which took hold in the wake of the "lost half-decade" of 1998–2003. Their plans to nationalize privatized industries were a direct response to the rapid implementation of free-market reforms. Without the Washington Consensus—let's imagine, for example, that Latin American governments had opened up their economies slowly, gradually, and without the blessing of Washington—Chávez might not have become an economic radical, and Morales and Correa might never have been elected. These leaders responded to the widespread discontent with free-market reforms by "reclaiming" industries that had formerly been in state hands and by nationalizing companies in other sectors they deemed to be strategically important to the functioning of the economy. Given the history of the Washington Consensus, many in the region approved of this policy. But free marketeers urged them to stay the course. While the radicals argued that the lost half-decade had been caused by the Washington Consensus, they contended that the reforms had not gone far enough. The true Washington Consensus, they said, had been implemented at best partially, incompetently, or halfheartedly, and the region needed to press on with increasingly free-market economic policies. But the Washington Consensus brand and its accompanying planks—such as privatization—had been irrevocably damaged. Arguing for a return to the "true" Washington Consensus sounded a bit like those die-hard Marxists who contended after the fall of the Soviet Union that true communism had never been tried. The fact was that back in the world of political reality, South America could not easily again be persuaded to become a laboratory for the economic think tankers of the developed world.

4

Resource Nationalism

I arrived in Caracas in March 2007 to discover that my hotel was being nationalized.

The place was living its final months as a Hilton. It showed. The room was shabby and drab. The ceiling tiles in the bathroom were filthy, and water was dripping through from upstairs. The furniture looked like it had been purchased thirty years earlier. The carpets were threadbare in some places. The TV was an old clunker, with peripatetic cable channel reception. The hotel occupied a vast double-tower complex in the center of town and had clearly once been very grand, one of the finest places to stay in the capital, I was assured. Now its cavernous conference halls and ballrooms were mostly empty—except for the few days during my stay that it was used for auditions for *Latin American Idol*, the TV pop-singing talent show. The central location had formerly been highly desirable. Now the area was seedy, and the guests were warned to take great care walking around, even during the day. The Venezuelan state owned the lease for the building and had told the company to pack up and leave by that May. Government officials often used the hotel when they needed accommodations in Caracas—Danny Glover, the American movie star, had apparently once stayed there as a guest of the Venezuelan state—and now they had clearly decided they were fed up with paying the Hiltons for the privilege.

The fate of the Caracas Hilton summed up the mood in Venezuela. Hugo Chávez had recently been reelected president for the third time, and he had decided to move his Bolivarian revolution up a gear. All around Caracas, giant red posters reminded people of the "five motors" of the revolution. Images of Chávez were everywhere, from the ubiquitous graffiti to the "twenty-first-century socialism" wristwatches on sale in the street markets. After eight years in power, Chávez was moving to expand the power of the state over the Venezuelan economy. He was in the process of extending government control over facilities in the Orinoco River basin—one of the richest sources of hydrocarbons in the world—which were under the control of foreign energy companies. That would give Caracas complete power over the entire oil sector. At the same time, the government was gearing up to nationalize the telecom and electricity industries.

Although it was hard to believe it in the heat of the revolutionary fervor gripping the capital, Chávez had not always been like this. When he was first elected president, he had struck a decidedly moderate tone. Unsure of his intentions, foreign oil companies had put some of their investment plans on hold. The president-elect had rushed to reassure them. "We are going to instill confidence, and that's my first message to investors," he told the Venevision TV network as the results of his first presidential election victory streamed in on December 6, 1998. "You, the investor: if you have capital abroad, bring it here." In a world where the menswear is the message, Chávez ditched his fatigues and red paratrooper's beret for a sober business suit and tie. He declared himself a follower of the "third way" between free-market capitalism and state-dominated socialism, an idea promulgated by another young, charismatic new leader—Tony Blair, who had been elected British prime minister a year earlier.

Venezuela's oil industry was already in state hands. The government had been actively involved in the sector since 1943, when it determined that all oil revenues had to be split 50–50 between the state and the foreign companies that controlled the pumping. In 1976, Venezuela's president, Carlos Andrés Pérez, nationalized the oil sector and created Petroleos de Venezuela (PDVSA), the state-owned energy company.

By the time Chávez took over the country twenty-three years later, PDVSA had grown dramatically. Its proven oil reserves had increased by 420 percent and its natural gas reserves had grown by 360 percent. It had a world-class research center and had expanded well beyond Venezuela's borders, with ownership stakes in refineries in Germany, Belgium, the United Kingdom, Sweden, and the United States. PDVSA owned the Citgo chain of thirteen thousand US gas stations, giving it 10 percent of that market.

While this expansion had earned PDVSA a reputation as an important player in the global oil industry, many on the Left thought the state company had become more interested in pursuing international linkups and collaborations with foreign oil companies in Venezuela than in making money for the state. The critics pointed out that the amount of money per barrel of oil that actually went to the government's coffers was about half the amount that Brazil's state oil company returned to its government, and a quarter of the amount Mexico's state energy company produced for its political masters. Partly that was because many of PDVSA's international ventures and partnerships with foreign companies were taxed at a relatively low rate. Partly it was because the kind of heavy crude oil found in Venezuela was expensive to process and required a lot of investment to keep fields productive.

This wasn't really about money, though, since PDVSA still supplied the government with about half of all its revenues. Really it was about the company's relative autonomy. Even from his earliest moments as president, Chávez signaled that this was a problem, saying that PDVSA's budget and operations should be determined by national political interests rather than corporate goals. "It cannot be seen as a state within a state," he said over and over again in media interviews following his 1998 election victory. Chávez, who was later to emerge as the Great Nationalizer, even floated the idea that some of PDVSA's operations and overseas assets could be privatized. So as he took office, the stage for a confrontation was set. Three years passed before Chávez and PDVSA finally took each other on, but when they did so, they battled over much more than just oil revenues: the very future of Venezuela was at stake, and the conflict would be suitably violent and bloody.

Politics Trumps Economics

In the early years of his presidency, Chávez's economic policy was not especially radical. Nevertheless, the political uncertainty that had clouded his early days only grew worse as time passed. Deep tensions opened up between the government and much of the rest of society.

Chávez's political reforms, such as the new constitution, mixed with his confrontational rhetoric, had earned him many enemies in Venezuela—particularly in the business world, among much of the media, and the Catholic Church. By early 2002, the Venezuelan economy was in bad shape, hit by the low price of oil after 9/11 and the withdrawal from the country of billions of dollars by private companies and individuals who did not trust Chávez. The president responded with economic orthodoxy: cutting the government budget, reducing its borrowing plans, and letting the currency float freely. In his first few years in office, he had made various attempts to take a firmer grasp of PDVSA but had always been stymied by its management and powerful unions. Now Chávez decided it was finally time to bring control of PDVSA within his grasp. In February, he fired some top staff at the state oil company—including its chairman, a well-respected army brigadier whom Chávez had installed but who had rebelled and taken the company's side against the government.

PDVSA openly turned on the government. Its management, which had previously enjoyed the private sector–like status that had enabled it to focus on making a profit, said it was tired of being treated like an ATM. The government was not paying its energy bills and, its senior management said in an extraordinary press statement in late February 2002, was "pushing the company to the verge of operational and financial collapse" by imposing political rather than commercial criteria.

Chávez responded by firing more of PDVSA's top executives. The next day, the country's main trade union body and the biggest business association began an indefinite general strike against his government, saying they would continue their work stoppage until Chávez stepped down. Two days into the strike, violence broke out as hundreds of thousands of people marched in support of the sacked PDVSA managers and encountered Chavista protesters, who were shown on live TV firing into the crowd. Some Caracas police officers returned fire, and in the exchange nineteen people were killed. As the violence raged, Chávez ordered the army to put down the protest. When his top generals refused, the game appeared to be up. The generals told Chávez they would help him flee to Cuba. And so in the midst of the popular protests against the president, the military effectively overthrew him.

It was perhaps the worst-organized coup of all time, in that the military hadn't actually thought about who would take Chavez's place. This led to a bizarre coup within a coup: Pedro Carmona, leader of the business association that was behind the general strike, was installed as president and immediately began to alienate his former allies. First, he installed a cabinet of his ultra-right-wing business friends, failing to include any of the unions that had also planned the strike. Second, he announced he was immediately shutting down the National Assembly and the Supreme Court, and he scrapped the new Chavista constitution, approved by a large majority of Venezuelans two years earlier. This annoyed not only residents of the *ranchos*—shantytowns on the hillsides surrounding Caracas—who were still loyal to Chávez, but many others as well, including the generals who had forced him out. There were more mass demonstrations as the country now mobilized against the new regime. Carmona did not have long to enjoy the feel of the presidential sash: within a few days, he was out and Chávez was restored to power by sympathetic army units.

The momentary coup once again reinforced the power of the street, which had unseated two presidents in three days, and of the military. It strengthened the president's hand: loyal forces on the street and within the military had won the day, enabling him to purge disloyal officers within the ranks. By contrast, the failed coup exposed how ill-formed was the plan to depose Chávez and how inept the plotters. It also further tainted the reputation of the United States, which in the mind of Chavistas had orchestrated and collaborated with the coup. Washington might not have played such a direct role, but it had certainly known of the impending coup and had been painfully slow to condemn it. But the coup had left unresolved the issue that had started it all: the relationship between the government and PDVSA.

By December, the fight was back on. This time, PDVSA's management joined a national strike, and oil production by Venezuela, the world's fifth biggest producer of oil, was reduced to a trickle. The strike dragged on for two months. In a country whose economy was propped up by oil revenues, its effect was disastrous. One of the most oil-rich countries on earth was forced to import gasoline. People waited in long lines of cars for hours—and sometimes days—at filling stations to pump their ration of gasoline. The lines got so bad that a market for places in line even sprang up. Black-market vendors went from car to car, offering gas for fifteen times more than the usual price. Few observers could believe that the standoff between the strikers and the government could last so long. The Venezuelan economy, starved of its only real source of income, was on its knees. The government was forced to introduce exchange controls to offer some feeble protection to its currency, which lost about a third of its value in one month. The strikers held out, apparently gambling that Chávez would either resort to violence against them—risking the army's support in the process— or that he would be forced to negotiate. Both sides hardened: the strikers now simply wanted Chávez to step down rather than face a referendum on his rule. They called him a dictator and an autocrat; he called them fascists and oligarchs.

Internationally, there was enormous interest in how this grand arm-wrestle would end. The world was also paying a price for the deadlock in Venezuela: the paralysis in production had helped add five dollars to the price of a barrel of oil. With a US attack on Iraq looking increasingly likely, oil analysts fretted about how much higher energy prices would go if conflicts broke out on two fronts.

Ultimately the oil strike ended not with a bang but a whimper. First, the government managed to persuade tanker pilots to return to work, so ships already loaded with oil could be moved. Then, a few weeks later, the striking oil workers trickled back to work. The opposition had underestimated Chávez again: his government had simply showed it had more stamina than the strikers. As he had done with the military, the president rooted out his opponents within PDVSA, firing almost half of the company's forty thousand workers.

The coup and the strike had not only failed to dislodge Chávez, they had reinforced his rule. He had defeated his opponents twice, he had established control over the military, and he had brought PDVSA's precious revenues within his grasp.

Chávez's attitude toward foreign oil companies at the time was reasonably friendly. Although he had reversed Venezuela's policy of allowing majority private stakes in oil production, he had opened up refining and the gas industry for private investors. Rather, the strike had been about control. The resources were already in the hands of the state. But PDVSA acted at arm's length from the government, and for Chávez that meant it was effectively pursuing its own autonomous interests and no longer necessarily serving those of the country. The oil industry had been nationalized to give the people of Venezuela ownership of their nation's natural resources, not to create a corporate behemoth that was primarily concerned with its own growth and development. Just as private oil companies were charged with maximizing profits for their shareholders—their ultimate owners—so, he reasoned, the state oil company should concern itself with returning as much money as possible to the government of the day. Just as important, Chávez now had complete control over *where* oil could be sent—and most of it was going to supply the United States, accounting for 14 percent of Americans' needs. Now Chávez could somewhat credibly claim to have a knife pressed to Washington's throat. He would soon begin to threaten to cut off supplies to the United States. Were the threats credible? After all, Venezuela needed the US market as much as the United States needed Venezuelan production. Nevertheless, they still sent a shudder through Washington. With Chávez in charge, it was perfectly clear that economic concerns could be subjugated to political ones if necessary—regardless of the consequences—so no one could ever be completely sure of his intentions.

Chávez's battle with PDVSA set the tone for the policies of resource nationalism that would stage a comeback in South America in the coming years. Strictly speaking, this wasn't a nationalization, because officially the state had always been in control of PDVSA. But like the policies of economic nationalism that were to follow, Chávez versus PDVSA had been a political struggle. He had succeeded in securing the very basis of resource nationalism—the use of natural resources to pursue political ends. Similarly, as governments in the region moved to expand government control over the economy (particularly those parts that dealt with natural resources), it wasn't that they had an economic goal in mind—such as securing more investment in extractive industries or boosting the production of oil or gas or precious metals—but rather that they sought to seize government control of these industries to fulfill a political purpose. They were going to take over these parts of the economy regardless of the consequences. The primary motivation of Chávez, Morales, and Correa was political, not some long-term economic strategy. This is a critical point, because those who criticize economically nationalistic leaders usually try to do so with economic reasoning—that what they are doing will scare away foreign investors, that it will harm output, that it is economically unsustainable. But for the resource nationalist, long-term economic sustainability is less important than asserting immediate political control over the country's economic levers, even if that comes at a considerable cost.

When PDVSA was semiautonomous, the size of the pie may have been growing, but who cared if all you got were crumbs? With the state company in government hands, output might be less, but it was completely at Chávez's whim. Economic success may be measured in terms of revenues and profits, but political success is judged in terms of power and control, popularity and election victories. By taking control of PDVSA, Chávez could use its revenues to increase social spending and pump funds into popular government programs, even if they weren't remotely sensible in economic terms. The year after the oil began to flow again, he faced a recall election, a key demand in the early days of the strike. Some 58 percent of Venezuelans voted for Chávez to stay. Few had expected the president to survive a coup, a devastating strike, and a recall vote. In doing so, Chávez had proved that winning the battle for control of resources was the key to political success.

A South American Tradition

Nationalization was hardly new for South America. Some three decades earlier, the continent had undergone a previous convulsion of resource nationalism. On seizing power in Peru in 1968, Juan Velasco, a left-wing general, had taken over the International Petroleum Company, which was owned by Standard Oil, the US energy giant (and the predecessor to today's ExxonMobil). He went on to nationalize vast swaths of the economy—mining, fisheries, telecommunications, and energy—and to expropriate large landholdings, which he broke up and gave to the rural poor. In 1969, Bolivia nationalized the facilities operated by Gulf Oil of the United States. In the 1970s, Salvador Allende in

Chile nationalized the copper mining and banking industries, while in Venezuela, Carlos Andrés Pérez oversaw the nationalization of the oil industry.

Economic nationalism in the region had a much longer and richer history. In the 1930s and 1940s, Latin American economic nationalism was aimed at industrializing what remained largely agrarian societies, with the goal of increasing domestic manufacturing to replace goods that had to be imported from abroad. The argument was similar to an economically nationalist sentiment you often hear in contemporary America: that reducing dependence on foreign oil imports will make the country freer to make policy in terms of its own interests. Latin American economic nationalists argued that they were doubly dependent: both on imports and on the export of commodities like oil, metals, and coffee. Only industrial self-sufficiency, they thought, would give them genuine national sovereignty.

Such protectionism spurred the rapid growth of cities, as peasants left the countryside in search of industrial jobs. Since the industrial jobs never really materialized, that in turn caused unemployment, which in due course led to the street protests that were ultimately to propel Chávez and friends to power. It also meant that although global trade increased in the decades after the Second World War, less and less of it flowed through Latin America, since exporting manufactured goods was seen as acting against the spirit of economic self-sufficiency.

Because the state was now effectively sponsoring industrial production and playing a large role in the economy, economic nationalism also aided corruption, since there were now all sorts of favors that business needed from government and was prepared to pay for. To avoid mass protests, leaders also tended toward populism, lavishing cash ad hoc on short-term measures to win the support of the urban masses. So in its own way, economic nationalism contributed to urbanization, corruption, and populism in Latin America.

The resource nationalism of the first few years of the twenty-first century was different, in that it was much more of a reaction against the shock therapy of the Washington Consensus. At the same time, in the broader historical context, the economic policy pendulum in Latin America had often swung back and forth between a state-dominated economy and a free market. Neither nationalization nor economic shock therapy solved the essential Latin American problems of inequality, poverty, weak political institutions, and corruption, so when one failed to work, the pendulum had a habit of swinging back in the opposite direction.

But if the region had long lacked the sort of broad-based economic development that would help a lot of its population to drag itself out of grinding poverty, and its democratic governments had been weak since birth, why did the pendulum happen to swing in the middle of the first decade of the twenty-first century?

The answer may have more to do with Asia than South America. By the turn of the century, the emerging markets of that continent— particularly China and India—were industrializing fast. As they did so, they sucked in resources like never before. The commodities that South America produces—oil, metal, soybeans—soared to prices that were not only historical highs, but had never been imagined before. As the value of their exports rose dramatically, the people of the region naturally became impatient to experience the benefits. At times, as in the mining areas of Peru, they would demand that foreign companies spend more in the actual regions where they were removing the natural resources. More often, they demanded that their governments take a larger share of the profits the companies were making. So resource nationalism was often more impelled from below than imposed from above. Before Evo Morales and Rafael Correa became presidents, their countries' legislatures were threatening tax hikes on foreign investors and seizing privately operated facilities. By the time they won office, the groundwork for the state taking more control over the economy was well set.

The bare-knuckle fight between Chávez and PDVSA had been a historic tussle for Venezuela, but apart from concerns over the effect it would have on oil prices, it was primarily a domestic issue. But when resource nationalism exploded in the Andes, the really contentious bit was the treatment of foreign-owned companies. When they got squeezed, the rest of the world started to pay very close attention.

Defying Count Dracula

Evo Morales's nationalization of the Bolivian gas industry was probably the moment when that happened. But the declaration capped years of political strife in the country over the gas issue. In 2003, the administration of Gonzalo Sánchez de Lozada was brought down by massive street protests against a gas export plan. The following year, his successor tried to defuse the issue by holding a nationwide referendum on the gas issue, in which the country overwhelmingly authorized increasing taxes and royalties in the gas industry to 50 percent. But the debate over how to arrive at that figure spurred more mass protests, and the new president also fell. By that point, it was clear that the gas industry would have to be nationalized—so clear that all three main candidates for the presidency promised to do so. In fact, Morales had originally supported the idea of raising taxes rather than nationalizing, but he had seen which way the wind was blowing and changed his rhetoric accordingly. Once he'd put in motion the gas nationalization, he subsequently announced plans to nationalize the mining industry, telecommunications, and the electric power sector.

While Bolivia's political leaders were tussling over raising taxes in the gas industry, Ecuador's president (Correa's predecessor) also said he wanted to raise taxes on foreign investors in his country's oil industry, from 20 percent to 50 percent. The following year his government slapped a 50 percent tax on the "extraordinary profits"—the difference between the price of oil at the time the original contracts were drawn up and the current oil price—being earned by foreign oil companies. A few weeks after Morales made his gas nationalization decree in Bolivia, Ecuador kicked out Occidental, a US oil company that was the biggest foreign investor in the country, saying it had violated the terms of its contract, and seized $1 billion in assets, handing them over to Petroecuador, the state energy company.

Later that year, Correa was elected president. Although he did not pledge to nationalize anything and stressed that he wasn't interested in having the government run the entire oil industry, the following year he decided that the foreign oil companies still operating in Ecuador weren't being squeezed enough and raised the tax on extraordinary profits from 50 percent to 99 percent. Understandably, the companies weren't too happy. A French company, Perenco, got involved in a dispute with the government about back payments, and by July 2009, it had left Ecuador in a huff, with the state seizing its assets. Along the way, Correa had also taken control of the local subsidiary of a Brazilian construction company, saying a hydroelectric plant it had built was not up to snuff. So although he was not officially pursuing a strategy of nationalization, under Correa the state extended its control over the economy. The following year, Correa gave foreign oil companies four months to agree to shift from production-sharing agreements to pure service contracts. The state would own the oil and gas produced and the multinationals would simply receive a fee for their work. Noble Energy, a US firm, pulled out rather than accept the terms, while Petrobras, Brazil's state-owned company, refused to operate its oil fields under the new arrangement.

Back in Venezuela, although Chávez had been squeezing international companies, he caught on relatively late to the idea of nationalizing them. In 2006, as Morales was taking on the international energy companies in Bolivia, the Venezuelan president raised taxes on foreign oil companies, but he only really got going the following year. First up, Chávez retook government control of the telecom industry and snapped up two electricity providers that had been owned by US corporations. Not bad for a warm-up. But the main course was to secure state control over operations in the Orinoco belt—a region that Venezuela claims may contain up to 300 billion barrels of oil, giving the country the biggest oil reserves in the world, which would be even more oil than in Saudi Arabia. The oil there is a kind of extra-heavy crude, which is both tricky and pricey to extract, so in the 1990s the area was opened up to private companies, which supplied the necessary investment to get the black gold out. All through Chávez's rule, the price of a barrel of oil had been rising. In 1999, when he first won the presidency, crude was hovering at just above $10 a barrel. By 2007, it was at about $55 and rising, pumping revenues into the state's coffers.

Chávez now decided to use the cash to buy the rest of the oil industry, and told the companies they would now have to take minority stakes, with control being handed over to PDVSA. Most of the companies agreed, including Chevron of the United States, the British oil giant BP, and France's Total. Two American companies—ConocoPhillips and ExxonMobil—refused the new terms, packed their bags, and threatened to pursue Venezuela in court.

That failed to sour Chávez's newfound taste for nationalization. The following year he took over a dairy producer, a cold storage company, the cement industry, the country's biggest steelmaker, and Banco de Venezuela, one of the nation's largest banks, which had been owned up to that point by Santander, the Spanish banking group. The year after that he nationalized or closed a string of smaller banks, took over a rice mill owned by Cargill of the United States, a tuna cannery, a pasta factory, two coffee-roasting companies, and a sugar mill, saying they were helping to cause food shortages. When the owners of Aeropostal, the Venezuelan airline, were arrested by Interpol for drug trafficking, Chávez said he would take over the airline as well. In 2010, he expropriated the local subsidiaries of Owens-Illinois, the US glassmaking company; Gruma, the Mexican food group; and a steel company. In Bolivia, Morales extended his nationalization policy to the electricity industry and even suggested nationalizing the Bolivian soccer team after they failed to qualify for the 2010 World Cup.

In some cases, these nationalizations were paid for, albeit with the amount of compensation usually set by the government and with the balance sometimes not actually being settled for years on end. Thanks to China and India, the high price of commodities had given South American countries the resources to pay. Those that were not paid for were simply expropriated outright. Although Correa shied away from using the term "nationalization," Ecuador frequently confiscated assets formerly owned by foreign investors. However, probably its biggest appropriation—that of Occidental— had been carried out before Correa became president.

In spite of the traditional rhetoric employed by the "new Left" about South American unity, their nationalizations showed little favor to companies from neighboring countries, even when they were state-owned. Bolivia had angered Argentina and Brazil with its gas nationalization. Correa's Ecuador seized the operations of Odebrecht, a Brazilian construction firm, and threatened to expel Petrobras. In Venezuela, Chávez expropriated the assets of Cemex of Mexico and took control of Sidor, a steel producer owned by Techint from Argentina.

Relatively few foreign companies were expelled or withdrew altogether from the region. Although they grumbled, many international investors chose to stay on, even though they were now paying much higher taxes or were relegated to operating as junior partners.

In a region where the opening up of markets had failed to bring economic development to those who needed it most, where the politicians who had first struck the deals with foreign companies were hopelessly discredited, where the vast profits being reaped from natural resources were being spirited out of the country, resource nationalism was popular. Most people might not have shared the ideological justification behind extending state control, but they instinctively thought the repatriation of profits from a poor part of the world was plain wrong, in the same way that American or European voters tend to get indignant about companies and wealthy individuals avoiding taxes by moving their investments offshore. In Venezuela, the nationalizations only boosted the standing of Chávez, who portrayed them as liberation from bloodsucking multinationals. "We were tired of all our oil going to Count Dracula," he told the leaders of the African Union at a summit in Banjul, Gambia, in July 2006. "Now Venezuela is free and we have recovered control over our oil." In Ecuador and Bolivia, resource nationalism preceded the leaders who would become associated with it. They did not win power and then impose a program of economic nationalism. On the contrary, they won because they promised to extend government control. After the failures of the Washington Consensus, the economic pendulum had swung very firmly back toward the state.

Economic Xenophobia

If the nationalizations of the early twenty-first century caused a hullabaloo, at least they didn't start a war.

On Valentine's Day in 1879, Bolivia seized the assets of the Antofagasta Nitrate and Rail Company of Chile, after it refused to agree to the tax hikes La Paz was demanding. The company was extracting saltpeter, a nitrate deposit used to make explosives, from the northern Atacama Desert in Bolivia's Pacific coastal region. The Chileans reacted furiously, sending troops to occupy the main local town. Within a few weeks, the two countries were at war. Peru, which had made a secret pact with Bolivia, threw in its lot against the Chileans.

The War of the Pacific—or the "Saltpeter War"—dragged on for five years and ended with a rout of Bolivia and Peru. For Peru, defeat was humiliating. Chile occupied its two southernmost cities, returning only one of them in 1929. For Bolivia, it was devastating. The nation was forced to give up its coastline and the valuable nitrate and copper deposits that sat underneath, becoming the landlocked country it remains today.

Unsurprisingly, this caused profound resentment in Bolivia and Peru. What is viewed as a deep historical injustice remains an open wound. One of the central and abiding pledges of Bolivian leaders is to regain their coastline. Bolivia continues to press Santiago through international organizations. Its own influence on Chile is somewhat limited: the two countries cut diplomatic ties over the issue in 1978. In 2009, Chilean architects put forward a plan to bore a ninety-mile-long tunnel under Chile to the ocean. The plan was ingenious, but it also indicated how remote Bolivia's coastal aspirations remained. Bolivia retains the biggest navy of any landlocked country, with more than five thousand personnel and over 170 boats stationed on Lake Titicaca, more than 150 miles from the Pacific. When Bolivia plays Chile at soccer, the Bolivian fans wave plastic boats. Bolivia still marks a poignant "Day of the Sea" every year on March 23, the date of the war's first battle, in which heavily outnumbered Bolivian soldiers and civilians resisted the Chilean army's advance. The day is marked with a five-minute silence, during which Bolivians listen solemnly to the sounds of the sea piped over a PA system. The navy marches, the president of the day vows to regain the country's coastline, and the crowd merrily burns the Chilean flag.

So when in 2003 Gonzalo Sánchez de Lozada, the Bolivian president, took up a proposal to export Bolivia's precious gas reserves by building a pipeline through Chile (the historic enemy) to be exported north to Mexico and the United States (another historic enemy), the reaction back home was not exactly warm. At first, protesters demanded that the gas be piped through Peru instead—even though that was likely to make the proposed pipeline $600 million more expensive to build. Ultimately the protests escalated, collecting all sorts of grievances against the government, until Sánchez de Lozada sent in troops to confront the demonstrations, dozens of people were killed, and the president was forced to hotfoot it to Miami. Largely because of the deaths and the successful ousting of a pro-free-market president, the "Gas War" is seen by the Left as a heroic struggle against the pillaging of the country's natural resources and the pivotal moment at which the demand for nationalization took hold nationwide. But it is reasonably clear that one of the protests' main motivations was hatred of Chile. On that score, even deeply divided Bolivia is reasonably united.

The case of the Gas War underlines something that many sympathizers of Morales, Chávez, and Correa prefer to ignore: that the nationalism part of resource nationalism is strong and ever-present. One of the key motivations for economic nationalism is present in any kind of nationalism—xenophobia.

When social problems arise in South America, it is usual to blame foreigners—after all, why would the locals make trouble? Venezuelans and Ecuadoreans take a dim view of Colombians. Brazil has tense relations with Argentina. Peruvians do not really trust any of their neighbors. And the Chileans are pretty much disliked by everyone else. Of course, these are all gross generalizations, which is why they are accurate more often than not.

When tensions are high, conflict can break out fairly easily. In 1932, Bolivia and Paraguay, its southern neighbor, went to war over postage stamps. Bolivia issued a stamp featuring a map of its territory that included the disputed border region of Gran Chaco. Paraguay responded by issuing a larger stamp, including Chaco in its map. The stamps became bigger and bigger until the two sides eventually went to battle over the region. (Bolivia lost the three-year conflict, ceding much of the Gran Chaco region to Paraguay.) Peru and Ecuador have fought three wars over their border, most recently in 1995.

The militaristic side of this nationalism remains—particularly when former military officers such as Chávez and Ollanta Humala get into politics. Under Chávez, Venezuela undertook a huge increase in military spending, sparking concerns about a "new arms race" in South America. Some of this saber-rattling was aimed at the United States, some at regional rivals such as Colombia and Chile. Superficially, there may seem little to connect an economic policy of expanding state control and a defense policy based on massive increases in military spending. But at the heart of both was nationalism.

Evo Morales's standard presidential campaign speech in rural areas included a vow to stop imports of cheap Peruvian potatoes from entering the country, a pledge usually greeted with ecstatic cheers. Similarly, in an address in Gamarra, Lima's garment district, I heard Humala promise to stop China from dumping low-cost textiles in

Peru. And of course, one of the favorite themes for the radical Latin American Left has always been anti-Americanism, which encompasses xenophobia, anti-imperialism, and hatred of "neoliberalism."

Nationalism has a long history in Latin America, dating back to the struggles for independence from Spain and Portugal, and had proved itself to be politically ambidextrous: right-wing military juntas employed nationalistic rhetoric as much as left-wing governments. Unlike in racially homogeneous states such as Chile and Argentina, in Andean countries with large indigenous populations, nationalism and xenophobia were often a way to divert attention from ethnic and class tensions.

But the indigenous population also produced a different kind of nationalism—one based on indigenous identity and resistance to the national political and economic systems that had kept them at the margins of power. This movement was particularly strong in the Andes, tracing its roots back to at least the eighteenth century, when indigenous resistance fighters such as the Peruvian Túpac Amaru II and the Bolivian Túpac Katari fought against the Spanish occupation of their countries. In the modern era, indigenous campaigns tended to focus on the defense of land and resources, increasing indigenous representation or influence in decision making, and protecting practice, culture, and language.

By the late twentieth century, this was translating itself into mainstream politics. Ecuador's indigenous movement was perhaps the best organized in the Americas. CONAIE, the main indigenous organization, helped topple three presidents since its formation in 1990. In 1996, it formed Pachakutik, a political party whose leaders went on to hold senior government ministerial positions. In 1997, Evo Morales and three others from the forerunner to his MAS (Movement to Socialism) party won seats in Congress for the first time. By the time Morales was campaigning to be president, the *wiphala*, a multicolored indigenous flag, was far more common at his rallies than the Bolivian flag itself. In Peru, the indigenous movement was weaker. In 2001, Alejandro Toledo became South America's first indigenous president, although the optimism surrounding his election quickly evaporated as it became clear that consuming Johnnie Walker Blue Label, an expensive blended Scotch whisky, was a higher priority for him than confronting poverty. Nevertheless, the flexing of indigenous political muscle was increasingly obvious in countless local and regional protests, which highlighted how international companies were exploiting traditional land rights or damaging the environment of native farmland. Globalization enabled these groups to find international allies among environmentalists, human rights activists, and antipoverty campaigners.

So nationalism—both of the conventional and indigenous varieties—was an important part of the radical South American project. To be sure, a primary motivation of resource nationalism was the ideological opposition to capitalism and globalization. But it was also about good old-fashioned national pride—and in South America, that included a healthy dose of chauvinism and animosity toward one's neighbors.

Return of the State

Had the nationalizations in the Andes been isolated incidents, the world might have been able to dismiss them as aberrations, the twitchings of the lifeless corpse of socialism or antiglobalism, historical irrelevances doomed to speedy failure.

But they were far from the extreme margins of history. Indigenous politics might have lent a unique flavor to the Andean version of economic nationalism, but it was at the forefront of a global phenomenon, with echoes in Asia, Europe, Russia, Africa, the Middle East, and yes, even the United States. Particularly in resource-rich but economically poor (or at least historically poor) countries, governments increasingly tightened the terms on which international companies could operate, forcing on them joint ventures with state institutions and on occasion expelling them altogether. As oil prices crept ever higher—by July 2008 they hit a high of more than $147 a barrel—the pressure on foreign investors grew stronger. At the same time, the world saw the reemergence of the state as a financial force, with China's state-owned institutions buying everything from access to resources to stakes in Wall Street banks and swaths of the US commercial property market, and sovereign wealth funds snapping up high-profile assets in Europe and the United States.

Within South America, economic nationalism spread beyond the Andes. When Brazil discovered huge amounts of oil and natural gas in a deep offshore reserve hiding beneath a layer of salt, the country's leaders proposed creating a new wholly state-owned oil company to exploit them—unlike Petrobras, more than 60 percent of whose capital is held by minority investors. In 2010, when Brazil issued $67 billion worth of stock in Petrobras—the biggest share offering in history—it structured the deal so as to give the state stronger control of the company, as its share of the oil firm's capital rose from 40 to 48 percent (the state had, in any case, always retained a majority of the voting stock). Argentina's government renationalized the airline Aerolíneas Argentinas, took over a military aircraft company from the US defense contractor Lockheed Martin, and seized control of the country's private pension system. In 2010, Chile increased the top royalty rate on mining companies from 5 percent to 14 percent.

The state was also making a triumphant return elsewhere in the world. Libya hiked tax rates on foreign oil companies and threatened to nationalize them. Kazakhstan forced foreign investors to reduce their stakes in its oil fields and hand them over to the state energy company. Algeria expelled Repsol, the Spanish oil and gas multinational. The United Kingdom raised taxes on international oil companies operating in the North Sea. The United States moved to close a loophole that exempted oil from royalty payments for drilling on the outer continental shelf.

Perhaps the most high-profile case was Russia, where Gazprom, a company formed from the old Soviet Ministry of Gas, became one of the Kremlin's favorite foreign policy tools. In 2004, a decade after it was partly privatized, Vladimir Putin, Russia's formidable president, retook state control of the company, which was growing into the biggest extractor of natural gas in the world and one of the world's most valuable companies. In 2006, Moscow turned off the gas tap to Ukraine for three days at the height of winter over a price dispute. In the years that followed, Russia regularly threatened to repeat the shutoff. In 2007, it warned it would cut supplies to Ukraine just as pro-Western parties were poised to win power in Kiev. In 2009, it cut supplies again. Russia's meddling in Ukraine might not have been such a big deal had the pipeline that flowed through it not gone on to supply European countries such as Austria, Germany, and Italy. That underlined how not only former Soviet countries but also Europe, once a bulwark against Russian expansionism, had become the Kremlin's economic captive. Just as the United States had come to depend on Venezuelan oil, so Europe had come to depend on Russian gas. "Gazprom's monopoly-seeking activities cannot be explained by economic motives alone," Richard Lugar, a US Republican senator, wrote in a statement to the Senate Foreign Relations Committee in the summer of 2008. "Clearly Gazprom has sacrificed profits and needed domestic infrastructure investments to achieve foreign policy goals."

The expansion of state control over natural resources has left some three-quarters of the world's oil and natural gas reserves in the hands of state-owned oil companies, while the "big five" energy multinationals—ExxonMobil and Chevron of the United States, Anglo-Dutch Royal Dutch Shell, BP of the United Kingdom, and France's Total—control just 9 percent. Outside the United States and a few European countries, the model in which private companies owned oil fields was withering. The trend looked set to continue: Abu Dhabi notified the oil majors that privately held concessions due to expire in 2014 and 2018 would not be renewed. This was resource nationalism, pure and simple. It may not have been aimed at the type of socialism that Chávez and Morales preached, but it was far from pure free marketeering. Rather, it was a kind of politicized capitalism, where the state now played a central role.

At the softer end of the same continuum was protectionism, a milder form of economic nationalism but one that still prioritized political considerations over purely economic ones. Mexico, whose oil industry was already nationalized, hiked tariffs on US imports in retaliation against Washington's termination of a pilot program allowing some Mexican truck drivers access to US roads. The United States blocked an attempt by the Chinese National Offshore Oil Company to buy Unocal, an American oil company, and prevented Dubai Ports World from buying some US ports. A Chinese company backed away from investing in a Mississippi steel mill after the deal was attacked on Capitol Hill. Rio Tinto, an Anglo-Australian mining group, walked away from a proposed $20 billion investment by Chinalco, a Chinese metals company, after ferocious opposition by Australian regulators.

Australia's government blocked a bid from Singapore to buy its stock exchange. China rejected an attempt by Coca-Cola to take over Huiyuan Juice, its leading juice maker. France, Luxembourg, and Spain united in an attempt to block a bid by India's Mittal Steel for Arcelor, one of the world's biggest steel companies, and only rolled over when New Delhi threatened to wage a retaliatory trade war. Canada blocked a $39 billion bid by BHP Billiton, the Anglo-Australian mining group, for Potash, a fertilizer company, saying a takeover would not be in the country's best interests. The French and Spanish governments pushed big energy companies to merge to avoid takeovers by firms from other European states. (Dominique de Villepin, France's prime minister, said this was not so much resource nationalism as "economic patriotism," which sounded a lot nicer.) Australia said foreign investments in its big companies should be capped at 15 percent. British workers went on strike to protest the hiring of foreigners. France told its carmakers to buy components at home, and Spain urged its consumers to buy Spanish. When the Obama administration formulated its $787 billion economic stimulus package in 2009, it inserted a "buy American" provision.

As well as countries becoming more economically nationalistic, the shifting power structures of the global economy meant that countries in which the state played a big role in the national economy were coming to the fore. The economic rise of China, India, and Russia meant that in an increasing proportion of the global economy, national governments played a central role. What's more, the attitudes of these new economic superpowers were different. China, for example, preferred bilateral trade deals with other countries—struck with political considerations in mind—to multilateral ones that helped create the groundwork for greater trade with all. Russia preferred to deal with companies of certain nationalities, such as Germans, over American and British investors.

Such state-dominated economies did not necessarily share a commitment to the global financial "rules of the game." In 2009, China's Assets Supervision and Administration Commission of the State Council said it would support some state-backed Chinese companies if they chose to renege on loss-making financial derivatives contracts with foreign banks that they had bought to protect themselves from rising commodity prices. The prospect that Beijing would so casually tear up international financial agreements sent a shiver through the world's big banks, which had been rushing to do business with China for many years.

Whereas the Washington Consensus had sought a general opening of markets for foreign investment, China's primary aim was to secure its own long-term need for energy and commodities, even if the markets it invested in remained relatively closed. Moreover, just as Western oil and mining companies were starting to respond to pressure from campaigning groups to behave better, some of their new Chinese, Indian, and Russian rivals were willing to cut deals with all sort of unsavory regimes to secure their strategic aims. Those aims were to ensure the continuation of the supply lines for the resources that had fed China's astonishing growth.

In 2004, Beijing began pressing state Chinese companies to snap up assets abroad to secure energy and raw materials. In 2008, Russia called on its biggest businesses to do likewise. The fast pace of growth in China and the huge increase in revenues coming into resource-rich countries led to an enthusiastic response. But for governments, being in control of their own economies was no longer enough. Instead, they wanted to use their riches to expand into the global economy. They created sovereign wealth funds—investment bodies owned by the state aimed at buying stakes in international companies. There had been a handful of these funds around for decades, but suddenly the idea of using state cash to buy assets abroad seemed to make more sense. At least nineteen sovereign wealth funds were created between 2005 and 2009—in China, Russia, Dubai, Saudi Arabia, Indonesia, Malaysia, South Korea, and Vietnam. Brazil set up a sovereign wealth fund. So did Australia. So did France, promising to protect strategically important national companies by any means possible. "What oil producers do, what China does, what Russia does, there's no reason that France should not do," said Nicolas Sarkozy, the country's president, at a press conference launching the idea in October 2008.

The sovereign wealth funds went out to buy up the world. The China Investment Corporation pumped billions of dollars into Blackstone, an American private equity firm, and Morgan Stanley, the Wall Street bank. Temasek of Singapore bought a big stake in Merrill Lynch, another Wall Street titan. Libya's sovereign wealth fund snapped up office space in London and took a 3 percent stake in Pearson, the media company that owns the *Financial Times*. (This became awkward in 2011, when civil war broke out in Libya, and Pearson was forced to freeze Gadhafi's shareholding.) Qatar took a stake in Volkswagen. Sovereign wealth funds from Abu Dhabi, the capital of the United Arab Emirates, bought big stakes in Citigroup and General Electric—the world's biggest company—in the United States, Barclays Bank in the United Kingdom, and the German carmaker Daimler. They took control of Manchester City—an English Premier League soccer team—and purchased a 90 percent share in the Chrysler Building in New York.

All this activity made sovereign wealth funds big players of their own on Wall Street. In mid-2006, Chinese holdings of US companies' shares were worth $4 billion. Two years later, the Chinese owned shares worth $100 billion. Sovereign wealth funds bought up more than 10 percent of the UK stock market.

The amount of the assets sovereign wealth funds controlled was vast—around $4.6 trillion by the end of 2007, a figure expected to double by 2013. These funds may have helped prop up the banking system in the United States and Europe when the financial crisis hit, but they also raised the specter of cross-border nationalization, in which companies in the developed world could become subject to the political considerations of governments in Asia or the Middle East. Western companies may have been enthusiastic about trading with China, but being controlled by its governing Communist Party was a different proposition. Just as the return of the state signaled a change in global investment attitudes, so the rise of sovereign wealth funds brought to the fore all sorts of big international financial players whose operations weren't transparent. The IMF grumbled, for example, that many funds were not even accountable to their domestic legislatures—no surprise since most came from nondemocratic countries. What's more, given that they were essentially the piggy banks of governments, their motivations weren't necessarily the usual profit and loss goals of private-sector companies, so one reason they inspired fear in the developed world was that it wasn't clear what their goals actually were. Hillary Clinton, then a US senator and presidential hopeful, expressed the frustration of many when she said of sovereign wealth funds, at a debate among the Democratic presidential hopefuls in Las Vegas in January 2008, "We need to have a lot more control over what they do and how they do it."

As the world was plunged into a global economic downturn in 2008, the return of the state became complete. When the financial industry crumbled and the rest of the economy followed, governments responded by ramping up public spending. In the United States, across Europe, and everywhere else that could afford it, governments lavished bailout money on banks, carmakers, airlines, industrial manufacturers. Usually the cash came with strings attached: it could only be spent within national borders. In many cases, the only way to avoid collapse was for the state itself to take a controlling stake.

For the previous three decades, policymakers in the developed world had rolled back the state and placed their faith in privatization, liberalization, and deregulation. Politicians of the center-left had also professed conversion to the new religion. In 1996, Bill Clinton had famously eulogized the state's role in the economy, declaring that "the era of big government is over." A dozen years later, big government was back. Advocates of free markets seemed to have been proved wrong. Banking chiefs were hauled, shamefaced, to plead their cases in front of legislatures. Peer Steinbrück, Germany's finance minister, wondered aloud if Karl Marx, the father of communism, had not been "all that incorrect" to prophesy that unbridled capitalism would inevitably implode someday. Even Alan Greenspan, the former Federal Reserve chairman, a disciple of conservative philosopher Ayn Rand and himself a high priest of capitalism, acknowledged he had made a "mistake" in believing that banks would protect their shareholders and institutions. Much of the new state interventionism was reluctant and intended to be temporary. At the same time, though, it was clear that since it would be politically tricky for the state to extricate itself from some of the industries it had supported, governments were likely to be involved in the economy for some time.

It was going far too far to suggest, as many did at the time, that capitalism had collapsed and died. It was an exaggeration to claim that the kinds of ideas expressed in the Washington Consensus had forced the world to the edge of disaster. But what was clear was that it would never again be as straightforward for the United States or other developed countries to persuade their poorer counterparts to open up their economies and to limit the role of government. It may have been an unregulated financial sector rather than capitalism as a whole that had proved a failure, but the distinction was likely to be lost on, for example, the average Andean voter. What they saw was that neoliberalism, once sold as a panacea for the ailments of developing countries, had finally dragged its own maker into an economic pit—and the rest of the world with it. Whatever the economic arguments, the Washington Consensus would never be the same again. "The question we ask today is not whether our government is too big or too small, but whether it works," Barack Obama told the world in his inaugural address in 2009.

Faced with economic disaster, America in fact turned to the same economic tool beloved of Chávez, Morales, and Correa. The US government nationalized the insurance company AIG, the mortgage agencies Fannie Mae and Freddie Mac, and General Motors. Lindsey Graham, the Republican senator, James Baker, Ronald Reagan's second treasury secretary, and Alan Greenspan all spoke up in favor of nationalizing US banks. "There are times nowadays when you think Hugo Chávez could win an election in America," a Washington insider told the *Financial Times* on March 21, 2009.

To Chávez, the turn of events was pretty funny. "Hey, Obama has just nationalized nothing more and nothing less than General Motors," he joked during a live TV broadcast on June 2, 2009. "Comrade Obama! Fidel, let's be careful or we're going to end up to the right of him."

5

Trading Oil, Drugs, and Insults

The painting was crude, garish, and poorly executed, but it was unmistakably a portrait of Osama bin Laden.

The image of the world's most famous terrorist adorned the back window of a bus going down a main street in El Alto, the indigenous capital of the Andes, thousands of miles away from Afghanistan. Bin Laden flanked one side of the window, while an equally clumsy depiction of Che Guevara accompanied him on the other side. In between them, the twin towers of the World Trade Center were portrayed, exploding amid the impact of an aircraft.

Seeing it shocked and confused me. Traveling in South America, you get used to viewing images of political icons daubed on walls—Che Guevara is the most common, but you also see historical figures—Túpac Amaru, Simón Bolívar, and contemporary heroes such as Hugo Chávez and Evo Morales. But Osama bin Laden? It seemed so incongruous and perverse to honor this man and the 9/11 attacks alongside perhaps the most celebrated of all South American political superstars—almost like the desecration of something holy.

But in a way the painting on the bus made perfect sense. It symbolized the strength of anti-Americanism among many in Bolivia, a sentiment so strong that the feeling of "my enemy's enemy is my friend" for some outweighed any other. When the twin towers fell and seemingly the entire world briefly united to condemn the attack on America, there were few voices outside the Middle East that dared buck the consensus. One was in Bolivia, where Felipe Quispe, a radical indigenous leader, told a reporter from Agence France-Presse, "I believe we need these kinds of actions to destroy the enemy." Another was in Venezuela, where Lina Ron, a militant left-wing activist much loved by Chávez, responded to 9/11 by burning a US flag in Caracas's main square. These were not mainstream views, of course, but neither could they be dismissed merely as the mere rantings of political crazies. After more than a century in which Washington's perception of Latin America as its rightful sphere of influence had driven it to plunder, brutalize, and manipulate the region, anti-Americanism had almost become part of the DNA in many countries. In societies that were deeply divided, anti-Americanism often served as a uniting lowest common denominator. Through Latin America's history, anti-Americanism had been far from the exclusive province of the Left. In fact, because the region experienced US interference long before Europe, Asia, or the Middle East, Latin America could be considered the birthplace of anti-Americanism. Sure, the region had originally liberated itself from European rule, but there was a widespread feeling that because it had grown up under the shadow of the United States' growing world power, it had never fully thrown off the yoke of imperial dominance. Both right-wing and left-wing nationalism in Latin America frequently took opposition to Washington's trampling of national sovereignty as its touchstone, in much the same way that African nationalism often defined itself as a perpetual struggle against British, French, or Belgian rule.

The anti-Americanism of Chávez, Morales, and Rafael Correa was in marked contrast to the scenes of hemispheric cooperation of the 1994 Summit of the Americas, when Latin American leaders had reacted enthusiastically to US president Bill Clinton's vision of a free-trade bloc "from Alaska to Argentina." But in the wider span of history, they were really returning to the region's form of political equilibrium—to defining their own nationalist projects in contrast to US dominance, their own sovereignty in opposition to US encroachment.

Morales and Correa could spout anti-American rhetoric as forcefully as anyone, but it was Chávez who made anti-Americanism his defining creed—and in return, anti-Americanism made Chávez world-famous. In a continent where the same message echoed in many countries, his virulent anti-Americanism enabled him to build a region-wide alliance and enhance his stature. And his status as an anti-American leader also enabled him at times to extend his alliance outside the region and play a walk-on part on the global stage. More than his vast oil wealth, more than his "Bolivarian revolution," more than his efforts to extend his political control over Venezuela, it was anti-Americanism that turned Chávez into a figure known across the world.

Chávez had come to assume the part only gradually. In the early days of his presidency, relations between Caracas and Washington were strained, but rarely downright hostile. While Lina Ron was burning the Stars and Stripes in downtown Caracas, Chávez was expressing "profound regret" at 9/11, describing the attacks as "cowardly, murderous," calling for a one-minute silence to honor the victims, and guaranteeing continued supplies of oil to the American people.

There were really two events that swung the Venezuelan leader more stridently against Washington: the US-led attack on Afghanistan in October 2001, and the US response to the 2002 coup that momentarily deposed Chávez himself. Chávez was not alone in finding both these events highly distasteful—not to mention the United States' invasion of Iraq the following year. As the target of multiple military invasions throughout their history, Latin Americans tended to look unfavorably on Washington's military adventures in the Middle East. When the United States assembled a "coalition of the willing" to attack Iraq in 2003, Colombia, the United States' die-hard ally, was the only South American country to sign up. Moderate, democratic, and centrist states such as Brazil and Chile stayed away.

When the United States also appeared to lend its support to the 2002 coup against Chávez and encouraged countries in the region to do likewise, that only aggravated the problem, reinforcing the idea that the United States was only interested in democracy if it led to the "right" outcomes and reviving the image of it as a continental giant trampling over the national sovereignty of others. Chávez's status as the region's most vocal opponent of US military adventurism—coupled with the fact that Washington had apparently thought him dangerous enough to support a military coup to oust him from power—smoothed the Venezuelan president's path to a kind of regional leadership.

Had the United States not botched its handling of the 2002 coup, and had Washington not ordered military attacks on Afghanistan and Iraq, Chávez's opposition to the economic aspects of the United States' Latin American agenda might have left him fairly lonely. To be sure, the shift to the left was a trend across the region, but it was far from uniform. In spite of the obvious shortcomings of the Washington Consensus, market skeptics in South America were still outnumbered by market enthusiasts, even if they leaned more to the left. But the coup and the United States' wars abroad brought back the worst kind of memories. In subsequent years, when Chávez increasingly poured vitriol on the United States, few other Latin American leaders would join him. But perhaps at times in private they felt some admiration for a regional president who dared to rebuke Washington so publicly and vehemently.

Chávez projected himself onto the bigger South American stage and his bombastic rhetoric set the tone for the region's relations with Washington. When *Time* magazine compiled a list of the world's one hundred most influential people in 2006, Chávez was the only Latin American to be included, on the basis that he was "Bush's loudest critic south of the border."

Petro-Diplomacy

In South America, Chávez, Morales, and Correa were only a gang of three—and the three countries they controlled were hardly the most important—yet the Venezuelan leader was able to buy friends beyond the Andes. In effect, he became an ATM for the Americas, doling out tens of billions of dollars not just to Ecuador, Bolivia, and Nicaragua but also to richer countries, including Argentina and Uruguay. He set up clinics in Peru. He supplied dozens of Caribbean and Central American countries with cut-price oil. When Antigua was rocked by news in 2009 that it had been hosting a $7 billion Ponzi scheme operated by Sir Allen Stanford, it was Chávez who came to the rescue with a $50 million emergency bailout. While the recipients of his largesse did not use the funds to build twenty-first-century socialism of their own, at the very least the cash bought Chávez the indulgence of the region's more powerful leaders, who shrank away from reining him in.

Foreign policy for South American countries typically goes little beyond securing trade deals and arguing about borders. But for Chávez, "petro-diplomacy" was critical to his entire government program. He stated that he was dedicating about 8 percent of his gross domestic product to these international arrangements. His opponents reckoned that his government gave away more than $60 billion to other countries. Caracas spent more in the region than Washington did, with one goal in mind: establishing Chávez's Venezuela as a counterbalance to the United States' traditional influence in the region. Chávez established a "Bolivarian Alternative for the Americas" as a response to Washington's plan for a Free Trade Area of the Americas. He proposed a South American development bank to eliminate the region's reliance on international financial institutions such as the World Bank and the International Monetary Fund. These were insubstantial initiatives, but at least they gave the appearance of something new and fresh.

Whether you liked him or hated him—and there were few who felt anything in between—by 2006–2007, it was Chávez who set much of Latin America's agenda. He was lucky with his timing. Rising oil prices had given him plenty of cash to splash around. At the same time, Washington was afflicted by hyperopia, farsightedness when it came to foreign policy that left it with a seeming inability to focus on the region nearest to it. Moreover, the Iraq war had stirred up anti-US sentiment in Latin America, further diminishing Washington's dwindling influence in the region.

The electorates of Ecuador and Bolivia had voted for like-minded presidents in part because they liked what Chávez had done at home and admired the way he thumbed his nose at the United States. The voters in Peru and Mexico similarly rejected radical leftists for fear of Chávez, while the Venezuelan president's perceived overinfluence prompted a coup in Honduras in 2009. A common claim was that Chávez was buying up elections and influence in the region. If so, he was only doing what the United States had long been engaged in, except that he didn't have Washington's historical baggage—and when oil prices were high, he had enough cash coming in to outspend the Americans.

Chávez's attempt to build an anti-American alliance didn't stop at Latin America. Instead, he behaved like the region's self-appointed delegate to what George W. Bush had called the axis of evil (or, as some wags called the more extended alliance of nationalistic oil-producing nations, the "axis of diesel"). No other head of state in the world traveled abroad as much as Chávez—he was on planes so often that you might wonder if an unhealthy obsession with collecting frequent-flyer miles was behind his single-minded pursuit of political power at home.

If Cuba and Bolivia were familiar destinations nearer home, Chávez appeared to feel equally comfortable with leaders such as Vladimir Putin in Russia, Muammar Gadhafi in Libya, Mahmoud Ahmadinejad in Iran, Alexander Lukashenko in Belarus (an arch-authoritarian widely known as Europe's last dictator), Zimbabwe's Robert Mugabe, and Bashar al-Assad in Syria.

Chávez regularly made a splash at meetings of OPEC, the oil exporters' club, by telling the organization that its role was to fight "imperialism" and "colonialism." In the absence of an ailing Fidel Castro, Chávez presided over a 2006 meeting of the Non-Aligned Movement—a grouping of nations principally from Latin America, Africa, and Asia, formed to reject the Cold War choice between Washington and Moscow. The organization had struggled to find a new purpose, but under Chávez's guidance it appeared to realize its twenty-first-century role: bashing the United States. In its final communiqué, the conference called for a unified front against Washington in favor of Iran's right to nuclear technology.

Other than the vanity aspect, the Iran issue illustrated why America cared that Chávez had widened his international social circle. Not only was Tehran's desire to develop nuclear technology something that Washington was trying to thwart through international consensus, but, more important, the axis of diesel—which most took to mean Russia, Iran, and Venezuela—regularly blocked the United States' foreign policy aims. Caracas and Tehran bought tens of billions of dollars' worth of military equipment from Moscow, and in return Russia helped thwart Washington's attempts to impose tough sanctions on Iran. At the same time, Iran was growing its influence in America's backyard, not only deepening ties with Chávez, Morales, and Correa but also with moderates such as Luiz Inácio Lula da Silva in Brazil.

The extent of Chávez's role in the anti-American alliance became clear with his memorable appearance at the United Nations in New York on September 20, 2006, when he lambasted the US president in front of the world, calling Bush—who had addressed the gathering a day earlier—a devil no fewer than eight times. It was an even more over-the-top performance than usual, but it helped him project his personal myth as the leader of the downtrodden of the world. "The president of the United States came to talk to the peoples of the world," Chávez said. "What would those peoples of the world tell him if they were given the floor? What would they have to say? I think I have some inkling of what the peoples of the south, the oppressed people think. They would say: 'Yankee imperialist—go home.'"

Whereas Bush's speech had received a polite but tepid response, when the Venezuelan leader was finished he was greeted with warm applause. He had piled derision on derision and the world had lapped it up. The spectacle perplexed many who witnessed it. Eric Shawn, a correspondent on the right-wing Fox News Channel, spluttered his disgust with the world in general.

"Here you have this anti-American, Marxist president who has aligned himself with terrorist supporters, with Ahmadinejad, with Iran and with Cuba—in effect, the enemies of America—and he got a much more warmer, enthusiastic response from the General Assembly," Shawn fumed. "The General Assembly today exposed itself for the world to see, to see how they politically align against America and against the administration by giving Chávez such warm, enthusiastic support. After this incredible anti-American rant, he was warmly and enthusiastically responded to by applause—sustained, continued, supportive applause—by the members of the General Assembly. What's happening here is that the Non-Aligned Movement, the 118 members of the General Assembly, more than two-thirds basically, have taken over the place."

Shocking though it might have been for some that a majority of countries would dare to criticize the global superpower, it would be exaggerating to say that they were a coherent group and that Chávez was their leader. Nevertheless, even his critics had to concede that Chávez had started to cobble together a global alliance. It may have been eclectic and bizarre—led by a hodgepodge of international devi-ants, outcasts, and other political lepers—but for the first time since the Cold War, it seemed, a group of countries from Latin America,

Asia, Eastern Europe, Africa, and the Middle East was starting to unite in opposition to Washington, and the Venezuelan leader had positioned himself in its vanguard.

Americans are not known for their general knowledge of the wider world, but few could say that they had never heard of Hugo Chávez. In 2010, Oliver Stone, the Hollywood movie director, released *South of the Border*, a hagiographic documentary charting the rise of the Left in South America, with Chávez starring as the film's hero. The Venezuelan leader was, as *Newsweek* magazine had announced in its May 28, 2006, issue, "the new rockstar of world politics."

Bankrolling Bolivarianism

US policy toward South America's radical Left has often revolved around trade: trading in oil and trading insults.

Bill Clinton, who was US president when Chávez first came to power, recast the framework for relations between Washington and Latin America as one based on trade. That was something of a departure from traditional US policy. When the countries of Latin America first achieved their independence in the nineteenth century, the United States largely viewed the region within its broader struggle to establish itself as a global power. The Monroe Doctrine, for example, aimed to prevent European countries, the superpowers of the Old World, from establishing strategic positions in Latin America that might threaten Washington's influence. Teddy Roosevelt's "gunboat diplomacy" extended that to include military interventions to safeguard US business interests. During the Cold War, Latin America became a proxy battleground between Washington and Moscow. Military interventions were officially justified on national security grounds rather than in terms of economic interests.

Clinton's 1994 proposal for a "Partnership for Prosperity" was different. Rather than reassert the right that Washington had historically claimed to meddle in the region for its own ends, trampling over the sovereignty of Latin American countries, it held out the promise of a regional agreement on economic development in which the United States and its neighbors would be equals. Clinton's vision originally sought to include a focus on democratic institutions as well as private enterprise and free trade. He promised to "change the lives of real people for the better."

But over the next decade, what was sold as a hemisphere-wide plan gradually came to a halt. The free-market reforms implemented in the region failed to improve governance or eliminate poverty. Unsurprisingly, South Americans were not keen on the idea of a Free Trade Area of the Americas—the Clintonian plan to extend the North American Free Trade Agreement between the United States, Canada, and Mexico south to the rest of the hemisphere. The United States ratified a regional trade deal with Central American countries in 2005, but in South America, Washington was left to pursue bilateral trade deals with individual countries.

In fact, the demise of the Clintonian Partnership for Prosperity dated back to the Clinton era. Congress did not warm to the idea of giving the president fast-track authority to strike trade deals, and multilateral negotiations were already starting to get bogged down. When George W. Bush came to office, he promised to reinvigorate Washington's Latin American agenda. "The best foreign policy starts at home," he told reporters aboard Air Force One three weeks after his inauguration. "We've got to have good relations in the hemisphere." Like Clinton, he promised to emphasize a twin track of both promoting democracy and opening up the region's economies—what he catchily termed "freedom and free markets."

But the Bush administration's definition of freedom did not always chime with others' understanding. When 9/11 diverted the White House's attention far away from Latin America, any connotation within the Bush policy of strengthening the fledgling democracies in the region was lost to a simplistic policy defined by a trade and antidrug agenda centered on military aid to Colombia. Latin American policy was left in the hands of officials who retained some aspects of Washington's Cold War perspective toward Latin America. The most obvious inheritance of that period was the Cuba embargo—a policy that since its full implementation in 1962 had failed to undermine the communist government in Havana and had instead earned the United States greater enmity within the region.

The US response to the 2002 coup against Chávez was another knee-jerk Cold War–style mistake. So was the warning, that same year, by Manuel Rocha, the US ambassador to La Paz, in a speech during a visit to the coca-growing Chapare region on June 27, 2002, that if Evo Morales won the presidential election it would jeopardize US aid to Bolivia since the candidate wanted Bolivia "to become a major cocaine exporter again." Both reactions backfired spectacularly. Chávez was soon back in power, stronger than ever and reborn as an anti-American firebrand. Morales, whose campaign had until then looked like a long shot, almost won the top spot in the 2002 election and publicly thanked Mr. Rocha, sarcastically calling him his campaign manager. His victory three years later was undoubtedly helped by that incident.

Given that background and the history of anti-Americanism in the region, it was perhaps not surprising that the governments of the radical Left so frequently made a show of attacking, ridiculing, and provoking Washington. From an American perspective, what was perhaps more alarming was that the United States on several occasions took the bait, elevating those governments' status as important enemies of Washington and confirming their arguments that the United States was working to unseat them. President Bush publicly fretted about the erosion of democracy in Venezuela. US officials blacklisted Chávez for not cooperating in the war on terror, accusing him of sheltering Middle Eastern terrorists and arming FARC guerrillas from neighboring Colombia. They accused him of manipulating elections in Argentina and Nicaragua. When Morales expelled the US ambassador to La Paz in September 2008, accusing him of fomenting protests against the government, and Chávez followed his lead, the State Department said in a statement the day after the expulsions that their moves reflected "weakness and desperation."

Attitudes toward the region improved somewhat in the latter years of the Bush administration when a vastly improved Latin America policy team opted to tone down the responses to Chávez's outbursts, and after Barack Obama became US president in 2009, but tit-for-tat incidents between Washington and the leftist governments in South America continued. Months after the Obama administration took over, it became embroiled in a dispute with Rafael Correa, who had been threatened by the Department of Homeland Security that it would withdraw $340,000 in aid to Ecuador's antidrug unit unless Correa gave Washington control over hiring at the agency. To make matters worse, the United States demanded the return of all furniture, cars, and equipment that it had donated to the unit. "Keep your dirty money, we don't need it," Correa responded during his weekly radio address. In 2010, Washington and Caracas became embroiled in another spat when Chávez declared he would refuse to accept Larry Palmer, Obama's nominee for US ambassador to Venezuela. Chávez, whose waning popularity had recently been confirmed in congressional elections, relished the opportunity to get into his favorite game of diplomatic Ping-Pong with the old enemy. He dared Washington to respond, and the United States duly did so, revoking the Venezuelan ambassador's visa in retaliation. In April 2011, Correa expelled the US ambassador to Ecuador after Wikileaks made public a cable she had sent to Washington in which she accused the country's most senior police officers of corruption and said the president was well aware of what was going on. The United States retaliated by ordering Ecuador's ambassador to leave Washington.

It was certainly true, as many observers noted, that as elsewhere around the world, focusing on the evils of America enabled the leaders of the radical Left to distract attention from problems at home. On the other hand, as these incidents suggested, the United States' actions all too often gave leaders of the radical Left precisely the ammunition they needed to portray their relationship with Washington as one of a struggle for national sovereignty, evoking the ghosts of former US interference in the region and further stoking the anti-Americanism that helped keep them in power.

At times relations between the radical Left in South America and Washington resembled more a school playground than the interactions of sovereign countries. This was important, particularly when it came to Venezuela, because when the back-and-forth rhetoric was stripped away, Washington and Caracas were intertwined in a firm embrace. Venezuela, sitting on top of the Western Hemisphere's largest proven reserves of hydrocarbons, was the United States' fifth largest oil supplier, and the United States was Venezuela's largest customer. Venezuelan oil was the main source of oil for refineries in the Gulf of Mexico, while the United States sucked in two-thirds of Venezuela's oil exports, providing in return about three-quarters of the South American country's export revenues and half of the government's income. While his exaggerated anti-American swagger had made Chávez a global figure, he was in the unusual position of being bankrolled by his main enemy. Their mutual dependence enabled him to threaten repeatedly to turn off the taps to the United States, while any serious observer realized that he needed American demand and was unable to do anything serious anytime soon. The United States was an oil addict, and Chávez—for all the insults and abuse—was one of its most important dealers. They were stuck with each other.

In the longer term, both Chávez's Venezuela and the United States wanted to loosen this embrace. The United States looked at alternative energy sources and more offshore drilling. As a presidential candidate, Hillary Clinton advised voters at a forum in Des Moines in March 2007 to combat Chávez by "turning off the lights"—not exactly a solution to the United States' energy needs. None of these seemed likely to cause a serious dent in the United States' need for Venezuelan oil. Chávez, on the other hand, did seem to be looking more strategically at lessening his country's need of US demand. It was nearly impossible in the short or medium term, but he cultivated the Chinese and ramped up exports to Asia, even though the long shipping route raised questions about the profitability of this setup. In 2006, Richard Lugar, the Republican senator from Indiana, had warned in a letter to the State Department, "Venezuela's leverage over global oil prices and its direct supply lines and refining capacity in the US give Venezuela undue ability to impact US security and our economy."

Building a long-term energy strategy on supplies from the Middle East was uncertain and unpalatable domestically, and it was at least credible that China and others would seek to establish a serious energy foothold in Latin America. Yet the United States seemed to lack a strategy on how to craft a realistic path to energy security that incorporated the biggest source of oil nearest to home. Its fretting about democracy in the Andes had a hollow ring to it. For one thing, Washington had focused on trying to forge trade relationships in the region, not on building democracy. Moreover, the United States was not troubled about democracy when it imported oil from Saudi Arabia or Kuwait.

The bipolar nature of US foreign policy became even clearer in 2006. In that year, Washington decided to restore diplomatic relations with Libya, a country run by Muammar Gadhafi, the dictator who came to power in a military coup in 1969. (Of course, in 2011, America would reverse that decision, joining NATO and the UN to support anti-Gadhafi forces in a civil war.) At the same time, the United States added Venezuela to its list of terrorist states that included North Korea, Iran, Syria, and Cuba, effectively banning Venezuela from all military sales and confirming the enmity between Washington and Caracas. In two fell swoops, the United States had elevated a despot with some oil while lumping in with a bunch of dictators a democratically elected leader with a lot of oil.

Was this prudent? Was it coherent? Was it consistent? Or in the case of Venezuela, was the United States unusually placing ideology above its own energy security? Stung by criticism and verbal barbs, was Washington letting its heart rule its head?

Coca Crops and Coups

If the main trade between Venezuela and the United States was oil, between much of the Andes and North America it was cocaine.

Apart from oil, cocaine was one of the most valuable exports from Latin America northward. If oil was the United States' most obvious legal addiction, cocaine was its most prominent illicit vice.

Cocaine is produced from the leaves of the coca plant, which grows on the eastern slopes of the Andes and in the highlands. For hundreds of years before the leaves were first refined to remove the pure drug, coca leaves were used by locals in religious and medical practices, and were chewed or brewed to ward off hunger and the effects of high altitude. The Incas held the plant in high regard. It had the same kind of role in their religion as wine and incense did for the Europeans, an integral part of their culture and way of life.

Coca's centrality to Andean life survived the Spanish colonization of South America. But it was not until the nineteenth century that Europeans began to enjoy the benefits of coca in their own way, after German chemists worked out how to develop cocaine from the leaf. For many decades, the cocaine trade was entirely legal and enjoyed licit demand from the United States and Europe. But as the twentieth century progressed, attitudes stiffened, and the coca leaf itself was swept along with them.

It was not until 1971 that President Richard Nixon declared a war on drugs, but US efforts to prevent the import of narcotics could be traced back to 1912, when the US government convened an international convention to control the production of opium and cocaine. In 1958, Nixon himself had gotten stoned in South America—although not in the psychedelic sense. On a trip to Caracas, his car had been set upon by a crowd of rock-throwing anti-American protesters. The then vice president escaped shaken but unhurt. In 1961, a UN convention determined that not only opium and cocaine but also coca leaf was a narcotic drug that should be prohibited except for medical and scientific purposes. It aimed to eradicate the cultivation and chewing of coca leaves within twenty-five years.

But in the 1970s, the United States' main concern was not cocaine but heroin and marijuana. In 1973, Nixon established the Drug Enforcement Administration to lead the country's antinarcotics efforts. But although the United States put pressure on Mexico to begin spraying plants with herbicides in order to eliminate marijuana, the war on drugs was largely a domestic affair, with law enforcement and drug treatment programs focused on stamping out the problem at home. It was not until Ronald Reagan's presidency in the 1980s that the international aspect of the war on drugs was stepped up, with the administration making antidrug policy a central plank of US foreign policy and declaring the issue one of national security. "We're taking down the surrender flag that has flown over so many drug efforts," Reagan declared on June 24, 1982, upon the launch of the White House Office of Drug Abuse Policy. "We're running up a battle flag."

Whereas previous efforts had focused on attacking demand for drugs, Reagan took aim at their supply. The United States poured money into the effort and looked beyond Mexico to the Andes to try to stamp out coca farming. It aimed to eradicate the plants, to persuade farmers to plant other crops, and to intercept drug traffickers. While Washington favored creating military or police antidrug squads in the Andes, the political leaders of Bolivia and Peru were initially hesitant to militarize the effort. Then, as now, growing coca was not strictly illegal in those countries as long as it was sold either to be chewed by locals or made into tea bags for the domestic market. Moreover, there were strong ties between the cocaine trade and the political establishment, who often enjoyed healthy bribes from traffickers. In 1980, General Luis García Meza seized power in Bolivia in the "cocaine coup," so called because he appointed well-known traffickers to his government, released imprisoned drug dealers, and refused to collaborate with the US war on drugs.

Being a supporter of the US policy in the Andes could be dangerous, as the drug traffickers assassinated politicians who supported the crackdown, bombed US embassies, and plotted to kill US ambassadors and drug agents. Nevertheless, Peru and Bolivia committed themselves to coca eradication efforts, although they were largely unsuccessful.

Under the Andean Initiative introduced by the elder President George Bush in 1989, the United States poured $2 billion worth of military aid into the region in order to crush the drug trade by force. The US military invaded Panama and ousted Manuel Noriega, partly because of his involvement in drug trafficking (he had also been moonlighting for the CIA throughout the 1980s, but the United States ignored this inconvenient bit of history when it ejected him). The US ambassador to Panama called the invasion "the biggest drug bust in history." (It was probably also the loudest: Noriega put up with a week of rock music blasted at his compound before surrendering.) Under Bill Clinton, the United States stepped up the militarization of the Andean front in the war on drugs. Washington helped Colombia smash the country's big drug cartels and assisted in crop spraying. It stepped up military training to neighboring countries such as Ecuador. It backed Alberto Fujimori, the strongman of Peru, who oversaw a bloody military struggle against the Shining Path (both the Fujimori administration and the guerrillas were heavily involved in the cocaine trade) and assisted the Peruvians in shooting down dozens of civilian planes suspected of carrying drugs—a strategy that backfired when the Peruvian air force downed an aircraft carrying an American missionary couple and their two children. In his final year in power, Clinton agreed to pour $1.3 billion into Plan Colombia, a two-pronged, mainly military strategy of curbing coca cultivation and drug trafficking while fighting the left-wing rebels of the Revolutionary Armed Forces of Colombia (FARC) and the National Liberation Army (ELN)—much of whose funding came from the drug trade.

After 9/11, these groups were neatly reclassified and lumped in with the enemy in the United States' global war on terror, bringing billions more dollars of aid from the administration of George W. Bush.

The war on drugs had found its perfect partner. Between them, the two wars capped a long-standing policy that had intensified conflict and militarized Washington's relationship with Latin America. The effort also came increasingly to define the United States' ties to the region. American aid to the region fell by one-third in real terms in the two decades following the Cold War, but more than half of it went to just five countries on the frontline of the war on drugs: Colombia, Peru, Bolivia, Ecuador, and Mexico. Military assistance to the region was similarly focused, with Colombia receiving more than 60 percent of the total.

The War on Drugs

In many ways, America's war on drugs encapsulated the essence of Washington's attitude toward Latin America. On the one hand, demand for drugs from North Americans had created the problem. Without American demand, there could be no drug trade. But rather than address the issue of demand, the United States chose to try to choke off supply, punishing the producing countries of the south for the addiction of the north.

Aside from upping the stakes in South America's military conflicts, the war on drugs also stirred up deeper historical struggles in the southern Andes. In Colombia, the US-sponsored efforts involved crop spraying—dropping devastating weed-killing chemicals on thousands of acres of farmland. But unlike Colombia, which the Incas had never conquered and colonized very extensively, in Peru and Bolivia, coca was an integral part of indigenous culture, making crop dusting there politically unacceptable.

Instead, the two countries gave their support to efforts either to pull up the plants by hand or to attempt to wean farmers off coca and toward coffee and other crops. The first approach was tiresome and ineffectual, and the second depended heavily on the fickle commodity markets, since coca was a cash crop that most farmers would have happily abandoned if other plants yielded better money. Either way, coca for personal use remained legal in Bolivia and Peru, and the eradication efforts—often implemented very halfheartedly by the governments of those countries—were widely seen as an attempt to placate the domestic US political agenda. The common view in the region was that because Washington was unable or unwilling to tackle the thorny issue of how to stop Americans from using cocaine, it had decided to fight the problem elsewhere. In the process, it had lumped the traditional use of coca—which went back centuries and helped to define indigenous culture—with the consumption of cocaine. Developed countries had created the cocaine problem and then punished others for it. The result was that the war on drugs in Peru and Bolivia became a de facto war on traditional Andean culture. This was not just about cash. It had become about history and conquest, the subjugation of indigenous people for hundreds of years at the hands of foreigners.

The collateral damage from the war on drugs was vast: it aggravated wars between the state and guerrillas in Peru and Colombia, killing tens of thousands of people and displacing millions more. By the end of the first decade of the twentieth century, after Mexico had become an easy gateway for US-bound cocaine, tens of thousands more would die on the streets of some of Mexico's biggest cities, as drug cartels kidnapped, tortured, shot, and executed one another, murdering countless civilians in the process. The wider effects of America's war on drugs were to exacerbate tensions between countries in the region, in particular between Colombia and its neighbors Venezuela and Ecuador. In March 2008, those tensions brought the region closer to a major war than it had been for decades after Colombia conducted a military strike against rebels camped out across the border in Ecuadorean territory. Venezuela deployed troops at its Colombian border in solidarity. The rage in Ecuador at the encroachment on its sovereign territory was only soothed after Colombia issued a wide-ranging apology and promised to respect the border in the future.

Politically, the war on drugs had the effect of isolating the United States and Colombia, its chief ally in the region. It forced Washington to define friends and foes according to their cooperation or lack of it with antidrug efforts. Those who were deemed "friends" on this score—such as Fujimori in Peru or Álvaro Uribe in Colombia—could be a liability elsewhere, since they tended to trample over human rights. For the United States' critics, the drug issue was a convenient stick with which to beat the American giant. Evo Morales, of course, had risen to prominence precisely because he represented the coca growers, who were seen as victims of Washington's crude lumping together of the traditional plant with cocaine. Hugo Chávez refused to collaborate with US antidrug efforts and was therefore banned from buying military equipment. Rafael Correa kicked the US military out of the Manta air base, its only installation in South America, refusing to sanction the antidrug monitoring as an infringement of Ecuadorean sovereignty. The Obama administration instead struck a deal with Colombia to increase US access to military bases there, a move that prompted concerns in Argentina, Brazil, and Chile and outraged condemnation in Venezuela and Ecuador. In any case, Colombia's own constitutional court ruled the US military deal unconstitutional in 2010. The episode hardly burnished Washington's reputation. Overall, the war on drugs further damaged the US brand in the region.

You might say the cost was worth it. After all, if Washington was to take the war on drugs seriously, it would have to treat it like a war—people would get killed, enemies would form alliances, political consequences were to be expected. But in other wars the United States employed a range of techniques in its efforts to undermine the enemy. In the Andes, the war on drugs came to depend almost exclusively on the thankless (and endless) task of eradicating the coca plant and supporting the Colombian government's war against the rebels. But the pertinent question, ultimately, was whether it was successful. Did the war on drugs actually work?

The answer was no—not because it was not prosecuted forcefully enough but because it was practically impossible to win. Coca cultivation displayed a balloon effect—when you squeezed it in one country, more would be produced elsewhere in the Andes. In the 1990s, production declined in Peru—then the biggest producer—and Bolivia. At the same time, Colombian output rose to make that country the biggest producer by the late 1990s. Plan Colombia led production to fall, but crop cultivation simultaneously increased again in Peru and Bolivia. By 2010, Peru was poised to regain its title as the world's biggest coca producer, according to the United Nations. While this was alarming, the United Nations also reported that the amount of land dedicated to growing coca had fallen by 5 percent. But that overlooked the fact that the seeds and coca-farming techniques had improved over time, so Andean farmers were able to squeeze a lot more coca leaf from of their plots than they had done in previous decades, even if the acreage given over to the crop was shrinking. By 2010, Andean coca was producing 521 tons of cocaine a year, having grown into a $72 billion global industry—more than twice the size of the heroin trade, according to the United Nations. So after more than three decades of the war on drugs, the amount of coca supplying the drug trade had increased over time, not diminished. In fact, the billions upon billions of dollars spent on antidrug efforts had little perceptible effect on drug availability and prices in the United States and Europe. Measured by its own aims, the war on drugs could only be deemed a dismal, costly, ill-conceived failure.

US policy toward Latin America had come to be defined around three areas: the war on drugs, the Cuba embargo, and the pursuit of more open trade. Both the antidrug efforts and the isolation of the Castro regime had failed in their basic aims. As far as the trade agenda was concerned, the rise of the radical Left had forced the United States to abandon its efforts for a Free Trade Area of the Americas and had forced it into a series of bilateral negotiations with governments in the region. The Bush administration signed trade agreements with Colombia and Panama but was unable to get them through Congress, both because of growing hostility to international trade within the United States and concerns about the Colombian government's trampling of human and civil rights in its war with the guerrillas.

Where South America was concerned, the United States had over the decades constructed a failed policy. To be sure, the war on FARC scored some big successes, but where its main goal of diminishing the flow of cocaine was concerned, the United States' efforts were both ineffective and counterproductive. Washington had no vision for its backyard, could issue no call to action, and had effectively abdicated its leadership of the Western Hemisphere.

Enter Obama

When George W. Bush was US president, it was easy to hate America—and most people did. After the surge of solidarity provoked by 9/11 faded away, global opinion surveys during the time of George II's rule regularly showed that the US president and his country were nearly uniformly loathed around the world.

That sentiment even helped Barack Obama's electoral victory in 2008. Many Americans who voted for Obama cited the United States' poor reputation internationally as one of their motivating factors. They wanted him to restore their nation's image in the eyes of the rest of the world. As a candidate, Obama's campaign document, *A New Partnership for the Americas,* had sketched out a wish for the United States to reestablish its "traditional leadership in the region—on democracy, trade and development, energy and immigration." This sentiment bore little relation to Washington's actual record in Latin America, but it at least signaled a desire to start over. As president, Obama went on to shake Chávez's hand at the Summit of the Americas in 2009 and reestablish diplomatic relations with Caracas. He pledged to close the detention center at Guantánamo Bay, the US base in Cuba, an affront to many in the region (and in the United States as well). He loosened the Cuba embargo. At a conference in Ecuador in 2010, Hillary Clinton, his secretary of state, talked about developing a "community of the Americas" that would be aimed at improving people's lives. In Obama's 2011 State of the Union address, he spoke of his intention "to forge new alliances across the Americas."

These were fine words, but the Obama administration gave little suggestion that it had developed a coherent policy approach that would address the popularity of the radical Left, the growing influence of rivals, and the entrenched political interests concerning Latin America back at home. Although softened, the Cuba embargo remained largely in place. Closing Guantánamo proved more tricky than planned, since it was politically difficult to bring Guantánamo prisoners stateside and to give them civilian trials. The administration's 2010 National Drug Control Strategy finally recognized that the drug problem was principally caused by demand from the United States. Yet the coca eradication efforts continued, although Morales, Correa, and Chávez refused to cooperate and even Alan García, Peru's US-friendly president, said he would not try to stop coca cultivation in large areas of the jungle where remnants of the Shining Path still operated.

The Obama administration's first real test in the region came in Honduras, where Manuel Zelaya, the president and a Chávez ally, was ousted in a military coup in 2009. Woken from his sleep at gunpoint and bundled onto a plane in the middle of the night, Zelaya was flown into exile still wearing his pajamas. The White House initially joined the rest of the region in condemnation. Obama called the coup illegal and said that as far as he was concerned, Zelaya was still president, while Hillary Clinton confirmed that the United States saw the action as a coup. Washington withdrew $16.5 million in military aid but refused to withhold $180 million in economic development aid (as it normally would in response to a coup) and, unlike other countries in the Americas and the European Union, did not recall its ambassador from Tegucigalpa. Moreover, it half blamed Zelaya for causing his own ouster, calling him a polarizing figure—a move that gave heart to supporters of the coup, who said the president had been defying the country's Supreme Court by planning an illegal referendum on changing the constitution to keep him in office beyond his single four-year term. But Washington still stood with the rest of the Organization of American States (OAS) in stating that Zelaya remained Honduras's president and that he should be reinstated to serve out his term. No matter that they had ideological differences, the US president stated at a press conference during his trip to Russia on July 7, 2009, his government subscribed to "the principle that people should choose their own leaders, whether they are leaders we agree with or not."

Interestingly, after years of telling the United States to keep its hands off the region, Chávez appealed to Washington to intervene. "Obama—do something! This is in your hands," the Venezuelan leader begged on his weekly television show a few days after Obama's statement, reflecting a widespread view across the region. The location had a potent symbolism for US relations with Latin America: in the 1980s, the United States had used Honduras as a platform for its invasions of Grenada and Panama and its meddling in civil wars in El Salvador, Nicaragua, and Guatemala.

But Obama dithered. With the United States apparently reluctant to take a leadership role, Brazil assumed the part of the dominant regional power, with Luiz Inácio Lula da Silva demanding that Zelaya be reinstated. (In the meantime, the deposed president had sneaked back into Honduras and was holed up at the Brazilian embassy enjoying Lula's hospitality, so the Brazilian leader might also simply have wanted to get rid of his new houseguest.) In the end, the United States decided to back a process of negotiations between Zelaya and Roberto Micheletti, the man the military had installed to replace him. Eventually, after several months, an agreement emerged under which both sides would respect the results of a new presidential election. "I cannot think of another example of a country in Latin America that, having suffered a rupture of its democratic and constitutional order, overcame such a crisis through negotiation and dialogue," Hillary Clinton said in a statement during a visit to Pakistan in October 2009. But the new election was far from clean. Zelaya had understood the deal to mean he would be reinstated until a newly elected government took over. He wasn't. Then the interim government stamped down on Zelaya's media supporters, shutting down two pro-Zelaya broadcasters. In the end, the deposed president called for a boycott of the poll, which was duly won by Porfirio Lobo, one of his center-right rivals. When Zelaya ultimately returned to Honduras in 2011, it was under a deal brokered by Venezuela and Colombia.

The result was far from satisfying, both for Honduras and the United States. The whole affair showed how isolated the United States was from other big powers in the region and how feeble its diplomacy could be. In backing down on its demand that Zelaya be reinstated, Washington had found itself alone in the OAS—the nearest thing the region had to the "community of the Americas" idea Hillary Clinton would champion. Had the United States been able to coordinate a common line with Brazil—and had it acted quickly and decisively— the two regional powers might have brought their combined influence to bear. The United States might have emerged not only as a leader in the hemisphere but as one that acted in cooperation with others. As it was, the Honduras coup did little to endear the United States to Latin America or enhance its influence, while the agreement that finally resolved the issue had been put together in part by Venezuela.

Washington's failure to build a forceful diplomatic alliance with Brazil was highlighted again in 2010, when Brazil and Turkey forged a deal with Iran to ship most of its low-enriched uranium to Turkey in exchange for nuclear fuel for a civilian research reactor. Since both Turkey and Brazil had seats on the UN Security Council at the time, the deal undermined the United States' attempts to stiffen UN economic sanctions against Tehran. "In our view, the agreement eliminates any ground for sanctions against Iran," Celso Amorim, the Brazilian foreign minister, said at a press conference in Brasília on May 17, 2010. Hillary Clinton was seething. "With all due respect to my Brazilian and

Turkish friends, the fact we had Russia on board, we had China on board and that we were moving . . . to share the text of that resolution put pressure on Iran that they were trying to somehow dissipate," she told reporters through gritted teeth a day later. In the end, Clinton got her way and the United Nations approved new sanctions. But the incident left a couple of important lessons. The first was that Iran's attempts to develop ties with countries in Latin America could eventually have real, concrete results. Second, Brazil desired to be taken seriously as a global political actor and was doing so by forging a foreign policy separate from that of the United States. In this case, the United States ultimately prevailed, but in doing so it highlighted how the fastest-emerging big power in the Americas was singing a very different tune from its own hymnal.

When it came down to it, the United States seemed more comfortable playing its own global big power games than working hard to cultivate its South American neighbors. That fed into a general picture that in broad terms, Obama's approach to Latin America was more characterized by continuity with the Bush administration's policy than a new approach. Most elements of the Cuba embargo remained in place. Not only did the war on drugs continue, but it became even more of a thorn in the region's side, after the United States opted to respond to Correa's closure of its base in Ecuador by hatching a deal with Colombia to give the US military greater access to Colombian bases for antidrug and counterinsurgency operations— a move that stirred Lula and Chávez to unite in opposition to it. The trade agenda was still in limbo, and agreements with Colombia and Panama remained unapproved, even if the White House did put more energy into persuading Congress to back the deals. Hyperopia continued to mark US foreign policy, with Latin America seemingly at the bottom of the agenda. Officials voiced some concerns about the growing influence of China, Russia, and Iran, but Washington did little to counteract the trend. Diplomatically, as Honduras had demonstrated, the United States remained isolated. When it came to the role of the Americas in the world, the region spoke with many voices, not one.

So much for a "community of the Americas."

6

Meet the Street

It was billed as the wedding of the century.

There were said to be more than five thousand guests, many of whom had been flown in by their hosts from as far as Tahiti, Italy, and the United States. The press recounted how they gorged on "a buffet overflowing with caviar, lobster and salmon" and imbibed thousands of bottles of La Grande Dame, Veuve Clicquot's premium vintage champagne, and Scotch whisky. The wedding planners even imported water from the Scottish Highlands to go with it.

Had you stood outside the church on February 16, 1989, and seen the young wedding couple—Gonzalo Fernández Tinoco y Zingg and Mariela Cisneros Fontanals—arrive in a Rolls-Royce, followed by twenty luxury buses for special guests, you might have assumed they were movie actors, pop singers, or soap opera stars.

But in fact, the ostentatious display of wealth was to celebrate more than a marriage of two people. Like a medieval royal wedding, it also marked the union of two of Venezuela's richest families. The bride's father, Oswaldo Cisneros, was one of the country's wealthiest people, having inherited the Pepsi franchise in Venezuela from his father, Diego. The Cisneros family controls dozens of companies in Latin America, the United States, and Europe, from the Miss Venezuela contest to Univision, the largest Spanish-language television network in the United States.

Just in case anyone missed any minor detail of the lavishness of the affair, *Diario de Caracas*, a Venezuelan newspaper, described the wedding bash in every lurid detail in a front-page story and on no fewer than nine inside pages stuffed with pictures.

Eleven days later, hundreds of poor Venezuelans would be shot to death in some of the most violent riots the country had ever seen. The clashes came to be known as *El Caracazo*—"the big one in Caracas." Of course, it would be going too far to blame the "wedding of the century" for the riots and the killings. It wasn't as if angry mobs had formed as the aroma of rich food wafted up into the shantytowns.

Rather, you might say that the wedding was merely the context—or at least one part of it. Venezuela was, and remains, one of the most unequal countries in the world in terms of wealth distribution. In the 1960s and 1970s, the country's oil industry did rather well. In 1973, more than a quarter of a century before Hugo Chávez was elected president, Venezuela voted to nationalize its oil sector, and completed that effort three years later. The 1970s were a good time to be an oil producer, with the 1973 Yom Kippur War and the 1979 revolution in Iran pushing prices up above $60 a barrel. The income from oil exports enabled the Venezuelan government to embark on something of a social-spending spree. Hitherto unheard-of amounts of money were lavished on health care, education, and transport. Wages for workers were relatively high and food relatively cheap, thanks to state subsidies.

While they had improved the lives of the poor, Venezuela's leaders had tied those lives to the international price of oil. In the early 1980s, when oil revenues were at their peak of $19 billion, that looked like a fine idea, but the price tumbled after that, and by 1988 oil exports had fallen to $8 billion. The result was that real wages in Venezuela dropped by 40 percent in six years. The worst-off suffered the most: in the early 1980s, about one-third of Venezuelans were living in poverty. By the time of the Caracazo, half of the country was considered to be poor. By the mid-1990s, two-thirds of Venezuelans were living below the poverty line.

At the same time as more and more people became destitute, the country's rich seemed bent more than ever on flaunting their wealth. As the new poor huddled in expanding clusters of ranchos—decrepit shantytowns on the hillsides around the capital that by the time of the Caracazo contained half the capital's population—the wealthy built ever more opulent mansions in the suburbs, as well as golf courses and country clubs. They imported luxury goods such as fancy American-made limousines, which Venezuelan law allowed them to bring into the country under the same preferential terms as medicine and food, as a perk to the elites.

During the boom years of the late 1970s, Venezuelans were the world's biggest per capita consumers of Johnnie Walker Black Label, one of the world's most popular blended whiskies. Given that the poor in Venezuela are enthusiastic beer drinkers (the country also has the highest per capita beer consumption in Latin America), the rich must have been drinking an awful lot of whisky—perhaps because it was imported under the same low-tariff regime as the sleek American automobiles. So at the same time as half of all Venezuelans were living in poverty, the Venezuelan state was effectively subsidizing the very Scotch the guests raised in a toast to the newlyweds at the Fernández-Cisneros nuptials.

"The Bomb That Only Kills People"

But the spark that lit the fire that led to the Caracazo riots was not in fact the wedding of the century. Two weeks before that event, Carlos Andrés Pérez had assumed his second term as president of Venezuela. His inauguration ceremony promised a new chapter for the country. For the first time in its history, the swearing-in took place not in the Congress building but in a large performing arts center in Caracas. Pérez had served his first term as president in the 1970s, overseeing the nationalization of the oil industry and the expansion of social spending during the boom years. He had become something of a regional leader, helping the Sandinista guerrillas to overthrow the Somoza dictatorship in Nicaragua, participating in the negotiations over the Panama Canal Treaty, earning the respect of US president Jimmy Carter, and sporting some of the finest sideburns in South America. All of this endeared him to the Venezuelan public.

In his inaugural speech, Pérez urged reform at home and more cooperation among countries in the hemisphere. If Afghanistan, Namibia, and Cambodia could solve their conflicts, why, Pérez asked, could the region not do the same? In the audience, Dan Quayle, the US vice president chiefly known for his inability to spell the word "potato," sat a few feet from Fidel Castro, Washington's longtime nemesis.

But the area in which people really wanted to know the new president's views was economic policy. When Pérez had first become president in 1974, oil prices were high and heading higher, and Venezuelan government revenues seemed limitless. As it increased all kinds of social spending, his administration gained a reputation for dispensing money freely and managing the public purse poorly. By 1989, the country was still as dependent on oil, but as the price had plummeted, living standards had declined sharply, inflation was running at 40 percent and rising, and the country had built up $33 billion of foreign debts (the fourth largest in Latin America), with interest payments amounting to about 40 percent of the revenues it earned from exports. The poor who were now the majority and had propelled Pérez to power remembered his rule as a time of plenty. But Pérez's place in history was about to be drastically rewritten.

Venezuela was broke. In the weeks after Pérez took office, bakeries ran out of bread as flour millers demanded higher prices from the government. Supplies of salt, sugar, rice, coffee, and oil started to run out. Teachers went on strike for more pay. The police morgue in Caracas even ran out of money to bury homeless people found dead in the capital. The police said they had forty bodies awaiting burial and did not know what they would do with them.

The International Monetary Fund was prepared to throw Pérez a $5 billion lifeline, but at a price. It demanded that he scrap the expensive subsidies and price controls that successive Venezuelan governments had put in place. The president had known this was coming. During his election campaign, he had warned the country that there would be tough times ahead and hard economic choices to make. He had talked about the need to reduce the government's deficit, devalue the currency, and remove price controls. On the other hand, he had also pledged his support for wage increases for workers and increasing subsidies and social programs for the poor. Also during his election campaign, he had described IMF lending as a "bomb that only kills people." But Pérez was in a bind, and he chose to accept the fund's terms. So on the same day that some of the country's wealthiest citizens were celebrating the wedding of the century, the president announced an austerity program that included the end of subsidies on basic food items, public services, and gasoline.

The protests began at the El Nuevo Circo bus station in Caracas. They weren't just caused by the removal of government subsidies, which resulted in an immediate 30 percent increase in fares. By the time the increase came into effect, Venezuelans had had a few weeks to absorb that shock. Rather, when people turned up at El Nuevo Circo, they found out that the bus operators had used the opportunity to hike up fares massively. In some cases, drivers were demanding that passengers pay more than double the previous fare and refused to honor the half-price concession cards carried by schoolchildren and other students. In Guarenas, a shantytown thirty miles east of the capital, workers trying to travel into town found that their fares had doubled, from 16 bolívars to 32—the equivalent of an increase from 41 cents to 82 cents. To be fair, the bus companies were facing their own price squeeze. Although the price of gas had doubled overnight, the government had instructed the operators only to pass on 30 percent of the increase to passengers. The smaller bus companies balked and simply doubled the fares.

Put it all together: the economic crisis, the fall in living standards, the hopes for a new government, the bus fare increases, the wedding of the century. That's how it began. In their frustration, angry passengers smashed the windows of the buses they could no longer afford to travel on, occupied the bus station, and set vehicles afire. It started with the buses, but it quickly spread. A common observation in Venezuela at the time was that one day the ranchos would explode, their residents flooding down the hillsides like molten lava to lay waste to Caracas. Now it was finally happening, shattering the relative calm that Venezuela had enjoyed since the 1950s.

Within hours, thousands of rancho residents had descended to the city and began a riot that spread to other cities across the country. Young people tore down lampposts to barricade the streets. Mobs marched on stores, looting everything from food to stereo equipment and setting fire to supermarkets. On some streets in downtown Caracas, virtually every shop was looted. Camera crews captured footage of people hauling away mattresses, furniture, large sides of beef and, yes, cases of Johnnie Walker Black Label. Just two blocks from the presidential palace, a bus lay on its side, burning in the street.

Chávismo's Foundation Myth

Although Pérez later said the riots were not unexpected, his government gave little early indication that it had a plan. That night, he called out the army to restore order. They came out shooting. At least twenty-six people were killed that day, including a pregnant woman in Guarenas and a police commander. The security forces blamed most of the killings on armed looters. The following morning, the police still appeared to lack a coherent strategy. In some areas, they fired automatic weapons at the rioters. In other neighborhoods, they actually agreed to permit looting—so long as it was controlled. The "looters" formed a line outside supermarkets and were allowed to take one armful of groceries each.

Alejandro Izaguirre, the minister of the interior, appeared live on TV to issue a call for calm. Unfortunately, he fainted and the broadcast had to be suspended in a hurry. By the evening, Pérez himself decided to appear on TV to announce that he was suspending civil rights and imposing a nationwide curfew from 6 p.m. to 6 a.m. The army went into the shantytowns, ostensibly to take on armed looters. In some cases, though, they opened fire on entire apartment buildings, in what effectively became an all-out war in which the ranchos were the battlefield. There were reports of police killing people in their own homes as they conducted house-to-house searches.

The violence went on for four horrific days and no one really knows how many hundreds of people were killed. The hospitals in the city were hopelessly overcrowded with injured people. More than eighteen hundred wounded were being attended to at the Hospital Pérez Carreño in southwest Caracas, which had only seven hundred beds. Clinics issued an urgent call for blood donations. Hundreds of bodies lay rotting in the capital's central morgue, which said it did not have enough staff to cope. Local residents complained about the stench. Some of the bodies were so deteriorated, and there was so little room at the morgue, that unidentified victims were buried in common graves. There was a shortage of coffins, so some dead were buried two to a casket.

On the Caracazo's third day, the government announced a series of measures apparently designed to soothe public anger, including wage increases for millions of public-sector workers and the reinstatement of subsidies for wheat, rice, flour, milk, medicine, and, of course, transport. "In this way, the national government believes it is interpreting the sentiment of the people and guaranteeing there will not be a drop in buying power," a spokesman said in a televised statement, apparently without irony.

The official death toll from the violence was less than three hundred. Press reports at the time put it at hundreds more, with perhaps thousands dead. Many people in Caracas will still tell you that three thousand died in the Caracazo. Rumors of large numbers of executed and disappeared prompted the excavation in 1990 of an area of the public cemetery in Caracas known as La Nueva Peste ("the new plague"), a historic mass grave for victims of an epidemic. They found sixty-eight bodies stuffed into plastic garbage bags, fueling a belief in the ranchos that this was just one of many such mass graves. Whatever the real number, Pérez's handling of the crisis had undoubtedly been appalling. Under his watch, the country's security forces had demonstrated their inability to impose order without the indiscriminate use of live ammunition.

The military initially blamed the riots on student radicals and jailed ten suspected ringleaders, but they were later freed. Then the government blamed illegal immigrants from Colombia, Ecuador, and Peru. They blamed the country's conservative opposition. Ultimately, though, it was clear that the Caracazo had not been an orchestrated event but a spontaneous uprising, expressing the frustration of those who had become more impoverished as time had gone on, who resented the vulgar profligacy of the rich and the logic that saw the price of essential goods double overnight in order for Venezuela to make interest payments on debts racked up by successive governments.

"There are those that sacked stores and they should seek pardon," Jorge Uroza Sabino, the auxiliary bishop of Caracas, observed during mass a few days later. "But there are also those—especially economic and political sectors—that have sacked the country for years. They should also seek pardon."

The Caracazo became a critical landmark in Venezuela's political history. It was the beginning of a slow death for Pérez's government, paving the way for the unsuccessful coup that Hugo Chávez was to lead in 1992 against the regime and for the president's impeachment on corruption charges the following year.

The violence showed what could happen when the Washington Consensus was applied without regard to the circumstances. Left-wing activists saw it as the start of the worldwide antiglobalization movement, which was to grab the world's attention again with the protests at the World Trade Organization meeting in Seattle in 1999. For Chavistas, the Caracazo was to take on legendary status, marking the start of their Bolivarian revolution, the point at which the old order was shown to be utterly discredited. Chávez, whose own revolt came three years later, was the heir of its martyrs. The Caracazo both shaped his outlook and provided a kind of founding myth for the ideological bent of his administration. The anniversary of the Caracazo in the Chávez era has become a national event, commemorated much as the United States marks 9/11.

In a country that had lived for three decades in relative peace, the Caracazo also showed the potential of street protest. The majority of Venezuelans now lived below the poverty line. It was in the Caracazo that they first flexed their muscles. It was a stark reminder of where political power really lay.

The seeds of what happened had been sown for decades. At least some of the blame for the Caracazo must go to the president who came before Pérez—Jaime Lusinchi. He left his successor a country with debts of $33 billion and only $7 billion in reserves, unsustainable subsidies, and a growing band of the poor and desperate.

When Caracas exploded, Jaime Lusinchi was relaxing at a spa in Florida.

Washington Contentious

The Caracazo had many sequels. In the coming years, South America would be rocked time and again by huge street protests in opposition to the free-market reforms of the Washington Consensus. John Williamson, the British economist who coined the phrase, first introduced it in 1989, the same year the Caracazo shook Venezuela. Throughout the 1990s, these two streams—the free-market reforms and the unrest against them—competed for supremacy. In many cases, when the reforms were introduced, mass demonstrations followed. In many cases, they ended in violence and death. In many cases, those in power were forced to reverse their free-market course. In several cases, governments were toppled.

The United States watched these mass mobilizations with horror. The demonstrators weren't chanting "death to America," trampling over the US flag, or burning the occupant of the White House in effigy (well, yes, on a very few occasions they actually were). This wasn't that kind of revolution. It was mainly about ideas. Even during the Cold War, Latin America had been more of an ideological battleground than a real war zone. After the Cold War ended, the United States' involvement in Latin America was founded on commercial interests. But even commercial interests depended on the success of American ideas—the ideas of open markets, free trade, and small government. Those ideas took shape in the policies of the Washington Consensus. Every time the mass protests took to the streets, free-market ideas became more discredited. In the minds of people in the region, economic reforms became associated with social strife, with turmoil, with death.

Within Latin America, the Washington Consensus became widely viewed as a way to formalize the expropriation of natural resources by foreign companies and justify it in the name of economic orthodoxy. The idea was to open the region's economies up to business— often meaning American corporations. They jumped at the chance to own infrastructure, such as water and power systems that had formerly been operated by the state—usually inefficiently, but with a low cost to the consumer that reflected their status as more public services than private businesses. US companies also welcomed the opportunity to get their hands on oil and gas reserves and the Andes' rich mining deposits. Such investments were more easily available and cheaper in Latin America than they would have been back home.

But the process of handing over water systems and mountains full of gold to private companies was bound to set a collision course between locals and foreign investors. Because they were foreign, the notion was revived that, as they had done since the earliest days of the colonial period, they were in Latin America to rape the continent and then leave. It also raised locals' hackles about sovereignty and the idea that natural resources that belonged to the nation as a whole were being exploited for the benefit of American shareholders. If foreign corporations were going to make a profit on investments in utilities, prices were going to have to go up, which would irk those who would suddenly have higher bills to pay. What's more, the Latin American governments that were privatizing their industries lacked the regulatory oversight to make sure that foreign investors were not harming the environment, bribing public officials, or treating their workers badly. The result was that the process of opening up Latin America's economies fueled anti-Americanism, stoking further the resentments founded on decades of Washington's military interventions and other meddling in the region. That sentiment was most strongly felt among those who benefited the least yet were most affected—the poor, the indigenous, and the politically marginalized.

In Latin America, the term "Washington Consensus" fell out of usage. If ever there had been a consensus about economic policy in the region, it was falling apart. Instead, the policies came to be known—particularly by their opponents—by the catchall term "neoliberalism," a reference to the revival of classical ideas of laissez-faire economics advanced by eighteenth-century thinkers such as Adam Smith. The word, used in the Latin American context, carries overwhelmingly negative connotations. It sounds esoteric and cerebral, but the term became instantly intelligible to those without any formal education. It is all the stronger for the fact that it is never clearly defined. But those who use it—and the term is ubiquitous—understand what it means. It symbolizes all the anger and frustration against the heavy-handed introduction of free-market policies by inept and discredited governments. It captures everything bad about the economic mismanagement of the Andean region: the enduring poverty and the disparities of wealth; the out-of-touch elites who control the economy and economic policy; the clumsiness of economic reform. Neoliberalism became a vessel for society's ills. By the end of the 1990s, if a politician condemned neoliberalism to a crowd of poor, angry people in some remote Andean village, every man, woman, and child would roar in agreement. If you had asked those same people what the term meant, no two would have given the same answer.

This had an important psychological effect on perceptions of the United States in South America. Not only was the United States a power that in times past had plundered, invaded, and meddled in the politics of the region, but it was also an imperial power that sought to impose its will not militarily, as in the past, but via economic policy. You might have thought that when the term "Washington Consensus"

was transformed into "neoliberalism," the United States would have
been less implicated in the perceived wrongs of free-market reform.
In fact, the opposite happened: neoliberalism was wider than simply
the reforms themselves, so the result was that Washington became the
source of all bad things. The distinctions between the faults of multilateral lending institutions and the shortcomings of the Washington
Consensus were blurred in the pool of neoliberalism. The gripes may
have been new, but the foe was familiar.

With the rising power of the street, South America was gripped by
a fresh wave of instability. The democracies in the region were relatively new, and they were weak and fragile. Whereas in the good old
days Washington could depend on military governments at least to be
somewhat durable, the new democracies were not entrenched, and so
the United States faced the prospect of political weakness, uncertainty,
and volatility in its backyard. This was less a temporary phase than a
permanent change in the order of power. The region's new political
elites had failed to include the most marginalized groups in society in
governing, and so the latter were starting to express themselves not
through the ballot box, where "the government always wins," but in
protests. Even when those protests were met initially by the full force
of the state, some still succeeded in ousting the government of the
day. Presidents had to weigh the international demands for economic
orthodoxy against the prospect of being forced to flee to Miami.

Just a couple of decades earlier, South American governments
had regularly been toppled by military coups. Now they were being
regularly toppled by mass protests. Shut out of the presidency, the
legislature, and the judiciary, ordinary people gathered for large demonstrations had effectively become the ultimate check and balance.
The street was now the fourth arm of government.

The Social License

I have never been to a more depressing place in a more beautiful
setting than Choropampa.

The village sits in an enchanting valley in the northern Peruvian
highlands, a magical, picture-postcard backdrop. Yet the town itself

is permeated by an intense sadness. Smiles are rare in Choropampa. The residents are highly reserved, as are many people in the Andean highlands when confronted with newcomers. But there is also a sort of universal weariness among the inhabitants, a weariness born of the endless recounting of their tragedy.

After climbing up and down the dirt streets to interview the village's residents, I stopped for a luridly colored fizzy drink and a chat at a street cart owned by Julia Guarniz, a big woman with several kids pulling at each of her powerful arms, at the side of a degraded road that runs through the center of Choropampa. Our conversation was interrupted by a sputtering drone that gradually became a deafening roar. Round the corner, jiggling up and down on the pockmarked street, came a huge juggernaut, a giant tractor-trailer that threw up clouds of dust and stones in its wake. It was followed by another and another—seven trucks in all, a caravan of dirt and noise. Each was plastered with a sign on the side bearing the warning: HAZARDOUS MATERIALS. The trucks were carrying toxic material from Yanacocha—at the time, the world's biggest gold mine by output—hundreds of miles south to the port of Callao, just north of Lima. As the earsplitting show thundered past us, Guarniz and I could do nothing but sit and stare at the vehicles. Her children hid behind her. Even though my mouth was closed, I could still taste the dirt the convoy coughed up.

After the trucks had passed, the noise had died down a bit, and the dust had begun to clear, Guarniz cleared her throat. "They scare me," she said quietly. "When I see them, I worry that it might happen again." There was no need to ask what she was referring to. Choropampa is one of those places overshadowed by a single event, an event that permeates almost everything else that happens there.

One night in 2000, a juggernaut spilled three hundred pounds of liquid mercury over more than twelve miles of the road that leads through the village. The residents of Choropampa did not know what it was, but they remember that it looked like "a liquid mirror," collecting in pools on the highway and reflecting the moon. They gathered it using spoons and took it home in cups and empty plastic bottles. Some people heated the mercury on their stoves, knowing that it had come from a gold mine and thinking that might help release some of the precious metal. Others drank it. Their children played with it. No one was aware that what they had brought into their homes was in fact a highly toxic substance.

Yanacocha's owner—Newmont, the world's biggest gold mining company, based in Nevada—initially botched the cleanup. It promised to pay for mercury that was brought to it, inadvertently creating a black market in the village for the substance. It gave the villagers medical insurance but refused to pay for their prescriptions. It pumped millions of dollars into cleanup and compensation but failed to soothe the anger in Choropampa. The residents told me that five years after the spill, they were still suffering from neurological and skin conditions. Hatred for the mine runs deep. Although many undoubtedly had received compensation, none admitted to it. That would have been a mark of shame. Instead, they keep the shame bottled up inside, adding to the sadness that pervades the village.

Choropampa is seen by many people as a powerful symbol of the environmental and social myopia among international mining companies. Like many oil companies in Latin America, these multinationals have all too often paid scant attention to the impact of their actions on local areas and communities.

In 2004, the full force of these frustrations hit Yanacocha, when Newmont decided it wanted to expand the mine by prospecting on Cerro Quilish, a mountain that according to locals feeds streams supplying the city of Cajamarca, the biggest city near the mine, with drinking water. The Quilish plan prompted thousands of protesters to block the road to the mine, forcing Newmont to helicopter in their workers and supplies. After two weeks, the company had had enough: it said it was abandoning Quilish and issued an unprecedented public apology.

Newmont still maintains that the science proves mining Quilish wouldn't have contaminated Cajamarca's drinking water, but that argument misses the totemic importance of the battle, which was fueled by a feeling among some locals that the company has not given enough to the community. "Quilish became an icon," Cajamarca's mayor Emilio Horna told me. Newmont had its official government license to expand the mine, but it had failed to secure what those in the mining and energy industries now call a social license from the communities affected.

From protests against oil exploration in the Ecuadorean and Peruvian Amazon to mining projects in the highlands of Bolivia, foreign companies have learned time and again that without a "social license" to operate, sooner or later they are likely to become the subject of violent protest. In recent decades, the number of nongovernmental organizations in the Andes has ballooned, and these groups—many of them funded by foreign governments or by private contributions from abroad—have helped to organize communities and to bring their concerns to an international audience. The protests tend to blame the companies for failing to work with the communities affected by their mines, gas pipelines, and oil wells.

That's perfectly understandable, but at the same time, you can see why the companies have historically not bothered to do so. After all, it is really the responsibility of governments to pass and enforce environmental laws, to protect land rights, to tax foreign companies, and to use the proceeds to aid development. But Andean governments have simply not done so. In many of the areas where extractive industries operate, the state effectively doesn't exist, so locals naturally look to foreign investors to provide the spending the government fails to do. International investors become, in short, a surrogate government. In some cases, the social license to operate means that the company is expected to build a local airport or to construct roads, schools, hospitals, and clinics. In other places, it means employing lots of people from all the local villages affected. In still other cases, it involves drafting local community leaders into the management structure. The point is, though, that the origin of the social license to operate is not a set of rules drawn up by the government. In practice, the idea of a social license only exists because of protests or the threat of them. That is often the only real power that local communities feel they have.

Yanacocha, like most other big mining projects in Peru, continues to be dogged by protests every so often. In 2006, a farmer was shot dead in protests against the company's plan to construct a dam, which locals said would contaminate their water. The following year, local farmers were arrested after seizing some of Yanacocha's heavy equipment in protest at what they said was the mine's unwillingness to pay them for construction work. Not every protest is successful, but in many cases they spur action from the central government. In part, the protests work because governments fear the domestic political consequences of social unrest. In part, they work because governments fear that such unrest will discourage foreign companies that might want to invest. Either way, people have learned that when traditional politics ignores them, protests get them attention. And the more violent they are, the more attention they get.

The Water War

In Venezuela, it had started with the price of bus tickets. In Bolivia, it was water.

Whereas the Caracazo had begun in the capital city, the protests that were eventually to pave the way for Evo Morales's ascent to the presidency started not in La Paz, the seat of government, or El Alto, Bolivia's indigenous capital, but 150 miles to the southeast in Cochabamba, the country's fourth biggest city. Cochabamba is a laid-back and pleasant place, located in the central Andes at a lower elevation than the Altiplano. Warmer than La Paz–El Alto and less steamy than Santa Cruz, it is known as the City of Eternal Spring. It nestles in a fertile valley that produces much of Bolivia's grain, poultry, fruit, and vegetables.

All this agriculture is one reason that water has long been such a highly politicized issue in Cochabamba. Another is the explosion of the urban population, the same process that saw hundreds of thousands of people move from rural areas to places like El Alto or the ranchos of Caracas. In 1976, Cochabamba had a population of two hundred thousand. In the past thirty years, that has tripled, and together with the surrounding towns, the metropolitan area now has about a million residents. With the demands of farming, deforestation, and the booming urban population, Cochabamba has long suffered a water shortage. Communities typically responded by drilling ever deeper wells, which meant everyone else had less water to draw from.

So water was already a source of conflict within Cochabamba and the surrounding towns long before someone had the bright idea of privatizing the water system in 1999. That someone was Hugo Banzer Suárez, a former military man who had been trained at the Armored

Cavalry School at Fort Hood in Texas and the notorious US Army School of the Americas in Panama. In 1971, when Banzer had been a general in the Bolivian army, the country started one of its periodic left-wing tilts. The president of the day was a sort of proto-Chávez: Juan José "JJ" Torres González, a general of partly indigenous heritage whose romantic socialist ideas were shared by neither the Nixon administration in Washington nor most of the Bolivian military. After just ten months as president, JJ was toppled in a bloody military coup led by General Banzer, who led the country for the next seven years. Banzer's time as a dictator is not exactly remembered as the good old days by most Bolivians. He killed hundreds of his opponents, including one of his own former ministers. He banned left-wing parties, closed universities, and shut down the trade union federation. Unsurprisingly, by the time Banzer stepped aside in 1978, he was not much loved, which was a shame for him, because he really wanted to be president again—this time around, democratically elected by the very people he had ruled as a dictator for the past seven years. Banzer's makeover took nineteen years, but in 1997 he finally won a Bolivian presidential election. The former autocrat secured just 23 percent of the vote in a highly fragmented field, but because the constitution handed the final decision to Congress, Banzer was able to build a coalition among lawmakers, enabling him to become Latin America's first ex-dictator to win the presidency via the ballot box—even if less than a quarter of the electorate had voted for him.

The two governments before Banzer's (second) administration had privatized whole swaths of the Bolivian economy formerly under state control, including the oil and gas sector, the electricity industry, the telephone system, the national airline, and the railways. Given his dubious past, Banzer felt under pressure from Washington to show he was both a democratic leader and a free-market thinker. He was easily persuaded by the World Bank, therefore, that the solution to the water shortages in Cochabamba was to privatize the system, so as to get private companies to come up with the investment needed to modernize it. At the time, water services in the city were run by Semapa, a municipal body that wasn't doing a particularly good job—unsurprising, as it was a paragon of corruption, an object of influence-peddling by local politicians.

As Cochabamba had grown, the water infrastructure had failed to grow with it, so that much of the city—particularly poorer neighborhoods in the south—lacked running water. Instead, these areas were served by local traders who sold water from creaking tankers that they drove around the shantytowns, charging up to five times more for their water than for the stuff that came out of the tap. The result was that even though the shantytown dwellers used much less water per family, they generally spent about 10 percent of their household income on expensive water from the tankers, whereas those hooked up to the system spent on average about 1 percent of their household income on water. Those who couldn't afford the price-gouging cost of the tanker water had to carry water in buckets, often filled from rivers and streams. Even if you had water on tap, the service was patchy, and the more water you used, the less you paid per unit—meaning there was effectively a built-in incentive to waste water. In the north of the city, middle-class *Cochabambinos* used sprinklers to keep their gardens nice and green, while in the southern districts entire families were making do with less than six gallons of water a day. The World Bank and the Banzer government saw Cochabamba as an excellent opportunity to show how a private company could improve efficiency, extend the network, and avert a water crisis in the city.

So Banzer set out his stall. On sale: the concession to run Cochabamba's water system. There wasn't exactly an enthusiastic response, but one company did express interest—International Water, a subsidiary of Bechtel, a huge private engineering company based in San Francisco that had helped build Nevada's Hoover Dam and the San Francisco rapid transit system. International Water entered its proposal in partnership with Abengoa, a Spanish company, and several smaller Bolivian firms under the name Aguas del Tunari, after Mount Tunari, the snowcapped peak that overlooks the city. Aguas del Tunari paid $1 million up front for the forty-year contract, promising to invest $180 million in the first five years and $140 million for the remaining thirty-five years. Within five years, they pledged, 93 percent of Cochabamba's residents would have drinking water and sewage connections. In return, the agreement specified that the company would be guaranteed an annual return of at least 16 percent on its investment.

One important character who had also been at the table when the Aguas del Tunari deal was being thrashed out was Manfred Reyes Villa, the suave mayor of Cochabamba. Reyes styled himself as a sort of Bolivian version of Tom Selleck in *Magnum P.I.* but actually looked more like Borat, the hapless fictitious Kazakh reporter. Reyes had one condition for allowing the privatization to go ahead: both the state and Aguas del Tunari also had to put money toward the Misicuni Project, a proposal to build a dam on a high plateau above Cochabamba and bore a twelve-mile tunnel through the mountain, at depths of up to thirty-three hundred feet, to bring water to the city. Constructing Misicuni was estimated to take ten years and cost up to $450 million. That made it more than six times as expensive and twice as long to bring online than another option, Corani, that would have brought water from an existing hydroelectric dam project just east of Cochabamba. The World Bank had condemned Misicuni as uneconomical, but Reyes was insistent. For one thing, he liked giant projects. Five years earlier, he had overseen the completion of a huge white statue of Jesus with outstretched arms on a hill in Cochabamba. Until Peru built an even bigger statue in 2011, it was the biggest Jesus in the world, a few feet taller than the famous figure that overlooks Rio de Janeiro. Second, Reyes's friends in the local business community stood to gain highly lucrative contracts from the Misicuni proposal. The mayor, who had just won reelection, was part of Banzer's fragile mega-coalition and the president wanted him on board. Reyes had vetoed an earlier privatization effort over the Misicuni issue, so it was understood that this was his price.

So Aguas del Tunari was promising to expand water coverage massively and help fund the Misicuni boondoggle, all while expecting a 16 percent yearly profit. It was clear that someone was ultimately going to have to pay for all this. The company was hoping it would be the citizens of Cochabamba.

But it wasn't just the price increases that sparked ugly scenes in the center of this charming city. It was also Law 2029, a piece of legislation passed hurriedly and without consultation that enabled the privatization to proceed but also gave the government the power to hand all local wells and rural irrigation trenches over to Aguas del Tunari. These waterworks had been built not by Semapa but by community organizations that sought to serve their own neighborhoods. The company was effectively granted the power to charge people for any water in the city from any source.

It was this law that first provoked protests by local irrigators. They formed the *Coordinadora*, an alliance with local unions, and started to organize protests against the privatization. The water rate increases came next, with average price hikes of at least 50 percent. The biggest price increases fell on the middle class, with some people's water bills tripling overnight. People instantly took to the streets, employing the impromptu roadblocks that are Bolivia's trademark tool of protest. In February 2000, armed police clashed with demonstrators for days in the middle of town. Cochabamba was united in opposition to the price hikes, with the middle class joining forces to protest alongside local peasants, workers, and students. It worked. The government intervened, saying the company would have to return to the old water rates, at least temporarily.

The protest leaders pressed their advantage: the mood had now turned so completely against Aguas del Tunari that they simply wanted the company out and Law 2029 revoked. In April, when protesters again took over the center of town, Banzer declared a state of siege, suspending civil rights and implementing a curfew. The protests only intensified, and in the ensuing clashes with security forces an army captain shot and killed an unarmed seventeen-year-old protester. It was a shocking, bloody climax to the whole affair. A few days later, the Bolivian government announced that Bechtel officials—who had watched the violence unfold on TV in their smart hotel room—had fled the country, effectively burying the contract. The World Bank–sponsored experiment in Cochabamba was over.

Evo's Lesson

Like the Caracazo, the Water War took on legendary status. For the first time, a street protest had forced a speedy U-turn of a privatization that had enjoyed the support of its own government and the big multilateral lending agencies in Washington. In the eyes of the world, Cochabamba showed that ordinary people had the will and the power to confront and defeat the accepted economic wisdom of the day. For six years, Bechtel pursued a $25 million claim against the Bolivian government for canceling the Cochabamba contract, but eventually it decided to walk away, calculating that the case was only harming its corporate reputation. The affair was a blow for the Washington Consensus, one that provoked some soul-searching in the US capital. If the Water War became a heroic and mythic event for the Left, for the World Bank it became something of a case study of how *not* to go about doing things. Communications professionals said the benefits of the project had not been made clear enough to residents. Governance experts blamed the choice of the Misicuni Project over the Corani option. Economists blamed the company for abandoning the project. Whatever your interpretation, like the Caracazo, the Water War had imprinted in people's minds the idea that free-market reforms inevitably led to violent social unrest. After what it went through, it would be hard for Cochabamba ever again to contemplate privatizing its water system. The water is back in public hands, and the corruption and mismanagement continue and much of the city is still without running water, but you would be hard pressed to find any residents who regret kicking out Aguas del Tunari.

The Water War also institutionalized in Bolivian politics the role of social movements—organizations that had been effectively excluded from political decision making, such as community organizations and peasant groups. If the Caracazo had established the street's role as the fourth arm of government, the Water War gave it a defined shape and a leadership. One of the key local figures on the streets in Cochabamba was Evo Morales, a coca growers' leader whose followers had their own beef with the government, since Banzer had promised the United States he would eliminate cultivation of the crop in Bolivia. Like everyone else who participated, Morales learned from the Water War an important lesson about the power of the street. Two years later, he ran for the presidency for the first time, effectively claiming leadership of the social movements. The following year, the Gas War exploded in El Alto, a backlash against then president Gonzalo Sánchez de Lozada's plan to export gas through Chile. Again, the social movements demonstrated their power: confrontations between protesters and security forces left dozens of people dead and forced the president to hotfoot it to Miami. His successor was also forced out by massive protests, setting up the election that put Morales in the presidential palace.

In just a few years, the social movements had unseated two presidents in Bolivia and had propelled Morales to power. The Caracazo had led to the ousting of Carlos Andrés Pérez in Venezuela and paved the way for Hugo Chávez's eventual rise to power. In Ecuador, violent street protests prompted Lucio Gutiérrez to flee the presidential palace in April 2005, making him the country's third head of state to be forced out of office early in eight years and setting the stage for the election of Rafael Correa the following year. In each case, the street movements preceded the men who later claimed to be their leaders. Without the mass demonstrations, Chávez, Morales, and Correa might well not have won power at all. But it was not they who prompted the protests, so much as the protests that prompted them. The power of the street came first, the presidential campaigns followed later.

As president, Evo Morales remained acutely aware that political power in Bolivia resided as much on the street as in the presidential palace. On one hand, that meant he had to be careful not to alienate the very social movements that had launched him into office. On the other hand, one got the impression that he never quite adapted to being the head of state. In April 2009, Morales was locked in a dispute with opposition lawmakers, who were refusing to approve elections mandated under Bolivia's new constitution. Frustrated by his old foes, the president reverted to type. He dragged his mattress into one of the staterooms in the presidential palace and declared to the world that he was going on a hunger strike. For five days, he wore the same black jeans and short-sleeved shirt and sustained himself by chewing on coca leaves. It worked: the opposition and the government eventually struck a deal.

Even as president, Morales had found, the official channels would only get you so far. The real way to get things done in Bolivia was to protest.

7

Evo, Evo Presidente!

As we descended painstakingly toward Morochata on a steep dirt track, Evo Morales told the driver to stop. He proudly pointed through the car window to a crowd of a few thousand people waiting for him in the village square below, savoring his triumphant entrance by delaying it for a few minutes.

It was a hot Sunday afternoon in November 2005 (the beginning of the Southern Hemisphere's summer), five weeks before the election that he would win with a historic landslide to become Bolivia's first indigenous president since the Spanish conquest. We were about thirty miles northwest of Cochabamba, deep in the stunning scenery of the high Andes. The air was thin, pure, and dry, and the sun was starting to burn my skin.

Evo, as he was known by both allies and enemies, loved being a presidential candidate. He seemed to possess boundless energy, visiting scores of cities, villages, and remote hamlets, and relishing every experience. He had little formal education and only eight years of congressional experience, but he possessed an acute strategic instinct and a natural sense of political theater.

In Morochata, he played the role of the returning conquering hero of old. Evo told the driver to stop the car on the edge of the little potato-farming village, where a brass band was waiting to accompany him on a jubilant march to the main square. A handful of local leaders anointed him with mounds of confetti that clung to his thatch of black hair. We walked through the town along dusty streets lined with crumbling stone houses. A group of men in red ponchos and trilby hats acted as an impromptu security team, forming a ring around Evo and those of us who were accompanying him. Every so often, villagers would come forward to hang a garland around his neck—some made of flowers, others of potatoes, beans, and coca leaves. The route to the plaza was marked by a series of wooden archways decorated with pink and white flowers. One was a goalpost that must have been plucked, cement bases and all, from the local soccer field. Crowds thronged the path, cheering, setting off homemade fireworks, and jostling to be near their future president.

The atmosphere in the main square was expectant, fueled by what smelled like ample amounts of *chicha*, the sour corn liquor fermented with spit that is ubiquitous across the Andean highlands. A reporter from the *New York Times* and I attracted attention, culminating every so often in what I assume were vague threats, though it was difficult to interpret the indecipherable drunken slurring.

Speaker after speaker introduced Morales as though he had already won the election. One described him as "president of the poor, president of the Aymara and Quechua peoples, president of this country." The order was important. Above everything else, Evo Morales won power because he promised fundamental change in economic management, vowing at every opportunity to end neoliberalism and reverse twenty years of Bolivian history.

Perhaps more than anywhere else, Bolivia became a laboratory for the policies of the Washington Consensus. Regardless of your political views, it would be hard to travel around Bolivia today and say with any conviction that these measures solved the country's basic economic problems. They failed to set the country on a sound economic footing or to tackle poverty. Life for most Bolivians remains intolerably wretched. Unemployment, lack of education, and child mortality are commonplace in South America's poorest country.

Much political debate in Bolivia revolved around the deep contrast between this abject poverty and the country's buried treasure: about 50 trillion cubic feet of natural gas, the second largest reserves in the region after Venezuela. After a decade of multinational energy companies successfully running the sector, and with global energy demand having pushed natural gas prices to historic highs, there was understandable frustration that the millions of dollars of profits collected by foreign investors were not seen to be benefiting ordinary Bolivians. It was this frustration that both prompted the elections of December 2005 (when interim president Carlos Mesa refused to approve the tax hikes on foreign investors in the gas sector) and the demand—picked up by all three of the leading candidates—to nationalize Bolivia's gas sector.

Morales had not originally favored nationalization. He only picked up on the demand after it became a popular call of mass protests. You often got the sense with Morales that he took his cue from the street—fitting for a man who adopted for his brand of Andean socialism a phrase borrowed from Roman Catholicism: "The voice of the people is the voice of God."

The closer the elections drew, the more foregone the eventual result became, although nearly no one expected it to be resolved in the first round. But on that day in Morochata, it was somewhat unbelievable that Evo Morales would soon become president. He was so profoundly ordinary. He looked ordinary, with his tubby body and hair like a center-parted black helmet, and he seemed to prefer joking around than talking seriously about politics.

In the Hands of Indigenous Peoples

Born near the city of Oruro in Bolivia's western highlands, Morales spent his childhood tending the family's llamas and cultivating potatoes. He described it as a daily struggle to survive and recalled running behind passing buses and scavenging the orange peels and banana skins passengers tossed out the window. Four of his six siblings died before they were one year old.

He dropped out of formal education several times and spent much of his teenage years flitting through a series of short-term jobs: bricklaying, baking, cutting sugarcane, playing trumpet in a traveling band.

His family moved periodically, settling in the 1980s in the Chapare region, in the highlands south of La Paz, where they farmed coca, a plant that has been used for centuries in the Andes as a traditional stimulant but which by then had taken off as an important export crop, thanks to the demand for cocaine on the streets of the United States and Europe.

In a sense, the US government gave Morales his first break in politics. After military service, he worked as a coca farmer and coach of a football team. As US-sponsored eradication efforts in the Chapare intensified, six local federations of coca growers united to defend their crops and elected him their leader in 1993.

From then, he began an extraordinary political ascent. He first organized the coca growers into a political party in 1995 to fight local elections. In 1997, his Movement to Socialism (MAS) won four seats in Congress. By 2002, aided by a backlash against derogatory comments from the US ambassador at the time, he came within a whisker of topping the presidential poll and MAS became the largest opposition party in Congress. By 2005, Morales pulled off a remarkable feat: a universally unexpected landslide, winning in the first round with almost 54 percent of the vote, an unprecedented achievement in such a politically divided country.

Left-wing and indigenous politics are not easily unraveled in the Andes, but for Morales, the former are at least as important as the latter. He rose not through traditional indigenous power structures and does not speak fluently either Aymara or Quechua, the two main indigenous languages. Other presidential candidates in 2005 better represented conventional indigenous interests, such as Felipe Quispe, an Aymara peasant leader with an Andean-wide vision of indigenous unity who ran against Morales (and whose virulent anti-Americanism had led him to celebrate the terrorist attacks of September 11, 2001).

But as a native Aymara who rose to political prominence as the leader of Quechua coca growers, Morales was able to present himself as a figure who could unite the two biggest indigenous groups, as well as a rural communitarian in touch with traditional methods of decision making.

More important, although he may have lacked some of the self-conscious trappings of indigenous leadership, Morales pledged to use the power of the state to reverse permanently the five-hundred-year-old marginalization of indigenous people from government. Since this historical injustice was codified in Bolivia's founding constitution, Morales pledged in every stump speech to convene an assembly to rewrite the constitution to include a greater say for the indigenous majority.

"No Aymara, no Quechua, no woman participated in writing the constitution in 1825," he told the crowd in Morochata. "What was created was a colonial state." Alongside the nationalization of natural resources, a new constitution was the other central plank of Morales's campaign.

He was careful to pay his dues to indigenous traditions at his swearing-in. The day before he officially took power, Morales became the first person in 513 years to be symbolically inaugurated by indigenous leaders from the high Andes in a ceremony at Tiwanaku, a spectacular pre-Incan ruin near La Paz.

Morales's victory was an important watershed in indigenous politics in Bolivia and beyond. In a country in which the Left had deployed a range of extra governmental practices, from terrorism to paralyzing roadblocks, he demonstrated that traditional forms of politics could be made to work for the indigenous majority. He showed ordinary Bolivians, traditionally alienated from the corridors of power in La Paz, that the mechanisms of governing the state could be theirs. "It is not I who have won power, it is the indigenous peoples of Bolivia," he declared before a massive crowd in Plaza San Francisco, the traditional rallying point for antigovernment protests, on the day of his inauguration.

Maximo Paredes, a traditional indigenous leader, told the crowd at Tiwanaku, "We now consider the Bolivian state to be in the hands of the indigenous peoples."

As we drove away from Morochata, Morales put on the car stereo a CD of songs entirely dedicated to himself and his forthcoming electoral victory, which we had already listened to several times on the three-hour drive to the village from Cochabamba. The CD had seventeen tracks, but Morales had a favorite that he played over and over, turning the volume high and drumming along on the dashboard. The song had a jolly, east European–style melody, and if you only half listened, it would not have sounded out of place at an Orthodox Jewish wedding, if not for the words:

Evo, Evo presidente! (Evo, Evo president!)
Todo el MAS *está presente!* (All the MAS is here!)
Evo, Evo presidente! (Evo, Evo president!)
Todo el pueblo está presente! (All the people are here!)

I remember listening and being overwhelmed by a strong sensation that the election itself would probably be a high point. There was a sort of tragic inevitability about Evo Morales's government. In the months after he was first elected, ordinary Bolivians expressed such high expectations about their new president that they were almost bound to be disappointed. I think Morales sensed it too. The goal of reforging the state, of overturning more than five hundred years of history, was a vast task, particularly for such an inexperienced leader. As election day drew closer, he inserted a section into his speeches pleading for patience and begging forgiveness for mistakes yet to be made.

Even as he was being inaugurated, you could see in his demeanor not triumph but trepidation. He looked overwhelmed by the task facing him, which only reinforced his ordinariness. As his vice president placed the sash of office around his neck, Morales burst into tears.

The Invisible

Since the time the Spanish arrived in South America, political power in the continent has usually resided in the hands of a tiny, cohesive, tightly knit political elite. The skin on those hands has tended to be pretty pale. In the early days of the European conquest, the Spanish themselves held the reins of power. Over time, their descendants—often the product of mixed marriages between those of pure European stock and the Incan aristocracy—maintained their control over the countries that eventually won independence from Spain in the nineteenth century.

Even when democracy finally swept the region for good, indigenous South Americans were largely excluded from power. In some parts of the continent, this was less obvious an omission than in others. In countries such as Argentina and Chile, for example, indigenous people make up a small proportion of the overall population.

This is partly because the governments of both countries dealt with their indigenous problem in the nineteenth century. From the 1860s to the 1880s, Chile fought a war against the Mapuche, an indigenous tribe that lived on the southern coast and had resisted conquest by both the Spanish and the Incas. The Mapuche were eventually defeated and either fled or were forcibly moved onto reservations. Their ancestral lands were confiscated, renamed, and given to European settlers.

A similar campaign was fought by Argentina between 1875 and 1884. Its mastermind was Julio Argentino Roca, a man who was to become president of Argentina twice and whose views made him lucky to have lived in an age before political correctness. "Our self-respect as a virile people obliges us to put down as soon as possible, by reason or by force, this handful of savages who destroy our wealth and prevent us from definitely occupying, in the name of law, progress and our own security, the richest and most fertile lands of the Republic," said Roca, in a speech to the country's legislature upon being named minister of war in 1877. Within about eight years, in the Conquest of the Desert, Roca "cleansed" Patagonia of indigenous settlements, with the help of breech-loading Remington rifles supplied by the United States. Again, the lands were seized and given to new immigrants from Europe.

As a result, Chile and Argentina are nowadays among the most European of South American countries, with indigenous populations estimated at about 5 percent for Chile and 2 percent for Argentina. So while indigenous rights activists continue to fight for the correction of these historic injustices in both countries, their marginalization from politics is not an electoral issue.

In Bolivia, Ecuador, and Peru, the situation is quite different. Although the Spanish fought and defeated the Incan empire, the authorities in those countries did not attempt the systematic wholesale slaughter of the indigenous population. The result is that although many people in the Andes are mixed-race mestizos who have both indigenous and European ancestry, there are large segments that have retained not only their indigenous communities but their indigenous culture and identity as well.

Indigenous peoples account for about 55 percent of Bolivia's population, 45 percent of Peru's, and about one-quarter of Ecuador's. In much of the Andes, therefore, they are a significant political force. Of course, they are neither a single group nor a united voting bloc. Nevertheless, they make up a large segment of the population—a segment that has historically been barred from power, regardless of whether the regime has been colonial, military, or democratic.

In some cases this marginalization has been a version of apartheid, as when indigenous Bolivians were barred from walking in certain areas of cities such as La Paz. In other cases, traditional languages such as Quechua, the language of the Inca, and Aymara, an indigenous tongue spoken in the communities of the high Andean plateau around Lake Titicaca, were not recognized by the state, denying their speakers a host of civil and political rights.

But in most cases the marginalization is a product of simply being ignored. For hundreds of years, people in the Andes had lived in civilized, well-organized communities, spoken their own languages, had their own leadership and legal code, and made their collective decisions through traditional power structures. In spite of the Spanish conquest, this way of life continued and still continues, yet the new republics that sprang up in the nineteenth century and fought for their independence from European control found little way of incorporating these traditions into their national power structures.

So where people were not barred and languages not banned, they were simply disregarded, pushed aside, overlooked, and undermined. The indigenous were made invisible: their leaders were afforded no power in the eyes of the state, their legal code was not incorporated into the law of the land, their language was unheard in the courts and the legislatures, and their words did not appear in the founding constitutions of countries such as Bolivia, Ecuador, and Peru.

Occasionally, the indigenous have been treated as if they really were invisible. When you think of indigenous people living in the Andes, you tend to conjure up images of blank, weather-beaten faces, of eking out an existence on the cold, high plateau by cultivating subsistence crops like potatoes and corn that can grow at high altitude. But large swaths of Bolivia, Ecuador, and Peru are the Amazon jungle, which contains many smaller groups of indigenous people who have either lived in the jungle for generations or have migrated down from the high Andes.

A small number of these jungle communities are uncontacted tribes, communities that live in isolation from the modern world, either because they choose to or because they have not yet come into contact with modernity and their lands have been protected from development.

Except that they haven't been very well protected. First, Andean governments have not acted firmly to stop logging in the Amazon, so loggers in search of valuable hardwood trees such as mahogany have ventured into tribal lands and cut down the forest, pushing the tribes into smaller and smaller territories and often causing conflict between them.

In addition, South American governments have often seen it as unfair that the natural resources under the ground have been monopolized by a tribal group simply because it has lived in that spot for hundreds of years. So in Peru, for example, the government has opened up the ancestral lands of indigenous communities in the Amazon for exploration by international energy companies looking for oil and gas—which, of course, pay a pretty penny for these exploration rights.

To back up this policy, the Peruvian state turned to a version of that thorny old philosophical puzzle: if a tree falls in a forest and no one is around to hear it, does it make a sound? In the oil-hunting formulation, it became: if the uncontacted tribes don't have any contact with anyone, how do we know they exist?

Cecilia Quiroz, a spokeswoman for Perupetro, a state-owned oil company, graphically illustrated this argument. "It is like the Loch Ness monster," she told the *Washington Post* in an article published on July 8, 2007. "Everyone seems to have seen or heard about uncontacted peoples, but there is no evidence."

A few months later, a Brazilian environmentalist flew over the ancestral lands of uncontacted tribes living on the Brazil-Peru border and captured rare evidence that although they were uncontacted, they were not fictional. The photos, which showed a couple of tribesmen painted in red war paint and threatening the aircraft with spears, grabbed the attention of the world.

Like the Loch Ness monster, the pictures caused a bit of a flap. Reports described the tribe as "undiscovered," which was not the case—they were known about but not in contact with the modern world. Nevertheless, some of the media condemned the whole thing as a stunt and a hoax, with a few even suggesting that the pictures had been staged.

That gave more credence to those who were more interested in exploiting the natural resources beneath their feet than in protecting the communities' traditional way of life. Alan García, Peru's president, wrote shortly after that those who protested the entry of the multinational energy companies into the pristine jungle were basically fantasists. "Against petroleum, they have created the figure of the 'unconnected' wild native, which is to say, something not known but presumed," he wrote in a column in Lima's *El Comercio* newspaper in October 2007.

Although this denial of a minority's existence is highly unusual, the general pattern of marginalization of indigenous peoples is of course a familiar story that could be told about the United States, Canada, Australia, and many other countries. The difference in the Andes was in the sheer number of people. Even when there were brief periods of democracy, the indigenous were essentially unrepresented in national decision making.

So when public money was being spent—on education, on infrastructure, on hospitals, on security—the voice of indigenous people was not heard. When laws that affected them were being drafted (such as the distribution of oil exploration lots), they were not consulted. When disaster befell them, relief was slow to come, if it came at all.

"No One Wants to Be a *Cholo*"

When people are far away, ignoring them is easy. But as hordes of indigenous people have left their hometowns in rural areas and moved into cities in recent decades, the active racism—as opposed to passive ignoring—of Andean societies has been thrown into stark contrast.

On a lazy Sunday summer afternoon in 2007, on a beach sixty miles south of Lima, hundreds of activists dressed in maids' uniforms paraded down the beach and plunged into the sea, disturbing the tranquility at one of Peru's most exclusive resorts.

It wasn't the local cross-dressing club out for a swim. The group was made up of civil rights campaigners protesting against what they said were informal rules at Asia, an upscale resort comprising a string of twenty-six private beach clubs and condominium developments. According to the protesters, the clubs' unwritten rules forced maids to wear uniforms and barred them from swimming in the ocean during the day. The claim was denied by local leaders in Asia, but in a country like Peru it was a believable allegation.

In 2005, I made my first and last visit to the Cricket and Football Club in Lima, an expatriate hangout so devoted to the joys of Merrie Olde England that a complete wooden pub had been shipped out from Britain and reconstructed there to impart an authentic flavor to the warm beer and soggy fish and chips. On the doors of the changing rooms was a sign warning: NO MAIDS ALLOWED.

One flashpoint where racism becomes most evident is at nightclubs. On one of my first nights out in Lima, a friend was stopped from going into a disco in Barranco, a hip neighborhood. The doorman told her he had been instructed to turn away people "whose skin is too dark."

This wasn't an isolated case. After years of hearing of such incidents, in 2007 the Peruvian government finally acted against the practice. It shut down Café del Mar, a chic nightspot in Miraflores, in south Lima, after undercover investigations revealed that mixed-race couples were being turned away from the club while whiter couples were being allowed in.

Café del Mar became the first nightclub to be forcibly closed because of racial discrimination. The case shed new light on ingrained practices in a society whose social, political, and economic elites have traditionally been dominated by lighter-skinned descendants of European immigrants.

After generations of intermarriage, most Peruvians do not fall easily into racial categories. The majority is mestizo and can trace its heritage back to combinations of indigenous, black, Chinese, and white ancestors. "Pure" indigenous Peruvians make up the majority in the high Andes, while there are much smaller numbers of whites and blacks.

This patchwork masks a deeply entrenched system of prejudices. Peruvians are acutely aware of a plethora of subtle social and cultural distinctions that are almost imperceptible to outsiders. These differences are marked by a complex mix of indicators such as race, height, facial characteristics, demeanor, dress, language, and accent. A European or North American might see two Peruvians and think their coloring looks about the same—but racial prejudice in the Andes is not a simple matter of skin color.

Discrimination is more than just an unfortunate stain on Andean society. It's actually a part of the cultural organization of society. To be white is the best of all possible worlds. To be mestizo is a little worse. To be a *cholo*—an indigenous person—is the worst, to the extent that in Peru, *cholo* is an insult, particularly when used by indigenous people about one another. As Ollanta Humala once told me in an interview, "No one wants to be a *cholo.*"

This mind-set has robbed many indigenous people of their self-respect. One of the most disturbing aspects of this is that European or North American male visitors to Peru are frequently approached by local women—particularly in the jungle region, which is less conservative than the highlands—whose aim is to get themselves pregnant by a white man.

Many ordinary Peruvian men and women also want to marry "whiter" than themselves—an impulse that can be traced back to the nineteenth-century idea of "improving the race," which provoked newly independent Latin American countries to send commissions to Europe to promote settlement in the region. Ollanta Humala again: "A *cholo* who becomes a bit whiter is often more racist than a white person."

"Give Them the Belt"

Imagine an American politician seeking national office and telling voters on the campaign trail that he wanted to go to Washington in order to continue the stellar work of the incumbent lawmakers on Capitol Hill. "Our government is doing a great job," the candidate would tell the assembled crowds, to rapturous applause. "What we need in our nation's capital is more of the same."

Or not. In real life there is only one way to win a seat in the US Congress—by promising to bring sweeping change, to shake things up, to confront special interests and do things completely differently.

But even the perennial-change candidates of US elections only take change so far. They propose to change the *way* of doing things, to improve the system and make it work better, cheaper, or more efficiently. What they don't do is suggest scrapping the whole system and starting again from scratch. Perhaps that reflects that at various points in their history Americans have been disgruntled with their government, but they have rarely been angry enough to throw out the whole thing.

In advanced democracies, when there is real anger and general disenchantment with politics and politicians, we call it a crisis. In 2009, hundreds of British politicians were found to have been claiming expenses from the taxpayers to pay for second homes, groceries, whirl-pool baths, pay-per-view pornographic films, and, in one case, to clear out a moat at a country estate. The understandable reaction of the general public was deep disgust. Perhaps the same sentiment met the abuses of power under the Nixon administration in the United States.

Now imagine that disgust rising up not just once in a generation but as a permanent feature of the political landscape. This ought to give a sense of the relationship between politicians and the public in much of the Andes. Ecuador offers a good example. Over the years, opin-ion polls have generally shown that less than 10 percent of the public approves of the Congress, even immediately after an election in which the former has just reelected the latter.

I got a taste of the general mood in Ecuador on the stump with Rafael Correa in October 2006. I followed his presidential campaign to Latacunga, a poor and dreary highland town about seventy-five miles south of Quito. It was a heavy, humid afternoon, Correa was three hours late, and the four thousand locals gathered in the town's shabby central square were starting to look bored. They listened politely as a precocious nine-year-old boy wailed bolero standards into a microphone. "We have waited all our lives for this revolution," pleaded one of the organizers between songs. "Please, let's wait a few minutes more."

When the candidate eventually deigned to turn up at his own rally, the bolero tape was hurriedly replaced with rock. Wearing a broad grin and clad in his campaign colors of lime green and blue, Correa bounced onto the stage to the anthemic heavy-metal strains of Twisted Sister's "We're Not Gonna Take It," wielding a brown leather belt, which he flexed along to the music.

The belt was to Ecuador what Evo Morales's sweater was to Bolivia. In Spanish, *correa* means "belt," and the candidate played on the connection with the slogan *"Dale Correa"* ("Give them the belt")—to signify his goal of whipping the country's politicians into shape. In television ads, a cartoon belt would appear in the corner of the screen and made a smacking sound to emphasize the point.

In front of the crowd, Correa was wildly energetic, jumping around to the music, pausing to wave to the crowd and to accept flowers, fruit, and a striped poncho. When he came to speak, the smile gave way to anger and a promise of vengeance. "The political and economic elites have stolen everything from us, but they cannot steal our hope," he told the crowd in Latacunga, speaking in Quichua, the indigenous language of the highlands. (The language is known as Quichua in Ecuador and Quechua in Peru and Bolivia.) "We will take back our oil, our country, our future."

The target of Correa's anger was not the country's government of the day, since the situation in Ecuador was similar to that in Bolivia before Evo Morales won office: the presidency was held by a hapless former vice president, a caretaker who had only stumbled into the top job after the elected head of state fled the country.

Instead, Correa declared war on what he called the *partidocracia* ("partyocracy"), the interminable rule by a cabal of discredited and widely loathed political parties. The line he took was similar to the old joke, "No matter who you vote for, the government always wins." The Ecuadorean people had been voting for "change" for decades, yet the same old parties, characters, and ideas seemed to continue to run the country.

The Outsiders Come In

Thanks to a year of his youth that he spent performing community service in a poor town, Correa may have been able to speak the indigenous language of the highlands, but he certainly did not have the ordinary credentials that Evo Morales boasted. He grew up not a rural peasant but a middle-class boy in Guayaquil, Ecuador's largest, richest city. Where Morales had almost no formal education, Correa had a master's degree from the Catholic University of Leuven in Belgium and a doctorate from the University of Illinois, both in economics.

Most obviously, Correa had no striped sweater. In fact, he was by far the best dressed of all Hugo Chávez's regional allies, appearing in a suit and tie for television interviews and presidential debates—although to retain some credibility with the disheveled Left, he claimed he had never actually purchased a tie and joked that his first presidential decree would be to ban them.

Still, Correa clearly was an outsider. He had spent some time as finance minister, of course, but it had lasted little longer than a stroll through the ministry's offices before he was shown the exit. Before that, he had been a university academic, whose left-wing views were well known to his colleagues.

The outsider status proved important. In much of the Andes, the more inexperienced you are, in many ways the greater your appeal to voters. (A notable exception to this rule was Colombia.) Evo Morales had spent most of his life with the coca growers of the central Bolivian highlands. Rafael Correa had spent much of his adult life safely protected from the pollution of Ecuadorean politics, tucked away in various universities around the world.

Before he was elected, Chávez was also the ultimate outsider. He grew up in poverty, his parents sending him to live with his grandmother because they were unable to support him, his younger brother dying because they could not afford medicine. Moreover, Chávez came from the military—an institution that still retains the respect of many in the Andes who have become disillusioned with the functioning of democracy. Even within the military, Chávez had a track record as an outsider, defying his superiors to launch an unsuccessful coup in 1992, in the aftermath of the Caracazo. As he was admitting defeat, Chávez memorably said in a televised statement that he was calling off the coup *"por ahora"* ("for the time being"), noting before being hauled off to prison that "new and better opportunities will emerge for us in the future."

In 1998, Venezuela's establishment tried everything it could think of to stop Chávez from winning the presidency. In a country that regularly wins the Miss World and Miss Universe competitions, it tried to make the presidential race into a beauty contest. At first it pitted Irene Saez, a blond, thirty-six-year-old former Miss Universe, to run against Chávez. In doing so, it set up the election as a choice between the beauty and the beast.

When Saez's candidacy stumbled, the mainstream parties united behind Henrique Salas Romer, a suave businessman. When that also failed to work, Chávez's opponents warned that his victory would lead to a certain military coup, since the armed forces feared a Fidel Castro–style regime taking power in Venezuela. Economic disaster would be inevitable, they said. "Think of what is at stake: your house, your family, your job—you could lose it all with the candidate of disaster," a foreboding voice cautioned in one anti-Chávez TV spot.

In Peru, Ollanta Humala had also been at the head of a failed coup—an attempt in 2000 to lead army units in rebellion against the government of Alberto Fujimori. At the time, some had declared him a hero of democracy. Humala was still considered an outsider when he won the presidency in 2011. As a presidential candidate, Humala tapped that vein. At a boisterous rally in Tacna, Peru's southernmost city, in April 2006, I watched him shouting in anger in front of a crowd baying for the blood of the politicians in Lima. "The powerful have stolen democracy from us," Humala roared. "They say I am 'antisystem.' Well, 'the system' is the poverty of our people! So yes, I am the antisystem candidate. I am more than that—I am a rebel!"

Being an outsider was not enough in itself. Political outsiders had come to office in Ecuador, Bolivia, and Peru in the past, but they had usually changed course once in power, abandoning their outsider status and failing to carry out the transformations they had promised.

So the focus of the new generation of radical Left leaders in the Andes was not just to change policies. It was to change fundamentally the rules of the game, the way that policies were made. Whereas politicians in the United States and Europe promised to change policy, the Andean radicals vowed to confront and defeat the system itself.

Rewriting Constitutions

To do so, they had to get at the heart of where they thought democracy had failed—the constitution. Since national constitutions had established the rules of the game that were now so discredited, one of their most important pledges was to rewrite their constitutions, to refound their republics with the aim of ridding them of the scourge of the former system.

"Venezuela is being born again," Chávez declared when he won the 1998 election with 56 percent of the vote, in spite of the best efforts of the political elite. In a taste of the rhetorical flourishes that were to mark his presidency, Chávez used his swearing-in ceremony to break with

the pledge repeated by every president during the previous four decades of Venezuelan democracy. "I swear before God, before the father-
land, before my people, and before this dying constitution, to fulfill the
necessary democratic transformations in order for the Republic to have
a new constitution, suited to the new times," the new president vowed.

Economic change would have to wait. First on Chávez's agenda
was political reform—specifically, Venezuela's stale 1961 constitution,
essentially a power-sharing agreement between the country's two
biggest political parties that enabled them to control Congress, the
judiciary, the civil service, trade unions, universities, and the military,
and to prevent the emergence of any serious opposition to their cozy
duopoly on power. In essence, the constitution enshrined the permanent rule of an old boys' club.

Chávez was calling time on this oligarchical arrangement. Within a
year, he had defied both the country's legislature (led by his opponents)
and its judiciary by tearing up the 1961 constitution and starting over.
Naturally, the new constitution was pretty favorable to him: it allowed
the head of state to run for two terms rather than one; extended the
presidential term from five to six years; expanded the president's
powers; scrapped one of the National Assembly's two chambers; took
away the legislature's power to appoint judges; and renamed the country the Bolivarian Republic of Venezuela after Chávez's hero. On the
other hand, the constitution had some more obviously progressive
elements, allowing for presidential recall elections and set up a regula-
tor to oversee the president and the National Assembly. Many of the
president's critics fretted that the country had now institutionalized his
power. But the public, glad to see the back of the corrupt old order,
backed the new constitution in a referendum.

By 2007, Chávez faced the prospect of only being allowed to
stay in the presidency for five more years and decided it would
actually be rather a good idea to get rid of presidential term limits altogether. Voters rejected, in December 2007, his first attempt
to pass the constitutional amendment, which was lumped together
with a plan to widen the powers of the state. But the following
year, Chávez felt confident enough to try again, in a vote held in
February 2009. This time the electorate approved the change. His
opponents balked again at the idea of him being allowed to continue

to run for election until 2021 (the president's stated aim, which he subsequently extended to 2031), but Chávez was nonplussed. "Ten [extra] years is nothing," he said at a press conference in Caracas. "I don't know what they're complaining about."

Where Venezuela led, Bolivia and Ecuador followed. In 2008, both countries rewrote their constitutions. Evo Morales succeeded in getting approval for a new constitution that strengthened his powers, weakened the judiciary, gave greater autonomy to indigenous communities, and increased the state's role in the economy. Rafael Correa secured a new constitution that substantially increased his power, placed the presidency above the legislature and judiciary, reclaimed monetary policy from the central bank, and allowed him to stand for two further terms rather than the one previously allowed. It gave the state more control over the oil and mining sectors, allowed the appropriation and redistribution of idle farmland, banned large land estates, and raised mandatory spending on health, education, and social security. It also made indigenous languages official and promised Ecuadoreans the right to *sumakkawsay*, Quichua for "good living."

These changes clearly paved the way for greater presidential control, prompting allegations that the new constitutions were "antidemocratic." Not that extending executive power was limited to the Left: in Colombia, the Congress had overturned the constitution in 2006, allowing Álvaro Uribe, the right-wing president, to stand for a second term. In 2010, he tried to extend that to a third term but was thwarted by the country's constitutional court. In New York, Michael Bloomberg, the Big Apple's mayor, secured a rule change that enabled him to stand for a third term in 2009.

The difference with the leaders of the Andean radical Left was that they also sought to recognize in the new constitutions historically marginalized groups such as the indigenous and women, and to institutionalize the redistributive economic policies Morales and Correa had promised to enact. This was also the significance of Ollanta Humala's insistence on being sworn in as Peru's president in 2011 on the country's 1979 constitution rather than that of 1993 constitution, which had curbed the role of the state in the economy.

On the other hand, the presidents could not be naïve enough to suppose the new constitutions would either change things permanently—beyond their own presidential terms—or even protect them while in office. After all, the new Ecuadorean constitution represented the twentieth time the country's founding document had been rewritten in its relatively short history.

What was equally as important as the practical matter of expanding their powers as president was the symbolic nature of refounding the state, of recasting it not as a club to protect vested political interests but as a reflection of the will of the people. At least that was the spin. As in all politics, everyone could agree that change was needed. But unlike most politics, change—at least symbolically—had actually come.

8

"For God and Money"

As he stood in line to take the oath of office, Gerardo Saavedra was nervous.

A portly landowner from northwestern Peru with bountiful eyebrows, Saavedra had recently been elected to Congress in the country's general elections of 2000. As he lined up with the other recently elected legislators to be sworn in officially, he found it hard to focus.

Perhaps the former police officer was overawed by the fading grandeur of the Congress building, so different from the sugarcane, rice paddies, and cotton fields of his rural estate in Lambayeque, a fertile region near Peru's northern Pacific coast. Back there, like most Peruvians, he was used to being called by his nickname, Cucho, affectionate slang for "old man." Here in Lima, he was *Congresista Saavedra*—a lawmaker, a national figure, a power broker.

Perhaps Saavedra was preoccupied with the tense atmosphere that had surrounded the country's 2000 general election. Alberto Fujimori, a Peruvian of Japanese descent who was nevertheless universally known in Peru as El Chino (the subtleties of different Asian nationalities can be somewhat lost on many South Americans) was running to be reelected as president. His regime, which had begun a decade earlier with promises of economic reform and the reestablishment of law and order, had descended into patent autocracy, repression, and hubris.

Fujimori was running for a third term in office, even though Peru's constitution clearly limited presidents to two terms. Undeterred, he pointed out that in 1993 he had torn up the previous constitution and had it rewritten in a show of strength that effectively transformed him from democrat to autocrat. Since the new constitution came into effect after his first election as president, Fujimori argued that he had actually only been elected once under the new constitution, and so what appeared to be a third term was in fact merely his second term since the new arrangements had come into effect.

It was a crude, absurd, childish argument—and it worked like a dream. His supporters in Congress ensured the passage of a "law of authentic interpretation" that allowed him to run again legally, while Peru's electoral authorities waved the decision through. Their actions showed how supine the state had become, malleable to the president's every manipulation.

If this were not deception enough, the election itself was a transparent fraud. Peru's military was drafted into a well-marshaled propaganda effort that involved defacing entire Andean mountains with huge pro-Fujimori slogans, painting campaign propaganda on walls, and destroying advertising by opposition politicians.

One of the political parties that supported Fujimori was revealed to have falsified names on the petition they used to register themselves, copying voters' signatures from official lists provided them by the electoral authorities. Officials who were supposed to be overseeing the conduct of the election were arrested before polling day, in possession of stolen voting papers already filled out in favor of Fujimori.

When Fujimori scooped just short of 50 percent of the vote—prompting the presidential election to go to a second round—the international observers who had flown in to monitor the election decided there was little point in lingering for the inevitable conclusion of the farce. They abandoned Lima, condemning Fujimori and leaving Peru to its own devices. In the second round, Fujimori supposedly won 74 percent of the vote, though no one believed it.

Gerardo Saavedra drove into the heart of this political maelstrom when he took the Pan-American Highway down to Lima to be sworn in as a congressman. Understandably, his state of mind must have been somewhat affected by the goings-on. He had won his seat as a candidate for Peru Posible, an opposition party whose presidential candidate, Alejandro Toledo, had called on voters to boycott the second round of voting. By entering the Congress, Saavedra was walking into a lions' den.

One by one, the legislators who had emerged victorious from this sullied election came forward to take their oath. The pledge itself was simple enough, with lawmakers swearing to carry out their duties *"Por Dios y la patria"*—for God and country. Some new congressmen added their own twist. "For God, for country, for the peasants, and for Fujimori!" declared one overenthusiastic supporter of the tarnished president.

But Saavedra's oath had an inadvertent twist of its own, one that would forever mark his place in Peruvian history. As he held up his palm, in a loud, clear voice he swore faithfully to discharge his office, not for God and country but *Por Dios y la plata*—for God and money.

Fujimori, Montesinos, and the Vladivideos

After his inauspicious start, Saavedra's career crawled to an inevitable, inglorious conclusion.

Within a year, Peru Posible was in power and the parliamentarian quickly settled into Lima's political culture. As president of the Congress's agricultural commission, he proposed a bill that would have made the state assume the debts of the farming sector. When it was revealed that he himself had $600,000 in farming debts, Saavedra responded that he was merely defending poor farmers.

On another occasion, Saavedra used his power to persuade the minister of the interior to tell police in Chiclayo not to prevent two local businessmen from illegally seizing control of Agro Pucalá, a sugar refinery, ostensibly on the basis that it owed them money. As soon as they had done so, the two businessmen paid Saavedra's wife $100,000 from the company accounts.

In January 2006, after one term in office, Saavedra was unceremoniously dumped by Peru Posible, after its presidential candidate demanded that the congressman be removed from the party list. Later that year, Saavedra died of cancer.

Shameful as Saavedra's legacy was—and as typically tawdry as the political careers of many Peruvian legislators—it was nothing compared to the man who stole the presidency the year that Saavedra swore an oath to God and money: Alberto Fujimori. Although Fujimori had stolen the second round of the presidential election— the one from which Alejandro Toledo, his principal opponent, had withdrawn—and was duly sworn in for a third time in July 2000, he had little time to savor his victory.

The following September, a devastating scandal exploded in Fujimori's face. A Peruvian television channel showed secret footage of Vladimiro Montesinos, Fujimori's right-hand man and the head of the country's intelligence services, handing over $15,000 to an opposition congressman in return for his defection to a pro-Fujimori party, something that would give the government a majority in the legislature.

It slowly emerged that there were a lot more of these "Vladivideos"— about seven hundred, in fact—documenting Montesinos paying money to all sorts of influential Peruvians in exchange for support for Fujimori's regime. Everyone of importance in the country had been purchased. If you weren't on the Vladivideos, you weren't worth buying.

As a house of cards constructed over a decade began to collapse fast, the newly reelected president was rapidly downgraded to the status of political outcast. Fujimori blustered for a month, then fled to Asia, turning up in Japan. Safe in the homeland of his ancestors and, presumably, the only country that would grant him citizenship outside Peru, he faxed his resignation to Lima. If nothing else, Fujimori secured his place in the history books by becoming the only president ever to have resigned by fax.

After Fujimori's regime collapsed, the full extent of his abuse of power began to come to light. Much of it was linked to Montesinos, a shadowy figure whose heavy eyelids, hawkish nose, and lank, combed-over balding hairstyle gave him the appearance of an archetypal James Bond film baddie out of central casting.

Montesinos saw the state and the power it gave him as his private business. He used his position to carry out a host of self-enrichment schemes—embezzlement, gunrunning, drug trafficking—and did much to keep the regime in power by bribing the country's top judges, politicians, bankers, and journalists.

He even held sway over Laura Bozzo, Peru's version of Jerry Springer. Her show, watched by some eight million people in the United States and many millions more in Latin America, normally saw Bozzo, an elflike plastic surgery devotee, welcome a never-ending stream of cheating love rats and preside over formulaic displays of on-air hair pulling, face slapping, and chair throwing on set.

Montesinos gave Bozzo $3 million, but she claimed the favorable coverage she gave him and the Fujimori regime was not the product of a mere bribe. She was quite open about her love for him, claiming later that she became obsessed. On her show, she blew him kisses and once even dressed up as Elvis to serenade him.

Officially, Montesinos was paid a state salary of $370 a month, yet his life was more like that of an international playboy than a civil servant. When police broke into one of his homes as the regime collapsed, they found more than a thousand identical Christian Dior shirts and $1 million in jewelry, including diamond-encrusted designer watches. Montesinos had life-size suggestive photos made of his secretary and displayed them in his bathroom, bedroom, and gym. Did the Rasputin-like figure fantasize about giving dictation in the bath?

He also habitually secretly filmed himself in the act of bribery, in the process creating the video library that contained the seeds of his own downfall and that of the Fujimori regime. How much money had Fujimori and Montesinos stolen during their ten years in power? Transparency International, a group that researches corruption, estimated that $600 million had been embezzled. Peru's own special prosecutor appointed to investigate Fujimori put the figure at $2 billion. Javier Diez Canseco, a Peruvian congressman who led a parliamentary investigation into government corruption, said the total loss to the country's economy was as much as $8.5 billion.

Whatever the truth, the amount that went missing was vast for a country like Peru. In 1995, at the midpoint of Fujimori's rule, the size of the country's economy was $53.6 billion. If we take the Peruvian special prosecutor's assessment that his regime stole $2 billion, the theft was equivalent to about 3.7 percent of gross domestic product.

To put it in context, that would be like a US president and his cronies stealing more than $500 billion from American taxpayers. It would be the greatest heist in US history. Such theft would surely do irreparable damage to the country, its economy, and the state itself.

Yet few Peruvians are really bothered about the money. In fact, even with both Fujimori and Montesinos in prison and undergoing drawn-out legal trials, the former president remains popular in Peru for two reasons—he saved the country from a severe economic collapse, and he fought a military campaign to stamp out the Shining Path, a vicious guerrilla group that waged war against the Peruvian state in the 1980s and 1990s.

His daughter, Keiko, was elected to Congress in 2006 with more votes than any legislator in the country. In 2007, Peru eventually extra-dited Fujimori (which they had been trying to do for years, somewhat ineptly), and the following year he was sentenced to a paltry six years in prison for abuse of power. And yet even then, local opinion polls showed he still had the support of about 30 percent of voters in Lima. In her first tilt at the presidency in 2011, Keiko won enough votes to graduate to the second round of voting in which she was defeated by Ollanta Humala.

Peruvians have come to accept that corruption is a way of life. It doesn't mean they like it or think it's acceptable. It's more that they have never known a government that was not tainted by corruption.

Latin Americans frequently point out that the developed world also suffers from corruption. But there is a difference: in Latin America, as in much of the developing world, corruption tends to be endemic, part of the system, the rule and not the exception. The figures involved in the example of Fujimori and Montesinos are mind-boggling, but in a sense they merely transferred to a national level the same behavior of the traffic cops on the streets of so many South American cities who stop motorists with phony violations in order to extract some petty bribe.

The example of Montesinos is important in another way. For all the money extracted from the state, the spy chief was not out just to get rich. In fact, he turned the notion of bribery on its head. Normally bribes are paid to public officials by companies or individuals; Montesinos paid bribes from the state's coffers to others in order to ensure that he had complete political control. In the Fujimori era, the entire system was not just infiltrated with corrupt practices but actually founded on them.

The Pervasiveness of Corruption

Every year Transparency International puts out a survey of how people view their own governments and ranks them from those states seen as the least corrupt down to the most. In 2006, for example (the year that South America jumped left), the list was topped by Finland, Iceland, and New Zealand, while Iraq, Myanmar, and Haiti came last.

The first appearance of a South American country was Chile, which came in at 20th place—a position it shared with the United States. Since it became a democracy in 1990, Chile has always been seen as a case apart in the region for its good governance and strong economy. In 28th place was Uruguay.

The rest of South America fared much less well. Colombia was in 59th place, Peru and Brazil were 70th, Argentina was in 93rd position, Bolivia in 105th, Paraguay was 111th, while Ecuador and Venezuela were in 138th place, below countries such as Russia, Zimbabwe, and Azerbaijan. (There were 163 placements on the 2006 list. In 1998—the year that Hugo Chávez won power—Venezuela was placed 77th out of 85 placements.)

It is difficult to measure corruption. The Transparency International data aren't perfect. They depend on various surveys of experts about how corrupt their countries are. You could argue that these views don't necessarily indicate how deep corruption is, so much as what people think it is. But opinions matter. Every year, Latin American governments embark on new anticorruption drives, yet when Transparency International asked people how they would assess their governments' actions against corruption, 42 percent of respondents said the state either doesn't bother fighting it or that it actually encourages corrupt practices—the highest such response of any region in the world.

So perhaps it's not accurate to say that South American countries actually are corrupt. But it does seem clear that very many South Americans think—rightly or wrongly—that they are. And if we are trying to work out what makes them jaded about free markets, globalization, and the functioning of democracy, it's the perceptions of ordinary people that matter.

Of course, it isn't just in South America that people think their politicians are corrupt. After my posting in the Andes, my newspaper sent me to be its correspondent in Chicago. The parallels with what I had seen in Latin America were pretty obvious. As I arrived in the city, Illinois's previous governor began a six-and-a-half-year prison term for racketeering. He was the third former governor to be jailed in recent decades. The following year, his successor, Rod Blagojevich, became infamous around the world when he was caught on tape by federal investigators apparently trying to sell President Barack Obama's just-vacated Senate seat to the highest bidder, among other misdemeanors.

So are North America and South America essentially the same when it comes to the ethical standards of their public servants? If so, why should voters in one region think of corruption as an aberration, an abuse of the system, while in the other they see it as an integral part of government? Certainly, corruption is not a rare occurrence in the United States. And in the Transparency International survey, 19 percent of Americans said their government actively encourages corrupt practices (more than in Africa, Asia, or the former Soviet republics).

But there are a couple of important differences. First, many Latin Americans come in contact with corruption every day of their lives. Drive through the Andes and sooner or later you will come to a police checkpoint at which you are expected to hand over some cash along with your identification. Many Americans and western Europeans have never experienced such a thing in their native country.

Transparency International found that in spite of their perceptions about corruption, fewer than 3 percent of American and European respondents to their survey had ever actually paid a bribe to a public official. In Latin America, about 32 percent said they had—a figure that still sounds conservative.

Perhaps it depends on what you think of as a bribe. Almost everyone from the Andes can tell you tales about their brushes with corruption. A Peruvian friend of mine recounts the time she was stopped by traffic police in Lima who told her she had just driven through a red light. The normal response would be to hand over enough banknotes to "pay the fine" and be waved on (as elsewhere, Peruvian police use this kind of technique to bulk up their paltry salaries).

But as it happened, on this occasion she actually had driven through a red light. So she decided to test the system. "You're right, Officer," she said. "You'd better take me to the police station and charge me." The policemen were unnerved by this apparent breach of street protocol. "No, no, you don't understand," one of them insisted, holding out his palm as discreetly as he could, "you drove through a red light." She was undeterred. "Yes, I did," she repeated. "You'd better arrest me and take me to the police station." The two policemen looked at each other. They were in a bind: they could either take her at her word and go through the rigmarole of booking, processing, and charging her without any guarantee of a backhander at the end; or they could stay on the street and use their time to try to get a bribe from someone more compliant. They waved her on.

Of course, these sorts of experiences are no reflection on the relative levels of the sort of grand corruption that politicians get sent to prison for, but they do indicate that in Latin America, corrupt actions permeate the entire system of government, from top to bottom, whereas for many Americans and Europeans, corruption is something that happens in the shadows of the corridors of power, far away from their day-to-day lives.

The other important difference between corruption in Latin America and in the United States and Europe is that in the latter, government in general functions well—or at least it functions. In spite of its (largely deserved) reputation for corruption, Chicago prides itself as being "the city that works." Public money might find its way into the wrong pockets, but buildings get constructed, new parks get built, garbage gets collected.

By contrast, consider a typical experience that happened to me dozens of times in different countries in the Andes: traveling on a road in the middle of nowhere that seems surprisingly well surfaced, I would ask my companions, "How old is the road?" They would respond that it was repaved in the past few years. Then, suddenly, it would feel like the car had driven onto an ancient track and the car would be shuddering like a jackhammer. "What happened?" I would ask. "They ran out of money" was the inevitable reply.

Whereas in North America and Europe, corruption often greases the palms of those who can get things done by bypassing the regular channels, in Latin America it all too often prevents projects from getting finished. Infrastructure schemes are always launched with great fanfare (it looks good on TV), but often the budget is shortly afterward exhausted and the road or train line or bridge never gets completed.

The consequence is that people in the Andes don't just come across corruption when a national politician or business figure's wrongdoing is exposed. They experience it every time they drive down a road—either because of the poor quality of the road itself or because of the police checkpoint along the way that is nothing more than an unofficial tollbooth.

To make things worse, much of the corruption that is exposed in Andean countries has to do with the very process of privatization that has proved so contentious. For example, in 2008 the Peruvian prime minister, the country's energy minister, the head of the state oil company, and several other officials were forced to resign after a scandal came to light about paying kickbacks in return for contracts for oil exploration. A TV station broadcast taped conversations apparently showing civil servants discussing how the ruling party had received bribes to grant five such contracts to a Norwegian oil company.

In Bolivia and Ecuador, it is common for state officials in the energy industry to transfer straight over to top-paying jobs with the same international oil companies that deal with their former colleagues, with few rules to prevent them from doing so.

More than a third of companies that do business with Latin American governments admitted they have paid bribes as part of government projects, saying the average bribe they have to pay amounts to 8 percent of the contract value (higher than in Asia or sub-Saharan Africa), according to the World Economic Forum, the international club for global business leaders.

The Washington Consensus didn't bring corruption to South America. The continent had a long tradition of corruption that predated the free-market reforms of the 1990s. But by getting South American countries to open up their economies to investment from overseas, the Washington Consensus unintentionally created a whole new and much more lucrative forum for bribery and graft.

Up until the 1980s, practices such as nepotism and profiting from drug smuggling were the predominant acts of corruption in South America. But with the Washington Consensus reforms bringing large multinational corporations looking to invest in the region's abundant natural resources, suddenly the opportunities to extort bribes mushroomed.

In other words, the economic changes that the United States, the IMF, and the World Bank were demanding didn't enhance democracy and governance, as their advocates had originally implied they would. Rather, they had the effect of helping to undermine democracy by placing all the emphasis on the fact of privatization rather than the mechanics of how economic reform was implemented. It's what you do that's important, they were saying, not the way that you do it.

Mind the Capability Gap

Woody Allen's *Annie Hall* begins with an old joke. Two elderly women are at a resort in the Catskill Mountains, the traditional retreat for Jewish New Yorkers. One of them says, "Boy, the food in this place is really terrible." The other responds, "Yes, I know—and such small portions."

For Allen, the joke encapsulated his view of life: full of loneliness, misery, suffering, and unhappiness, and all over much too quickly. It also parallels the Andean model of politics. Not only is government corrupt, inefficient, and ineffective, but there's so little of it.

All too often, a visit to a smaller Andean town presents a picture of a community that lives essentially beyond the reach of the state. Just as the dominance of informality in the economic system of Andean countries means that millions of people never pay tax, so large swaths of the population live out their lives effectively outside the state. Poor infrastructure, especially in the remote highlands, means their towns are physically isolated from the rest of the country. Often their health and education needs are scantily attended to. No police patrol the streets of their towns. Politicians do not visit to hear their grievances.

In the Andes, the bulk of indigenous people tended historically to live in rural areas, while most mestizos lived in the cities. Since political power remained in the hands of mestizos, it was also highly concentrated in the capital. This has created cities that have set themselves up as alternative power bases, often fueled by a resentful and suspicious attitude toward the capital and its political elite—Santa Cruz in Bolivia, Maracaibo in Venezuela, Guayaquil in Ecuador, and Arequipa in Peru. In each case, these "shadow capitals," some of them bigger than the actual capital cities, see themselves as the true drivers of the national economy, and are loath to send their taxes to be wasted in the honey pots of the political capital.

On a visit to Arequipa in 2006, I spotted a sign in the colonial city's grand central square that captured this sentiment. It sat among the newspapers festooning a rickety kiosk, above an official copy of the deal Peru had struck with Washington the previous year. In crude letters written on a piece of cardboard, the sign declared, "Know everything that the government is hiding from the country about the trade agreement signed with the United States."

It was the sort of sales pitch that goes down well in Peru's second biggest city, located about six hundred miles south of Lima. Among the million residents of Arequipa, attitudes toward the capital and central government run the gamut from deep mistrust to mere loathing.

Get out of the cities into the rural areas and the sentiment is even stronger. When the only contact you ever have with government is negative—such as the indifference of local government, the police or the army, a woefully underequipped health clinic or school, a road project that was never completed—it tends to breed a highly negative view of the state.

In recent years, the capacity gap—the inability of governments to govern and to serve communities outside big cities—has often been filled in part by nongovernmental organizations (NGOs). In countries such as Peru, Bolivia, and Ecuador, these groups have done terrific work in the areas of education, health care, literacy, and skill building. They have often brought dedicated people from other countries to remote areas to perform extremely valuable and much-needed work. But in their own way, these NGOs have also undermined the function of government in the Andes. They have attracted aid from foreign nations that might otherwise be channeled via the traditional arms of government and build capacity. They have employed some of the brightest local minds, who would prefer to work for an international development organization than their own government. They have enabled governments to avoid dealing with problems that should be part of their responsibility.

Similarly, foreign companies have also often been forced into the role of government by proxy. The need for a social license means mining companies operating in poor countries are now expected to build schools and clinics for local communities as well as provide jobs. When the locals are angry at the lack of such facilities, they often take their anger out against the company, the most obvious target in the absence of a government.

Andean governments have tended effectively to treat the majority of their populations as if they were minorities. As Enrique Mendoza, proprietor of *Arequipa al Día*, Lima's leading newspaper, told me, "Yes, they [Lima] are 27 percent of the population, but they should never forget that we are 73 percent." And yet every election cycle, aspiring politicians tour these remote communities and promise change, a new way of doing things, more investment, better services. The history of democracy in the Andes is a history of broken promises.

On the election trail in 2006, Ollanta Humala used to tell a joke that would raise a wry smile from audiences. A politician campaigning in Juliaca, a city in the southern highlands, promised that if elected he would build a school, hospital, and bridge. "But there's no river here," a local leader pointed out. "No problem," the politico responded, "we'll build the river first."

The Informal Economy

In 2006, I got in trouble with Fair Trade.

Fair Trade is an organization that certifies products from poor countries, ranging from cotton T-shirts and handicrafts to wine and chocolate, promising to pay the farmers there a better price for their goods than they traditionally receive on the conventional market.

The *Financial Times* published an investigation I had undertaken into how Fair Trade coffee was being produced in Peru, the world's top exporter of the stuff. My conclusion wasn't very flattering: not only was this "ethical" coffee actually being harvested by laborers paid below the legal minimum wage, but noncertified coffee was also being marked and exported as Fair Trade, and certified coffee was being illegally planted in protected rainforests.

To research the story, I had visited five small farms that were part of large cooperatives in two prominent coffee-producing areas of the

Peruvian jungle, all of which had Fair Trade certification and at least one other "ethical" mark. As part of their publicity, these certification groups would sometimes say that in harvest season, the farming families from the co-op would all help each other bring in the crop. That was utter nonsense. In reality, the farmers each hired twelve to twenty casual laborers, who came down to the farms from towns in the Andean highlands to pick their coffee. The farmers provided accommodation and food to the workers, which under Peruvian law allowed them to deduct 30 percent from their wages. After the 30 percent reduction from the legal daily minimum wage for casual agricultural workers of 16 Peruvian soles (which at the time was worth about $5), farm owners were still obliged to pay at least 11.2 soles a day. But in four of the five farms I visited, the pickers were receiving just 10 soles a day.

My aim in writing the story wasn't to attack Fair Trade. On the contrary, I support the principle of asking consumers to pay more and passing that extra on to producers in poor countries. Instead, I was trying to point out that policing such a system is near impossible in a country such as Peru.

The story caused something of a splash internationally. Fair Trade's US arm put out a letter saying I had exaggerated the issue. A local coffee producers' group issued a statement attacking my motives. Bloggers accused me of being a "neoliberal," free-marketeering scoundrel. I was uninvited to an international Fair Trade conference. The timing was tricky for US-Peru relations, since the Bush administration was trying to win approval from the US Congress for a bilateral trade agreement, but some Democrats opposed the deal. "These lax labor conditions are a major barrier to our trade relationship with Peru," Sander Levin, at the time the ranking Democrat on the House Ways and Means Trade subcommittee, told me in a phone call from Washington. (The deal was subsequently approved.)

But back in Peru, it was actually something of a snooze. No one was really surprised to hear that one of the country's premier export industries was paying below the legal minimum. In the story I quoted Eduardo Montauban, head of the Peruvian Coffee Chamber, a private exporters' group. "No one in the industry is paying minimum wage," he told me. "It's simply not feasible for producers."

It was a potent demonstration of the central role of informality in the economies of Latin America. In the United States, the informal sector is a significant part of the economy—one that comes to light whenever a company is busted for employing undocumented workers or a politician is outed for having hired an illegal immigrant to do domestic chores—but it is marginal and obscure. Across Latin America, by contrast, informality is central to the economy. About half of all urban workers in the region live in the world of illegal, cash-in-hand labor, according to the World Bank and the United Nations' International Labor Organization. In the Andes, informality is more dominant. Three-quarters of Peruvians of working age receive their income informally, according to the Peruvian Economic Institute, a think tank in Lima. Observers on the right of the political spectrum usually ascribe this to the cumbersome red tape needed to formalize a business and the overgenerous benefits the law requires employers to pay their workers. Those on the Left say the problem stems from a lack of job opportunities in the formal sector, discrimination against indigenous groups, and a weak education system.

Unlike in the United States, there is nothing covert about this world. In the center of Lima, the government has actually constructed a building to house Polvos Azules, which revels in the title of the largest black market in South America. It is, effectively, a giant shopping mall for pirated goods—fake designer clothes, illegal copies of music CDs, movies, and computer software, unauthorized prints of books. Polvos Azules is professional, efficient, and up to date. My friend Daniel Schweimler, formerly the BBC's South America correspondent, recorded a hilarious dispatch in August 2006 for the *From Our Own Correspondent* radio show in which he searched in the market for a copy of *Cars*, the animated film that had just come out. Instead, he was offered *Cars 2*, a movie that had not yet been released. Daniel questioned the vendor. "But that can't be," he said. "It's not been made yet. *Cars 1* is only being released in the cinema today." The vendor gave him a knowing look. "Not been released," he said, "but it's been made."

Such activity sounds nefarious and is certainly damaging to conventional business. In 2004, Royal Dutch Shell, the Anglo-Dutch oil company, sold its gas stations in Peru, saying it was being undermined by oil smuggling from Ecuador. In 2007, Blockbuster, the video rental chain, also pulled out of Peru. The company could not compete with the price it costs to buy a movie at Polvos Azules—about $1.

The preponderance of informality has a big effect on the state as well. In the final days of 2010, protests exploded in Bolivia after Evo Morales's administration removed government fuel subsidies, sending the price of gasoline up 73 percent and diesel by 83 percent. Morales said his hand had been forced because smugglers were exporting subsidized fuel across the border and selling it at an instant profit. This not only cost the country $150 million a year, but it also meant that organized crime had effectively become as much part of the public sector as the police and armed forces. In the face of the demonstrations, however, Morales was forced to back down and reinstated the subsidies.

If corruption is one main reason the state is so weak in Latin America, informality is another. Informal businesses do not pay business or sales taxes, and their employees do not pay income tax. Not paying tax is far from a phenomenon unique to the poor, either—the wealthy in South America have long since learned that they are highly unlikely to be investigated for leaving off significant amounts of income from their tax returns (if, indeed, they file a return at all). They can hardly be blamed when corruption is so rife. The result is that in countries such as Peru, tax revenue makes up only about one-eighth of gross domestic product. The implications are huge: when the state lacks funds, it lacks capacity. From a left-wing perspective, that is bad because it means the state is powerless to redistribute wealth to those most in need and thus speed the country's economic development. In Europe, some 45 percent of spending on children and young people is financed by government—through education, primarily—while about half comes from their families. In Latin America, the government accounts on average for about one-fifth of such spending, while families account for 73 percent, according to the UN Economic Commission for Latin America. From a right-wing point of view, the lack of state capacity can be blamed for the failure of the Washington Consensus, which in part reflected the lack of institutions to implement economic reforms. It also means that Latin American governments cannot tinker with the tax system to provide incentives in the same way as in developed countries.

There have been numerous attempts to reduce the size of the informal sector, and there are some indications that it is slowly shrinking. But it remains a central part of the economy of Latin America, and is likely to do so for some time.

Informality also has an enormous effect on ordinary people. The tens of millions of Latin Americans who work informally may not have to pay taxes, but they also receive no paid vacations or health insurance, are not protected by labor or consumer laws, and have no access to bank loans. When times are good, they tend to think that they are prospering because of their own hard work, and not because, say, the government has put in place economic policies that encourage growth and investment. This may help to explain why economic growth does not necessarily translate into support for the government of the day.

I once watched, entranced, as a group of men in Villa Maria del Triunfo, a shantytown south of Lima, poured cement to make a sidewalk on the dirt track that served as a street. Since the state would not do it, they were acting themselves, one resident explained to me. Informality had unleashed the collective creative consciousness of these men. In the absence of an active government, they had effectively created their own mini department of public works. I was struck with immense optimism at witnessing this. But what they were doing was removing them even further from the state. Not only did they work informally—now even their public sector was informal. Could such people ever think of the institutions of the state as worthwhile?

9

Power to the People

You probably haven't heard of the second biggest city in Bolivia. It may be one of the fastest-growing urban centers in South America, but it doesn't appear on many maps. Its status as the world's highest city is missing from the guidebooks. Although thousands of tourists fly into the city on their arrival in the country, almost none of them stays or even visits there.

That's a shame, because El Alto—situated on a plateau above La Paz, the capital—is probably the most interesting place in the Andes. For a start, the view of the city below is superb. La Paz is one of the most beautiful and underrated cities in South America. Nestled in a valley of naturally sculpted limestone, the temperate, mirror-bright city offers dramatic views of steep neighborhoods, roads that curlicue their way up and down hills, and skyscrapers that would feel at home in any big American city. On the basis of its scenery, La Paz could well be South America's version of San Francisco. The sun shines bright and strong at high altitude, and seen from El Alto, the Bolivian capital is stunning.

Moreover, El Alto's geography is unique. Every Latin American city is based around a central square, flanked by a cathedral, city hall, and other municipal buildings. Not El Alto. La Ceja, the center of the city, is a grimy, bustling commercial district of potholed roads, belching minibuses, street vendors, packs of stray dogs, and menacing huddles of teenagers. The air—thin and cold at 13,250 feet above sea level (or 4,100 meters—not that it's warmer in metric)—smells like poverty: a mixture of unwashed clothes, rotting vegetables, and urine.

On second thought, I can understand why the tour groups give it a miss.

The only sign of any civic presence—beyond the police checkpoints at the entrance to La Paz's international airport, located there because it is the nearest flat space in the mountainous vicinity of La Paz—is the burnt-out shell of what used to be the municipal building, a reminder of violent riots in February 2003. The mayor now works in a prefabricated office building in a distant residential district, presumably somewhat removed from potential angry mobs.

El Alto is often thought of as a slum, but it's very much a city in its own right. As a settlement that has grown organically in the past thirty years through migration from the high Andes, it may not have an architectural legacy or a colonial past. But it does have all the hallmarks of a twenty-first-century city: banks, restaurants, Internet cafés, a thriving cultural and sporting scene, three television broadcasters and more than sixty radio stations, some five hundred educational institutions including three universities, hospitals, pharmacies, factories, opticians, gymnasiums, and beauty parlors.

In 1994, the Vatican established a diocese there, giving El Alto its first bishop. In 2006, Peru even set up a consulate in El Alto, distinct from its embassy in La Paz, to serve the city's large Peruvian immigrant population. No slum in the world boasts a foreign diplomatic mission. Moreover, unlike a shantytown, whose residents typically travel into the center of the city to work, most of the 40 percent of *Alteños* who have jobs work not in what they call "the city below" but in El Alto itself. Many have little reason to descend the steep, winding road to La Paz, just as few *Paceños* experience El Alto more intimately than through the windows of a taxi to or from the airport.

Most important, El Alto has a distinct identity from the seat of government that sits in the valley below. It is strongly indigenous: about 80 percent of its residents are native Aymaras, mostly first- or second-generation migrants who speak Aymara, dress in traditional clothes, and retain close ties with their home villages in Bolivia's western Andean plateau.

"Most people live with one foot here and one in the country," was how Felix Muruchi, a former miners' leader and community activist who lives in El Alto, put it to me. "There is very little employment in El Alto, so people sell their agricultural produce in order to live in the city. They return to their villages often—particularly when it's time to sow and harvest."

The rapid migration of people from the countryside to the cities is a typical story in the developing world. Over the past thirty years, the world's urban population has gone from 1.6 billion to 3.3 billion. By 2008, for the first time in history, there were more people living in cities than in rural areas, largely because of the growth of urban centers in poor countries.

Within the next thirty years, cities in the developing world are projected to grow by another 2 billion. As in El Alto, when people move from rural areas to cities they tend to settle in poor neighborhoods on the outskirts of town—areas that lack the basic infrastructure of water and electricity supply, sewage systems, and roads. The United Nations estimates that by 2030, 2 billion people could be living in slums. Visit any big Latin American city and you will see the phenomenon, from the *favelas* of Rio to the pastel-colored ranchos of Caracas or the bamboo-and-tarpaulin shacks that pass for homes in the *pueblos jovenes* that dot the giant sand dunes at the side of the highway leading out of Lima.

Globalization has spurred the biggest movement of humans in history. Just as the Industrial Revolution in Europe led to the depopulation of the countryside there and the growth of industrial urban centers, so globalization has unleashed historic forces of internal and international migration, in which millions of people have left their birthplaces for cities either in their own country or abroad. The result is that while some cities depend on money sent back from abroad by their relatives who are often working without legal permission, other urban centers in the region have become overwhelmed by hordes of internal migrants, many of whom cannot find work.

Usually, migration to the city means abandoning the rural way of life in terms of work, family, and culture. But again, El Alto is different. "A migrant comes to Lima wearing a *pollera* [a traditional layered skirt] and the next day she's wearing blue jeans," Yvan Solari, the Peruvian consul in El Alto, told me. "Here, the migrant brings her traditions with her and imposes them on the city."

Accurate statistics are hard to come by and official data widely scoffed at, but intelligent estimates reckon El Alto's population at more than 1 million, having overtaken La Paz in size in about 2007 or 2008 to become Bolivia's second city after Santa Cruz. (Santa Cruz, located in the wealthy agricultural and gas-rich southeastern lowlands, itself only started growing seriously in the 1950s.) In the past twenty-five years it has been one of Latin America's fastest-growing cities: in the 1980s, it grew by an average of about 9 percent a year, although that has slowed in recent years to about 7 percent.

As El Alto has expanded, so has its political importance. The city is not only the indigenous capital of Bolivia or the poorest city in the poorest country in South America. El Alto is also the home of the pugnacious street protests that have toppled two presidents in recent years and propelled Evo Morales to victory. Morales knew his recent Bolivian history, and consequently appointed Abel Mamani, head of one of El Alto's powerful neighborhood committees, as his minister of water—the first *Alteño* to have a seat in the cabinet.

Roadblock Culture

"El Alto" has a double meaning in Spanish: the name can be translated as both "the high" and "the halt." It is an apt equivocation. In the past two decades, the world's highest city has brought Bolivia to a standstill countless times, with a will that has proved it cannot be denied.

In political if not climatic terms, El Alto enjoys a privileged location. All the main roads connecting La Paz to the interior and to neighboring countries run through it, as do oil and gas pipelines. The airport—the main international channel in landlocked Bolivia—is in the heart of La Ceja. For Bolivia, El Alto is a siege waiting to happen.

Roberto Charca, the laid-back news editor at *El Alteño*, the city's daily newspaper, put it to me succinctly. "El Alto is the distribution hub of Bolivia," he said. "It can shut the whole country down if it wants to—and it frequently has wanted to."

The main tool El Alto has used to apply this latent pressure has been the roadblock—a heavy scattering of rocks on the street, plus the odd burning tire, attended to by a neighborhood's worth of men, women, and children. They may be rudimentary, but El Alto's roadblocks are impermeable. On October 12, 2003, the city was on general strike in protest at plans by President Gonzalo Sánchez de Lozada to export gas through Chile, Bolivia's historic rival. A fleet of oil trucks attempted to drive through a blockade to relieve La Paz, which was running out of food and fuel. The result was a riot in which security forces killed sixteen people.

That day also saw a host of other confrontations, in which soldiers and police killed a total of seventy protesters. The government imposed martial law in El Alto but could not recover: five days later Sánchez de Lozada, a favorite of Washington, was forced from office and fled to the United States.

Some see El Alto's militant tactics as a long-established tradition. "Roadblocks have been used in El Alto since colonial times," Muruchi noted. In 1781, Túpac Katari, a young indigenous rebel leader, besieged Spanish-controlled La Paz from El Alto for more than a hundred days with an army of tens of thousands of indigenous peasants. In the nineteenth century, the high Andean plain around the city was an area of indigenous resistance to large landowners. The leaders of the 1952 revolution used El Alto as a base to take La Paz.

But these were rebellions launched from El Alto rather than by its residents. The current phenomenon of militancy has more to do with how the city came to be settled permanently. The first proper migration came after the 1952 revolution, when powerful mining cooperatives built housing for miners' families in an area that later came to be known as Ciudad Satélite, one of El Alto's oldest and now most prosperous neighborhoods.

The postrevolutionary government created neighborhood committees in the most marginalized areas of the capital, and the miners in El Alto secured the independence of their associations from those in La Paz. A large influx of miners migrated to the city following the 1985 tin crisis, when the price of the metal fell from about $14,100 per ton to about $4,800 per ton overnight and Bolivia's formerly thriving tin industry promptly collapsed.

With the migration of the miners, El Alto's distinct identity began to take shape. First, they were keen to establish their autonomy from La Paz, and through the neighborhood committees they became a central force in the battle to have El Alto declared a separate city, which it was in 1986. Second, the miners were already organized into a well-defined union structure that made organizing protests easier. Third, they brought with them an aggressive, radical, militant political stance and strategy, based around orderly marches punctuated by defiant blasts of dynamite, and giving rise to one of the city's legendary slogans: "El Alto on its feet—never on its knees."

The miners' penchant for protest was shared by peasants who streamed into the city from communities in the high Andes in the 1980s after a series of droughts. Many became affiliated to social movements such as the Regional Workers' Confederation or the Women's Federation, but the neighborhood committees remained strong.

The good organization these groups have provided has always been the backbone of social unrest in El Alto. "The neighborhood committees are very centralized," I was told by Juan José Munguia, who runs a youth leadership program in El Alto for CHF International, a US nongovernmental organization. "They tell people when to act and what to do. If you don't follow their instructions, they throw stones at your house or steal from you."

In practice, this means that roadblocks are officially called by organizations, which can paralyze the entire country within a few hours. When deals are agreed to, the blockades can be lifted very quickly. The recent history of Bolivia has reflected this—sharp increases in social unrest leading to brinkmanship between the social movements and the government, only for a last-minute accord to get life quickly back to normal. The country has lurched from crisis to crisis.

The Permanent Threat

Another reason cited by some for El Alto's militancy is its Aymara heritage. Rural villages have traditionally migrated to the city together, settling in one neighborhood and retaining their distinct cultural practices. Rural festivals, dancing, and music live on in the urban setting— and new forms of cultural expression such as Aymara-language rap music, film, and pirate radio have flourished.

Aymara culture tends to be tough and suspicious of outsiders. Centuries ago, the Aymara resisted the imperial expansion of the

Quechua-speaking Incas, just as they later fought the Spanish conquistadors and the big landowners who were descended from them. That culture of resistance lives on in predominantly Aymara El Alto.

At the same time there is a strong Aymara tradition of making deals with one's enemies, which also feeds into the strategy of brinkmanship. Militant, Aymara El Alto has shown its ability to work with outsiders to its own advantage, electing and reelecting as mayor in the 1990s José Luis Paredes, a nonindigenous, conservative *Paceño* businessman who improved infrastructure.

(During his time as mayor, Paredes had the idea of building a revolving restaurant in El Alto that would give patrons a chance to experience this spectacular view of the Bolivian capital while dining. This was like trying to make the Boston Tea Party into a *real* tea party, with scones and jam—a great idea except for the fact that it was located in perhaps the most radical and protest-prone city in the Americas. Paredes got as far as building a tower to house the restaurant, but after careful reconsideration—and a couple of roadblock-studded shutdowns later—the eatery itself was never built.)

In Bolivia, roadblocks work. The weakness of the central state and the viselike grip that El Alto can exert on Bolivia have meant that the blockades have usually secured victory for the social movements. The backlash against the violent crackdown attempted by Sánchez de Lozada led his successor, Carlos Mesa, to vow never to authorize the armed forces to fire on civilians. Within nineteen months, after weeks of roadblocks that left stocks of food and gas running low in La Paz, Mesa too was forced to step down, paving the way for the election won by Morales.

But while the roadblocks have proved a continued political success for El Alto, they have wrought economic devastation on an already impoverished city. While some civic leaders sought at one time to transform El Alto into Bolivia's economic capital, the campaign was never really more than a public relations exercise. Despite the cheapness of land and the abundance of low-cost labor, only a few international companies (such as Coca-Cola) have set up home in the city.

Those companies that have tried have learned that their business can be devastated by the social unrest that has come to characterize El Alto. In a matter of hours, protesters can (and often do) effectively close down the country by blocking roads to the airport, paralyzing the flow of imports and exports. Bolivia being a landlocked nation, the airport is important for international trade.

El Alto is perhaps an extreme example, but the slums that ring South America's main cities have also proved rich sources of support for radical, government-toppling politics. Like migration from Latin America northward and the creation of globalization's losers, internal migration toward cities, swollen with new shantytowns, is a secular process that has happened across the continent and across the world. Governments would have been hard-pressed to limit the flows of human traffic.

In La Paz, the resettlement has changed the reality of the city and the country. El Alto is no longer a shantytown on the edge of a big city but an entity in its own right. The governmental palace may remain in historic La Paz, but where does power really lie? That is a question that residents of the Bolivian capital must often ask themselves as they look heavenward toward the poor, radical, well-organized, and largely underemployed city that hangs like a permanent threat over their heads.

The Challenge of Democracy

Many South American countries enjoyed peripatetic bursts of democratic rule in the twentieth century, punctured by military coups. By the 1970s, most of South America was in the hands of authoritarian military governments. But in the final decades of the century an unassailable wave of democracy spread through the continent.

Ecuador returned to democracy in 1979. The following year, Peru had its first democratic elections since the 1940s. Fujimori's election in 1990 marked a swing toward authoritarianism, but free elections were restored after he fled in 2000. Argentina became a democracy in 1983. Uruguay's military ceded power to democratic civilian rule in 1984. Brazil and Bolivia emerged from decades of military rule in 1985. In 1989, Chile held its first free elections in nineteen years. Paraguay had its first free elections in four decades in 1993. The two exceptions to the trend were Venezuela, which has had democratically elected governments since 1958, and Colombia, which has had more elected regimes than military ones in its history, although it has also experienced periods of bloody internal conflict and dictatorship.

So by the early 1990s, this democratic wave had completely swept over the continent. For the first time in their history, the countries of South America looked unlikely to return to military rule. Democracy was entrenched.

But democracy did not bring with it stability—at least not for the Andes. In Ecuador, for example, the return of free elections failed to produce any certainty as to who was really in charge of the country. In February 1997, the country had three presidents in five days—a record that brings alive the adage that a week is a long time in politics. Ecuador's political institutions are weak and ineffective. Rather than acting as a check and balance on one another, as the republican constitution envisages, the three branches of government—president, Congress, and judiciary—have often engaged in full-blown conflict.

Having three presidents in five days is a good example. Abdalá Bucaram, a flamboyant, guitar-playing former Olympic sprinter, was elected president of Ecuador in July 1996. Six months after his victory, he was fired by the Congress for mental incapacity—perhaps the first time a president has been ousted ostensibly for being insane. (Though highly eccentric, Bucaram was not insane, but more on that later.) The legislature voted to replace him with its own chairman. The distinguished politicians had conveniently forgotten, however, that when a president is removed, the vice president is supposed to take over. So they grudgingly permitted the vice president to assume power—only for a day or two, mind, after which she would have to resign and allow them to have their way. Except that after a couple of days as president, Bucaram's former deputy decided that she quite liked the job and didn't want to step down after all. So the Congress just decided she would have to and that was it.

Almost every step along the way had been unconstitutional. First, the constitution allowed Congress to remove the president for mental incapacity, except that was a lie as he was perfectly capable. Then they ignored the traditional line of succession by imposing their own candidate as president. Then they forced out another president because she refused to abide by a prearranged backroom deal. The Congress's move against Bucaram was a popular one: by that point he had frittered away the 54 percent of the vote he had won in the presidential election and was down to a 15 percent approval rating.

It gave a big boost to the legislature, which was itself unpopular. But what did it do for the institution of the presidency and the constitution of the country? The military might not have been directly involved, but Bucaram was surely somewhat justified in claiming he had been a victim of a "congressional coup."

When Rod Blagojevich, the disgraced Illinois governor, was impeached by the state's general assembly in 2009, he similarly accused the lawmakers of illegitimate behavior, yet they acted in punctilious accordance with the state's constitution, achieving their goals within the established rules of the political game.

Frequently in Andean politics, the rules of the political game are ignored, undermined, and trampled. In fact, there is no real agreement on what the rules are or should be. When constitutions stand in the way of presidents or congresses, they tend either to overlook them or to try to rewrite the constitution itself. This lack of agreement over the basic questions of how government should function means that democratic debate often gets bogged down in bitter fights for power within the state, with presidents, legislatures, judges, and regional authorities vying for influence. This is either fiddling while Rome burns or rearranging deck chairs on the *Titanic*—pick your favorite cliché.

Amid this squabbling, the real business of government—governing, rather than endless debates about *how* to govern—gets lost. So when someone acts decisively, when things actually happen, electorates tend to be supportive. Hence the popularity of the Ecuadorean Congress's sacking of Bucaram.

In Ecuador, democracy may be entrenched, but the army remains a potent force in politics. In 2000, the country's president was overthrown in South America's last military coup. The army resisted seizing power for itself and instead handed the reins of government over to the vice president. It was a popular move that enhanced the military's reputation: three years later, the young colonel who orchestrated the coup was himself elected president.

That Latin America was engulfed by a wave of democracy was undoubtedly positive. But one of the main reasons that democracy did not necessarily lead to stability is that *democratic* government did not imply *good* government. The method of choosing leaders might have become more representative, but as the example of Ecuador shows, it also exposed the incompetence, pettiness, and abuse of power by those in elected office.

The United States had not always been on the side of democracy in Latin America. It had propped up unsavory dictatorships and helped to unseat democratically elected governments. But instability, corruption, and poor governance were not just America's fault. They also grew out of societies in which a small socioeconomic elite had been replaced by a small political elite. It was a classic case of "No matter who you vote for, the government always wins."

But the Washington Consensus reforms did little to strengthen the institutions of democracy. Instead, they raised the stakes for those in power, opening up the possibility that their struggling public utilities and their natural resources could be sold off to multinational companies. The corporations, in turn, were delighted at the opportunity and apparently unconcerned about the political risk that the governments that had sold them stakes in formerly state-owned enterprises might be overturned, changing the rules of the game against them.

The result is that the US economy has become ever more dependent on trade links with a region in which the "rules of the game" are still being negotiated. The "Latin American street" speaks with an increasingly loud and powerful voice. Democratic governance is weak. Institutions are unreliable and open to manipulation.

During the Cold War, the United States viewed Latin America as a possible political risk. The Washington Consensus transformed the region into a commercial risk as well, with all the implications that brings for American companies, American exports, and American jobs.

Winston Churchill described democracy as "the worst form of government except for all those others that have been tried." Many Latin Americans disagree. Every year, Latinobarómetro, a highly respected Chilean opinion pollster, puts out a fascinating survey of Latin American attitudes to democracy. In 2006, the year South America shifted left, only 55 percent of Peruvians questioned by Latinobarómetro said they thought democracy was preferable to any other kind of government. By 2010, that figure had risen to 61 percent, but it was still below the 63 percent who had said so in 1997.

While those figures do not suggest that democracy is in trouble, they also do not indicate that it is so established in the region as to be completely safe. The Latinobarómetro 2010 survey also indicated that more than 30 percent of Latin Americans thought an authoritarian government was either preferable or no worse than a democratic one. When asked how satisfied they were with how democracy functions, respondents were equally downbeat. In Peru, fewer than 30 percent said they were satisfied—the lowest in South America and the same as in 1996.

These responses are not hard to understand. They come from people who see that corruption is endemic, permeating the entire political system. Large chunks of the population have been permanently excluded from power. Government fails to reach much of the country. Politicians overpromise and underdeliver. Political institutions are unstable and ineffective. Informality means the state has little meaning to many people. When constitutions stand in their way, governments or congressional blocs break or remake them. Is it any surprise that so many people in South America think there is something deeply wrong with the functioning of democracy?

Community Power

It did not look much like a revolution.

Outside a brightly painted one-story house in La Vela de Coro, a sleepy town of twenty-one thousand people about two hundred miles west of Caracas, ten women sat around in plastic garden furniture chatting quietly about the health problems in their neighborhood.

But in fact, the group was at the forefront of Hugo Chávez's attempt to turn Venezuela into a socialist state. For Chávez, a central element of this project involved transferring power over local decision making and spending directly to small neighborhood groups. His government branded it "an explosion of communal power."

Along with constitutional, educational, and land reform, the development of thousands of communal councils—made up of between two hundred and four hundred families—was listed by Chávez as one of the "motors of the revolution" that formed the strategic plan for instituting "twenty-first-century socialism" in Venezuela.

As with almost everything in Chávez's Bolivarian Republic, attitudes toward the communal councils split Venezuelans into two camps.

To the president's devotees, they represented a new kind of direct democracy, in contrast to the failed indirect democracy of Congress. "This is central to the government's attempt to widen democratic participation," Maripili Hernández, Chávez's campaign manager in the presidential elections of 1998 and 2000, told me in Caracas.

To Chávez's opponents, they were as an extension of the president's autocratic ways, a scheme to concentrate more power in his hands by bypassing local government and transferring funds directly to the councils.

Whatever your perspective, there was little doubt that the policy was a priority for the president. "We, the constitutional power, should transfer political, social, economic, and administrative power to communal authorities in order to advance on the route to a social state," Chávez said in a big policy speech in 2007.

Sleepy it may be, but what took me to La Vela de Coro was that the small town on the Caribbean coast was at the vanguard of this policy, under the direction of Wilfredo Medina, the town's fiercely pro-Chávez mayor. Medina was friendly but businesslike, a no-nonsense, salt-of-the-earth foot soldier of the Bolivarian revolution. His office was a shrine to Chávez and twenty-first-century socialism, decorated with revolutionary posters and pictures of Che Guevara. On his desk, in pride of place, stood a Chávez action figure. The action figure was considerably more muscular than the real-life Chávez and lacked a beret-wearing parrot perched on his shoulder—or, for that matter, a string that you pull out at the back to make the doll deliver six-hour-long speeches.

If anyone was a real-life action figure, it was Mayor Medina. The mayor was so in step with the revolution, he was actually ahead of Chávez himself. "We have forty-nine communal councils here," he told me as he hurried me around the tumbledown, picturesque town. "We instituted this policy even before the president called on us to do so. We have now transferred 50 percent of our discretionary budget to their control—that's the highest figure in the country." The town's communal councils also received funds directly from the central government, giving them a total budget at the time equivalent to $400,000—an impressive sum for such a small place.

It was very fitting that La Vela was the place to pioneer in this aspect of Chávez's revolution. In this little town, Francisco de Miranda, a revolutionary who paved the way for Simón Bolívar himself, first raised the Venezuelan flag in 1806, an event that marked the beginning of the country's struggle for independence from Spain.

Bypassing Government

At the time I visited, the communal councils in La Vela were on the verge of gaining a whole new set of powers. Up until then, they had been focused on micro-projects such as repairing pathways and houses. But Mayor Medina would shortly transfer to them responsibility for larger projects, such as the building and repair of roads, schools, and sporting facilities, improving policing, and cultural activities.

The mayor told me that the councils had made local government more efficient, since residents knew exactly where money should be spent. There was something very presumptuous about this logic, but Medina had the air of a devout follower, with a definitive answer to any skeptical questions, so I let the matter rest. He also pointed out that the committees served to aid political education: "This teaches people to say what's important to them—they learn to articulate their needs," he said.

The women sitting on the garden furniture were the health committee for northern La Vela. I was told that each member of the committee—made up of representatives of the nine communal councils in the area—had surveyed the health problems in her neighborhood. "We are using this information to prioritize spending on health care and preventative medicine," said Josefa Gutiérrez, a doctor who was chairing the group from her plastic chair.

While the health committee was chiefly technocratic in nature, a few hundred feet down the road was a stark example of Mayor Medina's "political education." I was ushered into a building where I was told there was a meeting of the town's education committee. In contrast to the health committee, this had about as much citizen participation as a political discussion in Pyongyang. Party activists stood at the front of the room, reading out extracts from Chávez's speeches, while the locals sat vaguely listening in the sweltering afternoon heat, blank looks on their faces.

On the face of it, you couldn't really disagree with the idea of empowering local communities and of giving them a budget to tackle neighborhood problems. But there was clearly something very wrong about the propaganda exercise I had witnessed at the "education committee" meeting. Later I was told privately by some other locals that the leaders of the committees were chosen by the ruling party in closed meetings. Back in Caracas, lots of people complained that there was no real oversight of how the money was spent by the communities. Ricardo Gutiérrez, a senior pro-Chávez congressman, admitted that in practice there was plenty of corruption going on. "Congress, municipalities and states should all be more involved in monitoring spending," he told me.

But this missed the point entirely. Whatever your view of the communal councils, Chávez was clearly building them up not just as another arm of government but as a kind of separate, alternative, parallel state. The history of modern Venezuela had shown that the traditional arms of government did not work and should not be trusted. Chávez could change the constitution, he could win a big majority in Congress, he could install loyal judges, but deep down you got the impression that the president just did not trust the state.

The communal councils were Chávez's way of building a direct bond between himself and his supporters. In 1989, a decade before he became president, Venezuela had embarked on a process of political decentralization, devolving power down to states and city governments. On the face of it, Chávez was extending this policy right down to the level of the individual neighborhood, but at the same time he was completely bypassing local government, creating a vertical structure that seemed to link every community in the country directly with the presidential palace. Hence direct democracy or dictatorship, depending on your point of view.

It wasn't just communal councils. Chávez was building a series of political institutions that existed outside the traditional state, institutions with new or renewed clout that were loyal to him and derived their power directly from him. The president was avoiding the trap of governing through the old, discredited arms of government—even though he wanted to control them too. He was also buying himself a nice political insurance policy. If there was another coup, or Congress turned on him, or—as he was constantly warning—the Americans decided once and for all to get rid of him, the alternative state, the

Chavista state, would rise up and come to his aid. Sure, Chávez had been elected, but he had learned, so to speak, not to put all his political eggs in that basket.

For several years, for example, Chávez's pet project was the "Bolivarian circles," workers' councils that organized more than a million people in poor neighborhoods, both to undertake community development projects and to "defend the revolution" and the new Venezuelan constitution of 1999, the one that rebranded the country as a Bolivarian Republic. They also freelanced at intimidating critics of the government and clashing with anti-Chávez protesters. The communal councils were really the heirs of the Bolivarian circles movement, which fell apart after a few years.

Another important alternative institution was the military, which Chávez expanded massively, claiming he was only defending Venezuela from possible US aggression. Another was PDVSA, the state oil company, which under Chávez's watch gained all sorts of political, social, and cultural roles it had not had before.

The Revolution, Televised

Perhaps the most innovative parallel form of government Chávez came up with was *Aló, Presidente*, his live television show. At various times during his presidency, *Aló, Presidente* has been on once a week or more frequently, but whatever its frequency, the show is a hallmark of the Chávez era. To his most ardent supporters in the shantytowns of Caracas, *Aló, Presidente* is a chance for them to see their president at his most relaxed, his most informal.

American presidents have long had their weekly radio addresses, but those are a world away from *Aló, Presidente*. In a country known for its melodramatic TV soap operas, Chávez is a true performer, and more than anything else, the program is his stage. He sings, he tells jokes, he recites poetry, he flamboyantly attacks his enemies—"Mr. Danger," his gibe at George W. Bush, was an obvious favorite when the Republican was in the White House—but he also threatens his critics at home.

At times *Aló, Presidente* reveals Chávez's inner Oprah Winfrey. The twice-divorced president talks about his romantic life. He discusses his struggle with trying to lose weight. He has on celebrity guests such as Diego Maradona, the Argentine soccer legend, and Danny Glover, the American film star.

But what really differentiates the Venezuelan president's TV appearances from the sober fireside chats of his US counterparts is that for Chávez, *Aló, Presidente* is effectively a political institution. He uses it to announce that companies will be nationalized. He has fired officials live on air. He probably introduces more policy decisions on the show than anywhere else. Often his aides are left scrambling to catch up with announcements he makes spontaneously and without apparent preparations. Chávez requires his ministers to attend broadcasts, and he quizzes and rebukes them during the show.

In one memorable episode in March 2008, Chávez actually appeared to make military plans live on air, ordering his top general to send ten tank battalions to Venezuela's border with Colombia in response to a Colombian military strike in Ecuador. (The order was reportedly never carried out.)

Needless to say, the show does not follow the rules of normal programming. It lasts as long as Chávez feels like being on the air. This gets tedious—individual episodes have lasted eight hours, and in 2009, to mark *Aló, Presidente's* tenth anniversary, Chávez broadcast two full days of programming—but it is essential viewing. Politicians, diplomats, journalists—everyone must watch *Aló, Presidente*, otherwise they might miss a big move by Chávez's government. (Chávez also knows when not to broadcast: during the 2006 soccer World Cup, he wisely took a two-month break.)

Without doubt, *Aló, Presidente* gives Chávez an important regular platform to talk to the people directly. You might say it is the ultimate in transparent government—except for the lack of any opposition to question the president. It keeps everyone well informed on what is on Chávez's mind. It is also a fascinating window into the erratic workings of his psyche. It's car-crash TV, but with an entire country at stake.

But there is something very significant too about the whole notion of governing by television. Perhaps more than any other president in the world, Chávez really understands the power of the medium. After his failed 1992 coup—long before he became head of state—he had been allowed to concede defeat on TV and to warn that he had failed "for now." Under Chávez, the number of state television channels went from one to six in as many years and he set up Telesur, a region-wide Bolivarian equivalent of CNN. As well as *Aló, Presidente*, a 2004 law forced all broadcasters to carry live and in full Chávez's *cadenas*— marathon speeches devoted to commemorations, all-purpose propaganda, and, of course, invective against the enemies of the Bolivarian revolution. There are many countries where important announcements and presidential speeches are carried live on network TV, but Chávez's Venezuela took the cake: he made 1,816 such speeches in his first decade in power, talking for a total of 1,179 hours—or forty-nine days' worth of nonstop bombast.

Presidents use television advertisements to gain power and TV appearances to help them keep power. Leaders such as Churchill and Roosevelt grasped the importance of talking directly to their people. But no president has really transformed television into a political institution. In most countries, leaders call press conferences, make keynote policy speeches, address legislatures. Chávez governs live on air every single week.

Aló, Presidente is, then, perhaps the ultimate snub to Venezuela's established arms of government. It is Chávez's way of saying that what matters to him is not the formal due process of governing but taking his message directly to the people. The program is both an alternative form of government and a way for Chávez to show the people he is still one of them. In that sense, it is much like Evo Morales's sweater, Rafael Correa's belt, and the new Andean constitutions. When true outsiders win power, they continue to behave like outsiders.

In 1970, Gil Scott-Heron, the American jazz poet, famously predicted that "the revolution will not be televised." Chávez upended that idea. "Never has a revolutionary idea made use of a medium of communication with such efficiency," noted Fidel Castro in May 2009 in a column about the Venezuelan president syndicated in Cuba's official press. But Chávez has not only televised every step of his revolution, he went one step better: he made the revolution via television.

10

Hugonomics

The Subway in Las Mercedes was unlike any other I had ever visited. Admittedly, I am not a particularly dedicated patron of the international sandwich chain, having only visited just a handful of its thirty-one thousand locations. But on a visit to Caracas, I was attracted by the prospect of one of their famous foot-long sandwiches filled with a host of fresh ingredients of my choice. I was to be disappointed. As I was pondering my options at the Subway on the main boulevard through Las Mercedes, a swanky neighborhood that is the Venezuelan capital's primary shopping and leisure district, an unsmiling server pointed to a handwritten sign tacked on the front of the display case. It listed the sandwich fillings that were not available—no beef, no chicken, no peppers, no tomatoes, and no mozzarella cheese. Jared Fogle, an American student, once famously lost 245 pounds through a diet of Subway sandwiches. Had he lived in Caracas, he might well have lost even more.

The reduced menu at Subway indicated a very serious problem in Hugo Chávez's Venezuela. Even in wealthy areas, the shelves of the supermarkets were sorry-looking. In the low-priced state-sponsored supermarkets, items such as milk, eggs, oil, and sugar were often unavailable, or there was only enough to supply those at the front at the long lines that formed when they were in stock. A few weeks earlier, the country's National Supermarkets' Association had warned that inventories of basic goods were down by up to 35 percent. In many poor neighborhoods, Venezuelan staples such as meat and black beans were almost impossible to come by in shops. Supporters of the government accused the food producers of hoarding and speculation (a charge that led Chávez to nationalize a string of food-processing factories and supermarkets). Business leaders countered that by saying that price controls and import restrictions had hampered production. What was clear was that the food shortages were just one symptom of an economy distorted by foreign exchange restrictions, price controls, and subsidies. Gasoline, for example, was so heavily subsidized that it sold for a fraction of the price of bottled water. That resulted in a lot more cars in poor areas in Venezuela than you would see in the equivalent neighborhoods in other South American countries, and eternal traffic congestion on the streets of Caracas.

Another symptom was rampant consumerism. Down the street from the Subway in Las Mercedes, two US-made Hummers sat nose to nose outside Super Autos, a luxury car retailer. Chávez had won power in part because of outrage at a society in which ostentatious displays of wealth lived cheek by jowl with extreme poverty. Yet after a decade of left-wing rule, Venezuela had become the biggest importer of Hummers in the region. The sticker prices on the windshields of the Hummers outside Super Autos were the equivalent of about $100,000—some 50 percent more than what you might have paid for the vehicle at the time if you were buying it in the United States. I had a fascinating chat with Ricardo Díaz, the manager of the showroom. He told me Super Autos was the biggest importer of Hummers in Venezuela, selling between thirty and forty a year, but General Motors, which made Hummers at the time, would never send a boatload over, because it was worried that the Venezuelan government would confiscate such booty. Instead, GM exported the vehicles in batches of one or two, only after they had already been ordered and paid for by Venezuelan customers. So there never seemed to be enough Hummers—or other luxury cars—to satisfy buyers. "Demand for top-end vehicles has grown very quickly," Díaz told me. "Now it vastly outstrips supply."

Where was this demand coming from? On the one hand, it was coming from the wealthy. Many of them had left Venezuela when Chávez became president, or in the years that followed. (A joke once popular in

Caracas: Why did the rich schoolgirl want Chávez to win the election?
So she could move to Miami.) But many of those who remained did so
because for some businesspeople the Chávez era was actually a time of
plenty. Those who owned companies that had contracts with the military, for example, could make healthy profits. So could bankers: because
they were the only people the government allowed to trade using the
market rate for converting Venezuelan currency into dollars, they could
make a killing by exploiting the difference between official and unofficial exchange rates, lending money to the state at the official rate and
selling the bonds on to foreign investors at the unofficial market rate,
effectively tripling their money without doing very much at all. On the
other hand, the Super Autos manager told me, much of the new demand
for Hummers actually came from senior government officials or others
close to the regime—"boligarchs," as they were known in Venezuela.

A month earlier, one of Chávez's advisers had gotten an unexpected
response when he publicly criticized the growing number of politicians and their entourages who were driving around in luxury vehicles.
Luís Acosta Carlez, the pro-Chávez governor of Carabobo state, shot
back, "Don't revolutionaries have the right to own a Hummer too?"
(He wasn't joking.)

But it wasn't just the businessmen with government contracts, the
bankers, and the public officials who became wealthier under Chávez.
The Venezuelan leader had promised to help the country's poor, and
the massive increase in oil revenues enabled him to keep his word.
Even his opponents had to concede that the scale of redistribution
was vast—in terms of subsidies, public spending on social services,
and direct cash transfers. Much of this was lavished on the very poorest in society, such as the residents of the ranchos on the hills around
Caracas. Those in extreme poverty—about 53 percent of the population in 2004, according to Venezuela's National Statistics Institute—
saw their real incomes increase by 130 percent between 2004 and
2007. This led to a massive increase in food consumption among the
very poor, which, combined with all the other government spending,
helped drive up inflation. To combat the inflation, Chávez imposed
price controls. This worked to a degree, except that vendors stopped
selling meat, for example, in the shops, preferring instead to unload it
on the black market where the costs were much higher. The result was
that Venezuela's real inflation rates were far above those of every other

South American country, and prices were rising faster than the interest rate you could get by depositing your money in a high-interest bank account. So rather than holding on to money and watching the prices rise, poor and rich alike spent like crazy. The poor bought food and beer. The rich bought Hummers and champagne. In the topsy-turvy world of Hugonomics, the luxury vehicles went up in value as soon as they were driven away from Super Autos.

The whole situation was pretty farcical. Travelers to Latin America are used to things being chaotic, but this seemed completely out of control. It begged the question: how long could Chávez's "Bolivarian revolution" really last? Thanks to a constitutional change approved by a referendum in 2009, he could continue to run for reelection indefinitely. But how long would the economy hold out? Was Chávez a long-term problem for the United States, or could Washington hold its nose for a few years until the whole thing collapsed? How much longer would oil supplies be threatened, the war on drugs compromised, and US influence in the Americas undermined? Could Chavismo live on after its founder? Would the United States have to go in after and clean up the mess?

The spending frenzy gave Chávez's Venezuela the atmosphere of a wild party, an unexpected orgy of consumerism. If I hadn't seen it for myself, it wouldn't have been what I'd have envisaged from listening to either Chávez's supporters around the world—for whom Venezuela was at times portrayed as an Eden of shiny socialism—or his detractors, who depicted Venezuela under Chávez as a colorless dictatorship. In fact, the whole country was a bit like the political and economic equivalent of Studio 54 in the late 1970s. As long as the oil revenues continued to pour in, the party would rage on. But you were left with the distinct impression that Venezuela would wake up one day with the mother of all hangovers.

Production Problems

The history of Venezuela, Ecuador, Bolivia, and Peru is as much written on the oil-trading floors of New York and London as in Caracas, Quito, La Paz, and Lima.

Like South America in general, the economies of the Andes depend on the revenues that come from exporting natural resources. Oil is a volatile commodity. When prices in the trading pits soar, Andean economies tend to grow. When prices plunge, they struggle. When prices are high, politicians tend to splash money around and gain popularity. When they fall, governments often fall too. Datanalisis, a respected Venezuelan pollster, even found an 80 percent correlation between oil prices and public support for standing governments during the country's recent history.

Throughout their history, Venezuelan, Bolivian, and Ecuadorean politicians have often waxed lyrical about the need to diversify their economies, to create manufacturing bases that can help cushion them in times of low commodity prices. But ultimately, when the revenues flow again, such ideas are usually drowned out as the party music starts up again. The rise of China and India placed a new emphasis on the export value of natural resources, once again prioritizing raw materials within the economies of Latin America. By squeezing foreign investors or taking over their operations, Chávez, Morales, and Correa not only didn't end their countries' dependence on oil and gas, but they actually made them even more so. When commodity prices soared, so did the public coffers, and the state then built up spending commitments— rightly or wrongly—that could only be met by using oil revenues.

In May 2006, a few weeks after Ecuador's government unceremoniously kicked Occidental out of its oil fields, I went to see for myself what the locals made of the expulsion. The installation was near a town called Limoncocha, in a remote area of the country's eastern Amazon jungle region. On the way there, I imagined in my mind's eye the happy villagers, celebrating the exit of a hatred foreign intruder. Instead, when I arrived in Limoncocha—a pretty, tranquil village of faded pink-, blue-, and green-painted wooden huts less than a mile from the entrance to the oil field—I found them worrying about the future.

The community's fifteen hundred residents spoke both Spanish and Quechua, the main indigenous language of Ecuador. Most of them earned a meager living by selling cocoa beans, plantains, and corn at nearby towns. Very few had ever worked at the oil field. But one by one, they told me they had come to depend on the aid that Occidental gave to local indigenous communities and they were fearful about losing it. "Oxy helped us for twenty years—with infrastructure, educational scholarships, sports facilities, and vehicles," Jorge Grefa, president of the parish of Limoncocha, told me. He cast his arm around the village. "Pretty much all the infrastructure here was paid for by Oxy."

It emerged that the company had spent some $300,000 a year in local villages and had recently signed several new agreements with community leaders on social spending. Contractors who had agreements with Occidental also spent money in local villages, equipping the school at Limoncocha with an Internet-linked computer room. "Oxy was responsive to our requests," said Enoc Cerda, the school's rector. "We asked them to limit work at night and they did so. And they were pretty quick about responding to environmental problems."

By contrast, the villagers trembled at the prospect of Petroecuador, the state oil company, taking over. Residents from thirty-six local communities had demonstrated the previous week against the state company's taking over the field permanently. "We know how Petroecuador works," Cerda noted somberly. "They damage the environment and don't help local communities. Petroecuador has brought destruction wherever it has operated." When I asked about help from the government, they were also dismissive. "The local municipality doesn't spend any money here," Grefa said. "Oxy was almost like a replacement government for us. Now we've been left with no government, with nothing."

The Limoncocha trip surprised me at the time, but it highlighted how ordinary people who had seen firsthand the incompetence and mismanagement of a state company had come to fear it. This effect lay at the heart of some of the fears about resource nationalism. Leaving aside the ideological argument about whether the state or a private company should control natural resources, there was a great deal of concern about the ability of government-run companies to operate these extractive industries effectively.

Venezuela was another prime case. As a semiautonomous company in the years before it lost its 2002 battle with Chávez, PDVSA had been widely considered to be a professional, well-run state oil concern. But many of those who had held out for months against the Venezuelan president were technicians and administrators, so when he purged half the employees, at least some of that professionalism was bound to be lost. Two-thirds of managers and technical staff were let go, with an average service record of fifteen years with the company. The criteria for replacing them seemed to have more to do with their politics than their oil expertise. The payroll swelled massively as hordes of Chávez supporters were given jobs at the company. In 2009, Rafael Ramirez, Venezuela's oil minister, even said that PDVSA workers must support the government or be suspected of conspiring against the revolution.

PDVSA was also paying out much more of its revenues to the government and its social programs than ever before. Chávez roped PDVSA into funding all sorts of state schemes, including sponsoring free TV coverage for Bolivian viewers of the 2006 soccer World Cup. It was also obliged to pay into a development fund that the president controlled directly. As oil prices crept ever higher, PDVSA's fastest-growing division was Palmaven, its office that oversaw social spending.

Undoubtedly, much of this spending was on worthy causes—job creation, education, affordable housing, and so on—but it left PDVSA with less cash flow and therefore less money to invest in maintaining production, let alone increasing it. Since oil production involves depleting resources, an oil company must constantly replace its reserves. But PDVSA was spending more on social programs than on finding new sources of oil or maintaining its oil wells. When Chávez nationalized oil facilities in the Orinoco belt, PDVSA suddenly found itself with a controlling interest in all the area's oil installations. When ConocoPhillips and ExxonMobil quit Venezuela in protest at the nationalizations, PDVSA took over their facilities until new investors could be found, stretching the state oil company even thinner.

The result was that at fields controlled exclusively by PDVSA, production fell sharply under Chávez—although this drop was hidden by rising oil prices—so even though there was less oil being produced, revenues still increased handsomely. The lower yields were also masked by the government's official statistics, which tended to exaggerate how much oil the country was actually producing.

The other problem was that having had more taxes squeezed out of them and with their operating contracts changing several times, international oil companies were in no mood to make large investments in the Andes. They often preferred to do the minimum necessary to maintain their presence, presumably calculating that in the long term the government would change and they could reclaim more of their profits. With private investors leery, state-controlled national energy companies from China and Russia proved more willing partners for

Venezuela, although they could less easily be squeezed, since that might mean damaging relations with those countries. Moreover, they lacked the efficiency in production of private oil companies.

PDVSA had also been dragged into a host of international tie-ups that served Chávez's regional and global ambitions. He gave Cuba nearly 100,000 barrels of oil a day. A further 200,000 barrels a day of subsidized oil went to Central American and Caribbean countries. Through Citgo, Chávez even gave away free home heating oil to 180,000 poor households in the United States. The cost of this largesse added up (the US program alone cost $100 million a year). Some estimates put Venezuelan support to other countries—by direct payments, cheap oil, buying up debt, or building oil refineries—at a cumulative cost of more than $60 billion. Even for one of the world's biggest oil producers, this put considerable strain on Venezuela's budget.

In La Paz and Quito as much as Caracas, with the state fully in charge of the oil and gas industry, and with natural resources revenues driving the revolution, Bolivia, Ecuador, and Venezuela grew more dependent on oil than ever before. By 2008, oil accounted for some 95 percent of Venezuela's export revenues and about half of state spending. Of course, the problem was the fine print that mom-and-pop investors so often overlook: the "what goes up can come down" stuff. In 2008, when the price of oil plunged, the national incomes of countries such as Venezuela and Ecuador followed.

Chávez believed he could nationalize his way out of trouble, much as he had tried to do with the food producers after price controls had prompted them to cut back on their production, leading to shortages in the stores. At the end of 2008, cash-strapped PDVSA owed oil-services contractors $14 billion, according to a report to Venezuela's National Assembly. In response, Chávez simply nationalized the oil-services industry.

These problems were far from unique. From Azerbaijan to Nigeria to Saudi Arabia, big oil finds have tended to diminish other ways for countries to diversify their national income. In good times, oil led to corruption and lavish public spending, in bad times to economic crises and political instability. The resource nationalism of Chávez, Morales, and Correa sought to use oil and gas to pay for the massive redistribution of wealth, but in doing so, they made it likely that the money would run out sooner and tied their countries more closely to the notoriously volatile international commodity markets. Their natural resources were their salvation and their likely damnation. Not for nothing had Juan Pablo Pérez Alfonzo, Venezuela's oil minister in the early 1960s, observed that oil was not so much black gold as the devil's excrement.

Divide and Rule

The floor of the small synagogue in the center of Coro, the oldest Jewish house of prayer in Venezuela, is covered in a thick layer of sand.

The sand was intended to recall the Children of Israel's time wandering in the Sinai Desert, but it is also a symbol of the transience of Jewish settlement in South America. Jewish merchants first arrived in Coro—a small town in western Venezuela that was the country's first capital—from Curaçao in 1827. In 1855, a mob ransacked Jewish homes and shops, and almost all the community fled.

Over time, the Jews returned to Venezuela and enjoyed a more harmonious relationship with their compatriots. Argentina, the country with the biggest Jewish presence in the region, had long experienced anti-Semitism, with Jews disproportionately being "disappeared" by the military juntas of the 1970s and 1980s and the bloody bombings of the AMIA Jewish community center and the Israeli embassy in the 1990s. During the Shining Path era in Peru, Jewish facilities had been the target of bomb threats. By contrast, Venezuela's Jewish community had considered itself one of the best established and comfortable in South America.

But under Chávez, thousands of Venezuelan Jews once again fled the country, as they got the sense that they were on the wrong side of the Bolivarian revolution. More than half the community left the country. What happened to the Jews of Venezuela symbolizes how leaders of the radical Left often fueled confrontation and social division for political ends. The economy and the dependence on commodity prices was one source of instability. Encouraging societal strife was another. Through their history, Jews have often found themselves the targets of political leaders in trouble and looking for someone to blame.

To many observers, Chávez was simply a clownish, flamboyant populist given to outrageous outbursts and histrionic displays of mischievous wit. According to this view, the Venezuelan leader was entertaining but mostly harmless. But Chávez is more serious and has at times been more dangerous. While his supporters could justify his verbal attacks on the United States with reference to America's military interventions and other interferences in Latin America throughout its history, his attitudes to the Jews of his own country could not be so easily explained away. The Venezuelan leader was not an anti-Semite. Rather, his references to Jews were clearly an attempt to divide Venezuela, to scapegoat as a means of diverting attention from the shortcomings of his domestic policy—the failure of his Bolivarian revolution to solve the country's persistent problems and the madcap, chaotic nature of the government.

Things began to change for Venezuela's Jews in 2004. As Chávez started ramping up his Bolivarian revolution, they felt themselves to be in an increasingly hostile environment. That November, the Club Hebraica—a Jewish education, sports, and social complex in eastern Caracas—was raided by police carrying a search warrant issued by a pro-Chávez judge. The warrant, which came after the murder of Danilo Anderson, a public prosecutor, suggested that the Hebraica was being used to store weapons. This apparently sprang from rumors that Anderson had been killed with equipment from Mossad, the Israeli secret service. After searching the school and the club, the police left empty-handed. "Chávez must have known about it," one community member recalled when I interviewed him on a visit to Caracas a few years later. "In this society, nothing happens without his permission. There was a feeling that the government wanted to send a sign that no group was immune from its control."

The following year, Chávez said in his annual seasonal speech to the country on Christmas Eve 2005 that "the descendants of those who killed Christ" (along with the descendants of those who expelled Bolivar from Venezuela) had "taken possession of all the wealth in the world." Although the president subsequently reassured Venezuelan Jewish leaders that he had not been referring to the Jewish community, the comments added to the sense of unease. That was compounded by Chávez's growing friendship with Mahmoud Ahmadinejad, the

Iranian president who was not exactly a friend of the Jews. In 2005, Ahmadinejad called Israel a "disgraceful stain on the Islamic world" that needed to be "wiped from the pages of history." The following year he had hosted a high-profile conference of Holocaust deniers in Tehran. Unsurprisingly, the Jews of Venezuela were concerned about his increasingly close ties to their own president.

Things took a turn for the worse in 2006, when Caracas's official reaction to Israel's war with Hezbollah unleashed what Freddy Pressner, a prominent Jewish leader in Caracas, told me was "an explosion of anti-Semitism in Venezuela." Echoing Ahmadinejad, Chávez repeatedly compared Israel's behavior with that of the Nazis, a stance that prompted a wave of similar and even more vociferous comments in Venezuela. In a September 2, 2006, article in *Diario de Caracas*, a pro-government newspaper, for example, journalist Tarek Muci Nasir wrote, "The Jewish race is condemned to disappear, because if they continue marrying among themselves they will continue to degenerate; if they open their marriages they will racially dilute themselves, so the only resource they have left to stay united is to cause wars and genocides." Luis Cadenas, a Venezuelan writer, noted in *Diario VEA*, a state-owned newspaper, on July 4, 2006: "Undoubtedly the political, economic and military Israeli elites inherited the fascist weight of Hitler's Nazi Germany." Chávez's administration organized an anti-Israel demonstration outside the city's main Sephardic synagogue. When the protesters had gone home, the wall outside the synagogue was daubed with "Jews, killers—leave" and "Zionist baby killers." The following year, police again raided the Hebraica, apparently looking for concealed arms. Again, they left empty-handed.

When Israel invaded the Gaza Strip in December 2008, Chávez repeated his condemnation of the United States' "genocidal" ally. As he had done when Israel went to war with Hezbollah two years earlier, he cut off all diplomatic ties with the Jewish state. Once again, the pro-government media took his lead and unleashed a tirade of fury against Israel. But this time around, Caracas repeatedly linked the Israeli government's military offensive with the Jews of Venezuela. In an interview on VTV, Venezuela's state-run TV network, on January 6, 2009, for example, Chávez called on Venezuela's Jewish community to "declare itself against this barbarity" in Gaza. "Don't Jews repudiate the Holocaust?" he said. "This is precisely what we're witnessing." That attitude was taken much further by Aporrea, a pro-Chávez website, which urged the government to confiscate the property of Venezuelan Jews who supported Israel and donate the proceeds to Palestine.

In January 2009, Caracas's largest synagogue was broken into by eleven men, eight of them police officers. They desecrated Torah scrolls, spray-painted "Jews, get out" on the walls, and stole a computer database with the names and addresses of Venezuelan Jews. To be sure, the government denounced the break-in and brought charges against those who carried it out. But even when Nicolas Maduro, Venezuela's foreign minister, condemned the synagogue attack, in the same breath he attacked Israel's "criminal" government, suggesting the attack was not unjustified. "We respect the Jewish people, but we ask respect for the people of Palestine and their right to life," Maduro said on January 31, 2009, at a ceremony to welcome home two Venezuelan diplomats expelled from Israel in response to Caracas's cutting of ties.

Unfortunately, what had happened in Caracas was no isolated case. The attack on Gaza prompted a wave of anti-Semitic incidents around the world in which Jews were targeted in protest at Israel's actions.

It was far from clear whether the Caracas incident was really an anti-Semitic attack or whether it was primarily aimed at robbery, as the government claimed. Weeks later, thieves broke into Caracas's main mosque, destroyed sacred books, smashed windows, and stole computer equipment. A few months after that, there was a robbery at the presidency of the Catholic bishops in Caracas. What's more, one of those charged in the synagogue break-in was the rabbi's bodyguard, suggesting that it may have been planned by an insider.

Although Morales and Correa did not follow Chávez's lead of targeting their countries' (much smaller) Jewish communities, the radical Left in South America took a new approach to the classic strategy of divide and rule. As with Chávez's approach to Venezuela's Jews, when they set their fellow citizens against each other, they usually took up the cudgels for one side and demonized the other— the poor against the rich, the landless against the landholders, the comrades of the downtrodden against the allies of imperialism.

In Bolivia, for example, Evo Morales inherited a built-in geographic tension between the poor, indigenous highlands and the wealthier, ethnically whiter lowlands. The region of Santa Cruz, in the country's lush, gas-rich southeastern farmlands, had long been threatening to secede from the rest of the country. Although Morales didn't create this division, neither did he really try to overcome it. His supporters stressed that this was a "Croat enclave" (some of the elite in the area were ethnically Croatian), suggesting that the secessionists were not real Bolivians. Morales's economic and political reforms—which gave the impression to many that he was the "president of the indigenous" and not of anyone else—exacerbated the country's centrifugal forces, and other lowland regions elsewhere in Bolivia also started demanding more autonomy from the central government.

Much of this opposition coalesced around Morales's attempt to rewrite the Bolivian constitution. The president's instincts were to attack. He called his opponents racists, fascists, and traitors and accused them of working for the United States against the interests of Bolivia. "I am not afraid of the people, nor am I afraid of the empire," he said in a speech delivered to supporters from the balcony of the presidential palace in La Paz. "But some people don't want to submit to the people; they only want to submit to the empire." In the process, he alienated much of the urban middle class—many of whom had voted for him in the first place but were rapidly gaining the impression that he saw himself as just a president for the indigenous.

In late 2008, social tensions resulted in violent clashes across Bolivia, which left dozens of government supporters and opponents dead. A pro-government demonstration in Cobija, in the northern Amazon region, turned into a bloodbath with rival gangs exchanging gunfire. A subsequent investigation by the Union of South American Nations determined that the incident was a premeditated massacre of Morales's indigenous supporters by his opponents. The following year, hundreds of indigenous people attacked the home of Víctor Hugo Cárdenas, a former Bolivian vice president who had emerged as an outspoken critic of Morales. They beat Cárdenas's wife, children, and nephew with sticks and whips, putting them in the hospital. The qualified condemnation of Álvaro García Linera, Bolivia's vice president, was reminiscent of Nicolas Maduro's comments after the Caracas synagogue break-in. "Víctor Hugo Cárdenas should ask himself what harm he might have caused his neighbors for them to condemn him," he told Bolivia's *El Deber* newspaper on March 12, 2009.

Perhaps these confrontations were simply to be expected. To the government's thinking, this wasn't even necessarily a bad thing, since reclaiming power and resources for the historically marginalized majority was bound to ruffle some feathers. You don't make revolution without upsetting a few people. Besides, the opponents of Chávez had already shown themselves willing to overthrow him in a coup, while those seeking "autonomy" from the national government in Bolivia were masters of brinkmanship.

But in the Andes, where social unrest had so often propelled fragile governments into crisis after crisis, there was always a sense that deliberately provoking social confrontation might be both unnecessary and unwise. In the last few days of 2010, massive demonstrations forced Evo Morales to abandon his proposal to withdraw fuel subsidies. This illustrated how a leader who rises from the street would be forever subject to the will of the street.

In another telling moment in his presidency, Morales railed against opponents who had stormed government offices to press their case for greater regional autonomy. "Occupying state offices isn't democracy. Civil disobedience isn't democracy," he thundered in a televised address to the nation on November 28, 2007. Nothing better underlined the danger for Morales that the very tactics that had propelled the former protest leader to power could someday prove to be his undoing.

Borrowing Public Health

The lines at the Chacaltaya hospital started to form at 3:30 a.m. By the time the first doctors arrived to open the clinic at 8 a.m., those lines stretched the whole way around Plaza German Busch, a grubby square in Alto Lima, a neighborhood in El Alto. The people in line were some of the most downtrodden on the entire continent: Alto Lima is perhaps the poorest neighborhood of El Alto, the poorest city in Bolivia, the poorest country in South America.

Being so poor, they suffer from the kind of complaints you would expect: illnesses related to not having enough to eat or having a poor diet, or not having running water or sewers. But poverty is not the only reason the Chacaltaya hospital is so popular. More important, in 2006, it became the first medical facility in all of La Paz–El Alto to treat patients for free. Before Chacaltaya, even if residents of El Alto could afford medical care, they had to trudge down the mountainside to the crowded hospitals of La Paz to receive it.

Most of the cases at Chacaltaya were not serious—they required simple consultations, proper treatment for a wound, basic medicine, advice on diet, or, on occasion, a straightforward procedure. So when I visited in November 2006, even though Chacaltaya only had thirty-one doctors, they had attended to an astonishing thirty-six thousand patients in the three months since the clinic had opened. The doctors were all Cuban medics on a two-year volunteer stint. I had heard stories about Cuban doctors sent overseas, mostly negative stuff about how they were forced to indoctrinate their patients and how some had defected to the United States while abroad. True enough, one of the waiting rooms was postered with stories of the heroic legends of Cuban communism, but it was pretty mild stuff and none of the patients seemed to be look-ing at any of it (many were probably illiterate). When I spoke to the doctors, they were far from socialist propagandists. They came across as professional, educated, and committed, much like doctors from the United States or Europe who volunteer to work in war-torn regions for organizations such as Doctors Without Borders. I interviewed quite a few patients, to try to find out if they had been victims of Cuban indoc-trination. None seemed to have been, but I stopped asking after a while, as they saw my clothes and pale skin and assumed that I too was a Cuban doctor. Even as I shook my head vigorously and held up my press pass, they exposed various body parts to show me their ailments.

Chacaltaya's thirty-one doctors were part of a group of more than seventeen hundred Cuban medical staff working all over Bolivia. In Evo Morales's first eleven months as president, they had already made an impressive impact: Cuban doctors attended to more than 2.2 million Bolivians, a quarter of the country's population. The spread of Cuban medical staff in Bolivia echoed a much larger story that had been going on for a few years in Venezuela. In exchange for cheap oil, some thirty thousand Cuban medical staff, not to mention dentists and teachers, had flooded into the Bolivarian Republic since 2003. Caracas had traded subsidized oil for a ready-made social wel-fare system.

The wholesale importation of Cuban doctors into Venezuela and Bolivia (and a much smaller number into Ecuador) was perhaps the radical Left's flagship policy. It was also arguably the most positive part of Chávez's and Morales's rule. Whatever your view of "twenty-first-century socialism," it brought rudimentary health care to millions of people in the Andes who had never received it before. Not only was this a hugely significant achievement, but it also helped explain the enduring popularity of South American leaders like Chávez.

Actually, the strategy was not exactly new. If the history of South American politics shows anything, it is that presidential reputations are not built on winning wars or establishing sound institutions but on feeding the hungry—in the broadest sense. In that sense, Chávez was reviving the spirit of Juan and Eva Perón in 1940s Argentina or Alberto Fujimori in 1990s Peru as much as left-wing heroes such as Fidel Castro or Salvador Allende of Chile. (And, like Fujimori, he deployed the military in election campaigning on his behalf.) For all the hype, "twenty-first-century socialism" was a reheated version of a classic South American dish that had been served up to much acclaim many times before. Its essential ingredient was delivery. While previous governments had become bogged down by corruption, by fights between different political elites or institutions, by commitments to foreign debtors, by ineffective reform measures, the radical Left understood that the key to winning power was to convince the people that they would do things completely differently—and the key to staying in power was actually to deliver. The Chacaltaya clinic and the thousands of other new medical facilities across the Andes symbolized that. So did the huge amounts of money poured into education efforts, food subsidies and price controls, and soup kitchens in the ranchos.

The scale of redistribution undertaken by the Chávez government through subsidies and direct cash transfers was undeniable. The high inflation rate was partly a by-product of the fact that Venezuelans were buying a lot more of everything than they had before Chávez. And it wasn't only the poorest who benefited. In Venezuela, there were anti-illiteracy campaigns in the ranchos, but there were also more opportunities in higher education for some of those who were a little better off. The free medical and dental care reached more than just the very poor, so they helped Chávez win some support among the lower middle class as well. Morales and Correa also focused on improving education, which appealed to the lower middle class as much as the poor. In Bolivia, Morales introduced free school meals and cash payments for mothers who made sure their children went to school or who took their babies to health clinics. He introduced a noncontributory old-age pension. He handed out hundreds of free tractors. In Ecuador, Correa also started providing free school meals and abolished fees at state schools. Both leaders raised the minimum wage and increased the number of public payroll jobs.

Fidel Castro and Che Guevara had attempted to spread socialism through the continent by fighting with arms. Chávez, Morales, and Correa fought for hearts and minds. Their weapons were full bellies and basic services. They were lucky that the Cuban health care system produced doctors who were not only exceptionally well trained and used to working in straitened circumstances but were also committed to helping the region's poor. Selling oil to the Americans brought in US dollars to fill up the reserves, but giving oil and financial assistance to Cuba brought in a fully formed health care system, ready to service the poorest of society. It's unlikely that a homemade Venezuelan or Bolivian system would have been so effective or efficient.

Social programs provided real, visible results and they engendered devotion for the leaders who implemented them. In the ranchos of Venezuela, many people idolized Chávez. Some saw him as a benevolent father figure, others as a revolutionary South American legend like Che Guevara or Simón Bolívar. Some were even said to pray to his image. For all its finger-wagging, Washington, by contrast, had little tangible to offer poor South Americans. For decades it had been preaching the gospel of slashing state spending and eliminating subsidies, without much strategic thought on how to improve education and health care for the poor. In 2007, in a halfhearted effort to combat populism in the region, the United States equipped a naval ship to stop off at the ports of eleven poor Latin American countries to offer medical consultations for eighty-five thousand people—less than 4 percent of the number of Bolivians whom Cuban doctors treated in Evo Morales's first year in power.

The United States should really have understood better how to win people over. After all, delivery was also the foundation of American politics. No US senator who had not delivered big federal projects in his or her state would ever expect to be reelected. US budgets were always laden down with pork, unrelated spending tacked on to secure the support of individual politicians.

The strategy of Chávez, Morales, and Correa was really an updated version of the promise that had won Herbert Hoover the White House back in 1928: "A chicken in every pot and a car in every garage."

Popularity and Populism

Quite a lot of what the radical Left did was popular. As well as social spending, Chávez, Morales, and Correa understood the importance of showing in a host of other ways how they were on the side of the marginalized masses—hence the nationalizations, the rewriting of constitutions, the attempts at land reform, and other confrontations with vested interests. Partly it was ideology that prompted them to do these things. Partly it was simply because it was popular, and the leaders of the radical Left had built their whole political careers on doing what was popular—which could prove useful in distracting attention from areas where things weren't going well.

To some observers, doing what was popular spelled disaster. South American countries needed all kinds of reforms if they were to establish a base for solid long-term growth, they argued. By merely doing what was popular, the countries were wasting time, effort, and money on short-term policies that however laudable—you could hardly object to feeding and educating the poor—were not part of a long-term development strategy and so were simply unsustainable. In Lewis Carroll's *Through the Looking-Glass*, the White Queen had outlined a policy of "jam tomorrow and jam yesterday—but never jam today." Chávez, Morales, and Correa offered jam today but didn't give the impression of having thought a great deal about tomorrow.

As with the nationalizations, the priority of leaders on the radical Left was politics, not economics. Leaders in the past who had tried to do the "right thing"—like those who implemented the Washington Consensus policies—had all too often alienated the very populations they were trying to help. In Ecuador, for example, another young failed coup leader and left-wing military figure, Lucio Gutiérrez, had become president in 2003. Troubled by his rabble-rousing candidacy, many on the right urged him not to become like Chávez but to stick to the center ground. He followed their advice. Within two years he was forced out by massive street protests.

Chávez, Morales, and Correa enjoyed more longevity. They may have polarized their societies and provoked social divisions, but they were careful to keep the majority on their side. Although they took over during situations of political instability and institutional weakness, they provided what was, for the Andes, a remarkably stable period. They thrived during election campaigns, when they could go out and connect directly with the people, remind them why they hated the old order and why the revolution was worth defending. At times it seemed like the Andes were in constant election mode. Chávez first won office in 1998, then won a constitutional referendum in 1999, triumphed in another presidential contest under the new constitution in 2000, survived a coup in 2002, won a recall referendum in 2004, gained reelection as president in 2006, narrowly lost a constitutional referendum in 2007, won another constitutional referendum in 2009 and lost congressional elections in 2010.

If anything, his acolytes abroad were even bigger election lovers. Evo Morales first won office in 2005, won the biggest number of seats in an assembly to rewrite the constitution in 2006, secured victory in a recall referendum in 2008, won a constitutional referendum in 2009, and was reelected in 2009. Rafael Correa won office in 2006, won a referendum to establish an assembly to rewrite the constitution in 2007 as well as elections to that assembly five months later, won another referendum approving the new constitution in 2008, won presidential reelection in 2009, and won yet another referendum, this time on judicial and media reform, in 2011. The era of the radical Left in South America was the epoch of the permanent election campaign. That suited their style. It proved their enduring popularity. It gave a sense of a participatory style of democracy. It also played into the confrontational, brinkmanship style of their politics. After all, why work with your opponents when you can demonize them on the campaign trail?

When they won elections, that strategy worked well. When they went against them, things started to go awry. In 2008, Chávez was facing a revitalized opposition in regional elections. As the poll drew closer, 260 candidates—nearly all of them from the opposition—were arbitrarily disqualified from running. When the opposition won in the country's three most populous states and in most of Caracas, Chávez turned his attention to its leaders. The mayor of Maracaibo, Venezuela's second city, was accused of corruption and fled to Peru. One of Chávez's former defense ministers was imprisoned, also on corruption charges. The office of the mayor of Caracas was taken over by pro-government activist mobs and his recent election victory undermined when most of his money, staff, and powers were handed over to a newly created position handpicked by the president himself. Apparently no longer trusting even his allies in the regions, Chávez stripped state governors of some of their powers and funding, which was either transferred to Caracas or to local communal councils.

The president had not taken defeat well, and he would continue not to do so in 2010, when his party suffered a huge blow in congressional elections, losing its two-thirds majority and failing to win a majority of the popular vote. The leader's popularity, it seemed, was certainly on the wane. Even Petare, a once solidly Chavista shantytown in Caracas, elected an opposition deputy. Chávez once again seemed determined to undermine the election result. Before the new deputies were sworn in, his supporters in the lame-duck legislature rewrote congressional rules, potentially limiting the body to just four meetings a month and capping speeches at fifteen minutes (you may wonder how Chávez would have coped under such a restriction). They extended government control over universities and devolved more power to the communal councils. They approved the nominations of nine new pro-government Supreme Court justices. They passed a law enabling Chávez to rule by decree for eighteen months.

Fresh from inflicting their most significant electoral defeat of Chávez, the opposition was buoyant. But the real prize was the presidency itself. Ironically, Chávez's increasing authoritarianism seemed more than ever directed at winning another six-year term in 2012. On this score, no one would write him off. He had the tools of the state at his command, was a powerful campaigner, and the opposition lacked a clear uniting figure to challenge him.

From about 2002 onward, someone had always been forecasting Chávez's imminent political demise. When he revealed in 2011 that he was suffering from cancer, it gave renewed hope to his opponents that the president was too weak to campaign in his usual flamboyant style ahead of the 2012 elections. But the Venezuelan leader had often seemed to defy political gravity, and he could not be written off. More than anything else, his supporters' favorite chant was the soccer-style *"Ooh, ah, Chávez no se va"*—the equivalent of "Hell, no, Chavez won't go." Like all electorally successful political leaders, he was also lucky. Along with Morales and Correa, he oversaw historically high oil prices that enabled him to spend freely. He was blessed with a weak and divided opposition. He also recognized that electoral success hinged primarily on the ability to deliver. The radical Left had promised new constitutions that would end the old political order and they were good to their word. They pledged to squeeze foreign multinationals and they did so. They vowed to redistribute wealth and it actually happened. This may have been populism—the betrayal of long-term prosperity at the expense of "jam today"—but it won elections. For someone without much of a long-term strategy, Chávez's length of time in office was impressive. Although Morales and Correa did not seem as likely to endure as long, their electoral achievements were also significant. Their predecessors would have done anything to win the same kind of multiple poll victories.

Chávez's was a mixed record. He undoubtedly succeeded in bringing down poverty—the share of Venezuelans living in poverty nearly halved in his first decade in power, from about 67 percent to about 38 percent, according to official Venezuelan figures, while unemployment went from 18 percent in 2000 to 7.4 percent in 2009, before rising again to 12 percent in 2011. He had managed to provide more health, education, and cash to the poor. But the urban poor by and large still lived in horrific conditions in the ranchos, with no proper sanitation or waste disposal. Chávez failed to invest adequately in infrastructure to remedy these problems. Under Chávez, Venezuela became one of the world's most violent countries: the number of murders more than doubled in his first decade in power, to almost 15,000 in 2008. In Caracas, the government's own statistics showed there were 130 murders per 100,000 people—up from 63 per 100,000 in 1998. (As a comparison, South Africa, a country with a long-standing violent reputation, had a rate of about 36 murders per 100,000 people.) Dissatisfaction with these issues was a principal factor behind Chávez's election defeats.

Chávez was acutely aware that he needed to maintain his popularity. Even though the 2009 constitutional referendum had eliminated presidential term limits, he still actually had to win the elections to stay in power. He was jealous about criticism and paranoid about opposition. Having pioneered the strategy of "revolution via television," Chávez was particularly sensitive about hostile media.

The opposition-controlled private TV channels had earned his ire back during the 2002 two-day coup, when several appeared to cheer his overthrow and failed to report the massive popular rejection of the coup, instead broadcasting old movies and cartoons. As time went on, he felt emboldened to take on the antigovernment bias of some of the private channels. In 2007, he refused to renew the concession for RCTV—one of Venezuela's most popular channels, which he accused of backing the 2002 coup—and replaced it with a state channel. The state channel that replaced RCTV became the sixth government TV station.

Yet most of the public airwaves were still controlled by the private media, and in 2009, fresh from his referendum triumph, Chávez clamped down further. The government targeted Globovisión, the last stridently anti-Chávez TV station left in Venezuela, with investigations and ads on state TV that announced, "Globovisión doesn't inform, it makes you sick. Turn off the sickness!" He pulled the plug on thirty-four radio stations—many of them opposition broadcasters that quickly moved online—revoking the licenses of some and refusing to renew the permits of others. "Freedom of expression must be limited," Luisa Ortega, Venezuela's attorney general, told reporters on July 30, 2009, as she outlined plans to punish "media crimes" perpetrated by outlets deemed to be manipulating the news "with the purpose of transmitting a false perception of the facts." Chávez shut down RCTV—which had switched to cable—for good in 2010 after it refused to transmit his speeches live. The president of Globovisión was arrested for conspiracy and fled to the United States, seeking political asylum.

In the hyperactive lame-duck session following the 2010 congressional elections, Chávez's supporters in the legislature voted to criminalize Internet content that promotes social unrest, challenges authority, or condones crime. Meanwhile, Chávez enthusiastically embraced Twitter, tweeting under the name Chavezcandanga—"naughty Chávez."

Morales and Correa had not yet had to face significant electoral defeat, but they also showed tentative signs of tightening their grip on power. In Bolivia, Morales took power from the elected Congress and handed it to indigenous leaders. In Ecuador, Correa launched a full frontal assault on the hostile independent media. Correa attacked journalists as "rabid dogs," "liars," and "wild beasts." He regularly threatened to fine media outlets he didn't like and to revoke broadcasters' licenses. During a police strike in 2010, all TV and radio stations were required to broadcast only government-supplied information. The state extended its control to twenty media companies and banned banks from media ownership.

But Venezuela was entering a different class. Chávez hovered in the hinterland between autocracy and democracy. In spite of his supporters' observation that the government's loss of the congressional elections of 2010 proved Venezuela remained a democracy, Chávez had clearly trampled all over the results. On the other hand, in spite of what many opponents said, he was not a dictator. There was still a big difference between Venezuela and, say, Iran or Zimbabwe—or, for that matter, Cuba or China. Elections were still competitive: Chávez lost the 2007 constitutional referendum and the 2010 congressional election, and in the 2008 regional elections his opponents won in the country's three most populous states and in most of Caracas. Yet he was undoubtedly fond of power and patronage and had undermined Venezuela's (admittedly flawed) democratic institutions rather than strengthen them. Chávez had expanded the powers of the presidency and loosened the checks upon it. He had bypassed the legislature. He had expanded the Supreme Court and packed it full of pliant judges. He had beefed up the military and given it a new, expanded role in Venezuelan society. Morales and Correa exhibited the same tendency to concentrate power in their own hands—the nationalizations and constitution rewritings were partly about this—albeit in a much less extreme way.

What this suggested was that the leaders of the radical Left perceived their power to be fragile. The elections helped to beef up their legitimacy, but they needed to continue to deliver—and the ability to deliver was far from secure. In Bolivia, Evo Morales's attempts to reduce poverty were hampered by rising prices for basic foodstuffs and shrinking remittances, as the global economic downturn made it harder for Bolivians abroad to send money back home. In Ecuador, Correa's second term was marked by increasing tensions with the very groups that had helped propel him to power. Teachers and students demonstrated against his attempts to improve educational standards, while indigenous groups protested against the president's plan to centralize the management of water resources. When police took to the streets over benefit cuts, Correa confronted them personally, ripping open his shirt at one point and daring them to kill him. When they shot tear gas at him instead, he accused them of attempting a coup against him.

The initial progress Venezuela had seen with the arrival of the Cuban doctors also started to slip away. Ironically, the number of Cuban volunteers who had been sent to Bolivia had limited the availability for Venezuela. Other doctors had returned home; some even fled to avoid returning to Cuba. Chávez admitted in 2009 that nearly one-third of the original clinics has been abandoned. What's more, the country's public hospitals had deteriorated as public funding focused on the clinics. In the topsy-turvy world of Chávez's Venezuela, an impoverished state health system existed alongside a well-funded and well-regarded Barrio Adentro program using Cuban volunteer doctors.

Viva la Revolución

The radical Left had clung to power against the predictions of many commentators who had seen a string of Andean presidents come and go. But for their countries and their populations, the obsession with how much longer they could last was perhaps misplaced. The greater issue was whether their revolutions would endure after their time in office. To a greater or lesser degree, Chávez, Morales, and Correa all fostered a cult of personality and demonstrated paranoia. That made it difficult to foster heirs apparent, a new generation of leaders who would continue the reforms after them. Venezuela was a prime case: Bolivarianism looked set to live and die with Chávez alone, and when his cancer was made public, the lack of an obvious successor sparked power struggles within the governing party.

Because these leaders all had inherently confrontational styles, it also seemed quite likely that their periods in power would end with victory for their political opponents, who might promptly seek to overturn what they had done. They had rewritten their countries' constitutions, but it would seem foolish to bet that these constitutions would live on much beyond their presidencies. They had nationalized industries, but their successors might cash in by reprivatizing them. By coming to power through the ballot box, they had strengthened the democratic culture in South America. On the other hand, they had extended the power of the president at the expense of the normal checks and balances that make democracy robust, and Chávez had shown a tendency not to accept the will of the electorate. They had elevated citizens' groups and street protest rather than refounding, improving, and strengthening established political institutions.

Predictably, the radical Left did not abolish corruption. As money from the export of natural resources flowed in and government spending expanded, corruption flourished as before—albeit with the proceeds going into new pockets. In Bolivia, for example, the head of YPFB, the revived state energy company, was imprisoned in 2009, charged with arranging millions of dollars in bribes for contracts. In Ecuador, Rafael Correa's own brother—a businessman who had won some $167 million worth of government contracts during his sibling's first term in office— accused his administration of accepting bribes. In Venezuela, Chávez's science minister resigned in 2009 after his brother was arrested in a banking scandal. There were countless other such cases. In Transparency International's corruption perception index for 2010, Venezuela came in 164th—the lowest of any Latin American country—while Ecuador fared little better in 127th place, and Bolivia in 110th. Within those countries, the common view was clearly that corruption was flourishing as much as ever.

Corruption was aggravated by supreme incompetence. While government had never been particularly competent, the ineptitude of the radical Left at times confounded even its most ardent supporters. The most blatant example came in 2010, when 120,000 tons of food imported by the Venezuelan government the previous year was found rotting in warehouses. The incident was shameful in a country plagued with serious food shortages and a persistent lack of staple goods. According to one estimate, the wasted cargo could have met half the entire country's food needs for a month. Chávez blamed corruption and had the head of the relevant state company arrested, but a few months later another embarrassing revelation turned up. It came after Venezuela pledged a massive amount of aid to Haiti following the devastating 2010 earthquake. Chávez forgave Haiti $395 million it was owed for already subsidized oil and promised to give the stricken country a further $2.4 billion worth of relief aid—twice as much as the US government donated (although much of Venezuela's donation was to have been in oil rather than conventional aid). But one ship carrying 39 tons of food aid was returned because the food was spoiled. It was an episode that further underlined the government's inability to manage the day-to-day challenges of public administration.

The food debacles were only one example of the government's chronic mismanagement. The economy was shambolic; crime was soaring; supplies of food, water, and electricity were intermittent. Although they had boosted the power of the central government, the radical Left had done little to add to the state's capacity. In many cases, they had undermined it, seizing power or handing it to organizations that had not been given the tools and training to wield it. In 2009, the government was forced into rationing electricity and running water. Chávez blamed a particularly bad drought for both, since low water levels had a double impact in a country that relies on hydroelectricity for 70 percent of its power. His critics said the shortages demonstrated the government's incompetence. Blaming the rich for being wasteful, Chávez recommended that Venezuelans shower for no more than three minutes. "One minute to wet yourself, another to soap yourself, and the third to wash it off. The rest is a waste," he advised.

In many cases, the radical Left's record on corruption and incompetence wasn't worse than the governments that had come before—but dissatisfaction with this kind of behavior was one of the main gripes that had helped them to power in the first place.

The radical Left had started to tackle some of the worst problems of Andean society—poverty, the marginalization of certain groups, and the lack of basic services—but even their most enthusiastic backers would not claim that they had solved them, or even provided the institutions to do so. It seemed very likely that when they eventually left office, the fundamental issues that had propelled them to power in the first place would be as pressing as they had ever been.

Remember the Scotch whisky that the guests had quaffed at the "wedding of the century" in Caracas in 1989, the garish opulence of which symbolized how unequal Venezuela had become? In 2009, a decade after Chávez took office, the country remained one of the world's top whisky importers, with 77 percent growth on the prior year—the highest in the world. But not all of it was to be drunk. As inflation soared and Venezuelan currency became increasingly worthless, people instead put the liquor away in storage. Some were perhaps saving it to be broken out to celebrate when Chávez was no longer in power. Others were hoarding it in case he remained in power and things continued to worsen. Whatever happened, good Scotch was one asset that seemed sure to hold its value.

11

The Curious Death
of the Panama Hat

In the back corner of the store room at the Hormero Ortega factory in Cuenca, Ecuador, there is a locked, caged-off room containing about eighteen thousand of some of the finest Panama hats in the world.

I stood and inhaled the intoxicatingly sweet and fragrant smell of straw, while Ivan Maldonado, marketing manager at Hormero Ortega, secured the key from an administrator and unlocked the padlock. It felt like being let into the inner sanctum of some holy temple. We talked in tones of hushed reverence.

The difference between the Panamas in the caged-off room and the hundreds of thousands of hats in the rest of the storage area was immediately clear. Looked at close up, each woven row was perfectly straight and the weaving tight—so tight that some of the hats looked like they were made of off-white cotton.

For almost thirty years, one of Ecuador's most famous hat producers had been building up the stockpile, aware that the knowledge of how to make the very best Panama hats—the *superfinos*—was being lost. These superbly woven specimens were meant to extend the life of the company in preparation for when production of the Panama hat is no more.

"This is the most important stockpile of superfinos in the world," Maldonado told me. "We have it because we have to recognize that the art of weaving like this is dying out."

The Panama hat is one of Ecuador's most emblematic products: a signature of old-fashioned debonair elegance; the traditional summer headwear of US presidents, European leaders, English cricket umpires, and spies the world over; the hat worn by Churchill, Hemingway, Edward VII, and Al Capone.

The Internet and the rise of the global market should have been the savior of the Panama. Instead, globalization appears about to seal its fate: within twenty years it is likely that the Panama hat—at least *el superfino*—will be gone.

At this point, you are either reading smugly because you already knew that Panama hats don't actually come from Panama, or you are confused. The origin of the misnomer actually comes from the hat's widespread use by the workers who built the Panama Canal from 1904 to 1914. Unsurprisingly, in Ecuador they don't call them Panamas. They call them *sombreros de paja toquilla*, or hats woven from the straw of the *toquilla* plant, which grows in the swamps near the country's central coast.

That the Panama actually comes from Ecuador is not only the stuff of afternoon TV quiz shows: it is also partly responsible for the hat's demise. The headwear has been a *paja toquilla* hat for far longer than it's been a Panama: its origin goes back at least to the Spanish conquest in the sixteenth century and probably much further. But the anomaly has made it difficult to prevent other countries from producing hats and marketing them as Panamas. After all, if they don't actually come from Panama, why can't they come from, well, *anywhere*?

As with many other industries in the world, the biggest threat to Ecuador's Panama hat makers is China. No matter that their "straw" hats are actually woven from paper—few consumers would notice the difference. They are cheaper than the real thing, look as good to most people, and are more flexible. As one industry insider put it to me succinctly, "They have every advantage except authenticity."

Since the 1970s, China has swallowed much of the cheaper-end market once supplied by Ecuador, particularly to other Latin American countries such as Mexico and Brazil. China is the world's top straw-hat producer, exporting more than $1 billion worth a year—over 40 percent of the global market. Ecuador, in thirty-fourth place, exports about one-tenth of 1 percent of world demand, a few million dollars' worth each year.

"We cannot compete with the Chinese on price," Alicia Ortega, the elegant daughter of Hormero Ortega, and now the company's president, told me. "We can only compete on quality."

Exporting People

There is another strong reason globalization is killing the Panama hat. Young people in Ecuador, as in many poor countries, do not aspire to follow their parents into traditional occupations. Nowadays, the South American dream is to migrate and secure relatively well-paid labor in Europe—with Spain one of the most favored destinations, for ease of language—or the United States.

Kurt Dorfzaun made the opposite journey. Fleeing Nazi Germany in the 1930s, he ended up in Cuenca and built up his uncle's company to become Ecuador's biggest Panama hat exporter. When I met Dorfzaun, then approaching his mideighties and in poor health, I was keen to get the perspective of a man who had witnessed the industry slowly fade from the glory days of the 1940s and 1950s, when no self-respecting person would leave the house without a hat.

In heavily German-accented English, he told me a story that revealed a sardonic humor befitting a man who knew he would not be around to see the demise of the Panama. "An importer from Madrid called me and said, 'We need more hats!'" Dorfzaun gasped. "So I said to him, 'Put an advert in the paper—you have more weavers there than we do here.'"

Almost a quarter of Ecuador's 13 million people are estimated to live abroad, many of them without documentation. Cuenca, the country's third largest city, has been particularly affected by migration. A census a few years ago calculated the city had 400,000 inhabitants. The real figure is thought to be about 250,000, as people did not want to admit to government officials that their relatives were living abroad illegally.

So while globalization has enabled some cities, such as the booming new metropolises of China, to grow at a terrific rate on the back of exporting cheaply produced goods to Europe and the United States, the main economic export of cities such as Cuenca is, in fact, people.

To be sure, this process predates modern globalization. In colonial times, Cuenca was one of the most important cities in South America.

Since Ecuador gained independence in 1822, it has been steadily shrinking in size and stature, at first losing population to other cities in Ecuador—notably Guayaquil, a sprawling port that is now the country's biggest city—and more recently to migration abroad.

As a result, Cuenca's formal employment rate is high—about 60 percent, compared to about 40 percent in Guayaquil and about 50 percent in Quito. Local employers complain of the lack of skilled labor, and the city buzzes with illegal Colombian and Peruvian immigrants. But residents say the temptation to join relatives abroad remains strong. Ecuadoreans outside the country send some $2.5 billion a year to relatives and friends at home, helping fuel the economy of cities such as Cuenca.

Migration became an important issue in the election that made Rafael Correa president. I was in Cuenca—a picturesque colonial town set almost eight thousand feet above sea level in the southern highlands—in October 2006 to see him wrap up the southern part of his presidential campaign with a rally there. He devoted a whole section of his speech to migration, promising that if elected he would create a ministry for migrants and set aside six congressional seats to represent them: two each for Ecuadoreans living in the United States, Europe, and other Latin American countries. When he won the presidency five days later, Correa received his strongest support in Cuenca's home province of Azuay, winning more than 70 percent of the votes.

Correa's focus on the migrants was significant. For a start, they usually came from the poorest, most disenfranchised class—exactly the kind of people who felt most hostile toward the country's traditional political power brokers. Migrants, potential migrants, their families and communities—these were another rich exploitable national resource for insurgents such as Correa to use. What he was arguing in essence was that Ecuadoreans should decide their own fate, rather than officials in the corridors of power in Washington.

I drove north out of Cuenca, on a road punctuated with billboards warning about the dangers of migration. "If you are going to leave, inform yourself—people smuggling is a crime," said one. Another showed a picture of an overcrowded boat sinking. "Don't let your dreams sink in the sea," it warned.

When I reached Azogues, a town of about twenty-five thousand some twenty miles northeast of Cuenca, the signs of migration were everywhere. I was taken around by Betty Ruiz, who works for a local weavers' foundation. Five years earlier the association had five hundred members, she told me, a number that had dwindled to two hundred. All were women. The men had mostly left for the United States.

There was furious construction activity, and the hillside neighborhoods away from the center were peppered with half-built mansions that did not fit with the humble surroundings. The more we drove around the area, the more plush villas we saw—palaces of vulgar, garish opulence, with pastel-colored walls, orange roofs, imposing black gates, and pillars topped off with stone dogs, lions, and cockerels.

At first I assumed the mansions had been built by locals using money sent back by their relatives, but as the day wore on it became clear that most of them were unoccupied. "The migrants send back money to build the houses for themselves," Betty told me. "They say they'll come back to live in them when they've made some money, but they never return."

One of the Panama hat weavers we visited was working in the main room of one of the villas whose grand exterior belied an empty cement interior. Entering the house was like looking behind a movie set. She explained that the house belonged to her brothers, who were working in Chicago. They did not intend to return, she told me. So why did they need the house? I asked. "They're illegal immigrants," she said. "They could be deported any day."

The image of this woman sitting amid the dust behind an opulent façade was depressing, but what I saw next was even sadder. In Wilchacabamba, a poor, rural neighborhood, I met Elsa Coronel, a twenty-three-year-old weaver who lives with her mother in a small wooden house. She sat throughout our visit, quietly weaving a Panama hat, answering my questions in a barely audible whisper. She was married, she told me, but she hadn't seen her husband since he left for the United States eighteen months earlier. She hadn't even heard from him in the past few months and was unsure exactly where he was. Her mother and Betty, the lady who was showing me around, looked down awkwardly at the floor at this admission. Afterward, Betty told me Elsa's story was a common one. The men who leave behind wives and children hardly ever return, she said. Often they meet other women and marry again in the United States, she added, leaving behind migration widows and orphans who have no idea of where their husbands and fathers have gone.

Money Isn't Jobs

Elsa Coronel is one of globalization's losers.

It is easy to think of globalization's winners: the stores that can source cheaper products made in China; the companies that can outsource telephone call centers to India; the consumers who pay less for their purchases made in Asia.

The Panama weavers of Ecuador are like the car workers of the United States. Not only are they in an industry that is making a product that people no longer need (at least that would be true for the traditional gas guzzlers produced by the Big Three automakers), but they are also facing competition from powerful Asian manufacturers that can produce something that looks and feels the same at a fraction of the cost. Of course, the Ecuadorean weavers do not enjoy the benefits nor the government bailouts that the US car industry has had.

In the international division of labor that the globalized world economy throws up, countries such as China and India are increasingly becoming the world's producers, while countries such as the United States and Germany are losing their manufacturing sectors and becoming the world's service providers. Ecuador, like much of South America, has found its own role in this system—as a producer and exporter of raw materials. When the price of those raw materials—which in Ecuador's case means oil—is high, their economies tend to do relatively well.

As China's economy has opened up and grown, it has become increasingly hungry for the raw materials that feed its manufacturing base. Latin America has benefited. Ecuador and Venezuela have raked in revenues from oil, Chile from copper, Peru from silver and gold. Yet mining and drilling do not actually employ many people. Such extractive industries tend to be capital intensive, rather than labor intensive. There may be money coming into the nation's coffers, but that does not always translate to job opportunities.

In a global economy, the job opportunities are, in fact, global—even if they are not legal. So every year tens of thousands of Latin Americans leave their home countries and go to work in mostly low-paying jobs in Europe and North America. When governments in those countries tighten their border security and immigration checks, they can stem this tide, but they can never stop it for good until global economics changes. International migration is mostly economic, a product of globalization itself. The gradual freeing up of international trade in goods and services is an undeniable trend in recent decades. To expect that labor would not follow the same process of globalization would be naïve.

There is every indication that the movement of labor from Latin America to the Northern Hemisphere will in fact increase in the coming years. A Gallup poll in 2007 found that 35 percent of Latin Americans aged between fifteen and twenty-four said they would migrate if they had the means to do so. It is largely the young and ambitious who leave. For many people in Latin America, merely to get out is a mark of success. To stay at home, by contrast, is considered by many to be something of a badge of failure.

In Europe and the United States, the phenomenon of migration is talked about a lot. Our homes and public buildings are often built and maintained by migrants. The food we eat is harvested and processed by them. Our streets are often kept clean by them. Often when we talk about migrants, it is in terms of concern. We consider how their being here affects our societies—will Spanish or Polish or Arabic become the de facto vernacular in some areas? Are immigrants stealing work, or are they just doing the jobs that natives would refuse to do? How can we keep them out more effectively?

Consider what happens to the places and communities the immigrants come from. Cities like Cuenca lose many of their young people. Traditional family structures are broken up. To stay behind is to limit your life chances and those of your children. Sure, you can go to school and university, try to improve yourself, and work hard. But you can make more money as an unskilled laborer in the United States or Europe than you could as a skilled, educated worker at home.

The mass migration of people from poor countries to wealthy ones has accelerated rapidly in the past two decades. One way of tracking this is by looking at remittances—money sent back home by migrant workers. The value of global remittances increased by seven times between 1990 and 2006 to more than $200 billion, according to the World Bank. For Latin America and the Caribbean, remittances exceeded $69 billion in 2008, according to the Inter-American

Development Bank. Those figures mainly trace money flows sent via banks or international wire services (which have boomed as remittances have grown: one of the biggest such companies, Western Union, had eighteen thousand agents in 1990 but now has more than three hundred thousand). Experts say the real value could be twice as high, if you include all the unofficial ways of sending money abroad—with returning friends or relatives and the like.

This is more than just pocket change being sent back for birthday presents. For the recipients in poor countries, this is serious money that boosts their spending power. That spending has a significant effect on those economies. In Central America, remittances are worth more than traditional agricultural exports such as coffee and bananas. In some countries such as Jamaica and Haiti, the total level of remittances is greater than all their exports combined.

Welcome though these cash inflows are, they cannot compensate for the economic disruption caused by emigration—the brain drain of professionals such as medics and engineers whose skills are worth more abroad, or entrepreneurs and young people seeking opportunities elsewhere.

Although remittances can help reduce poverty, they can also create economic dependency. They also help governments in poor countries to ignore their own failure to generate economic development, since the economy of a city like Cuenca is buoyed by financial support from abroad.

What should we expect the Panama hat weavers of Ecuador to think about globalization? In Europe and the United States, most of us view it negatively. In a 2007 poll conducted on behalf of the *Financial Times*, more than 80 percent of respondents in Britain, the United States, and Spain said globalization was having a negative rather than a positive effect on their countries. The general response in the other countries surveyed—France, Germany, and Italy—was the same, albeit less emphatic.

If that is the mood in Europe and the United States (in a survey conducted *before* the world slipped into a global economic downturn), we can only imagine what the attitudes are among those who feel they have failed to see any benefit from the globalized economy, who are being undercut by cheap Asian products, whose youngest and brightest see escape as their only future.

In the last few months of 2008, as the world plunged into an economic recession, the amount of money migrants from Latin America sent home began to fall for the first time in recent years, according to the Inter-American Development Bank. But Luis Alberto Moreno, the bank's president, was clear that although unemployment in richer countries was rising and attitudes hardening toward migrants, large numbers of Latino expatriates would not be returning home. "They change jobs, work longer hours, cut back on spending, move to another city, and even dip into savings in order to continue sending money to their families," he said. "Going home is usually a last resort."

Going home would be admitting defeat. It would mean joining globalization's losers.

Decoupling

Luiz Inácio Lula da Silva, by contrast, was one of globalization's winners. In fact, when the global recession hit, the Brazilian president turned the accepted wisdom about globalization on its head, casting the United States as something of a loser in a process that had somewhat passed it by.

"People ask me about the crisis and I answer, 'go ask Bush,'" he told reporters in September 2008 as Wall Street looked about to topple over. "It is his crisis, not mine."

Lula's view encapsulated how Latin Americans were frolicking at the time in the notion that their economies had "decoupled" from that of the world's largest economy. For one thing, the countries in the region were not encumbered by the big debt burdens they had borne in previous crises. Ecuador, Venezuela, Argentina, and the like initially seemed pretty unaffected by the credit crisis—the inability to borrow money that characterized the early days of the economic downturn in the United States—since they were already pretty much frozen out of the international financial markets. Also, thanks to the strength of demand from Asia, fueled by the rapid industrialization of China and India, they argued they could withstand a slump in the US economy.

The financial crisis also pulled the rug a bit from under the feet of those who got so hot under the collar about the unsustainability of what

Chávez, Morales, and Correa were doing. Of course, the crisis didn't make their policies any more sustainable, but it did demonstrate that unbridled free markets—the kind that the Washington Consensus had recommended—were themselves pretty unsustainable. Subprime mortgages had been unsustainable. The credit default swap market had been unsustainable. The US budget deficit was unsustainable. The finances of Iceland, Greece, Ireland, Spain, and Portugal were unsustainable.

By 2008, it seemed that the decoupling might have been overstated. The economy of Mexico—the Latin American country with the closest economic ties to the United States—started to shrink for the first time in six years. On one hand, the radical Left in South America was delighted that the US economy was writhing in agony. On the other, it was bracing for the consequences. Hugo Chávez said the crisis heralded the downfall of capitalism and blamed the "irresponsibility" of Washington. Yet he admitted that even his government was not immune to the impact of the banking crisis, which he said had the force of "a hundred hurricanes." For all its talk of "twenty-first-century socialism," Chávez's Venezuela had also gambled on Wall Street. When the investment bank Lehman Brothers collapsed, Caracas was left holding more than $300 million worth of Lehman debt, and when oil prices plummeted in late 2008, it seemed the game was up for the radical Left. The entire project of the radical Left was based on the revenue from oil and gas, so surely they could not survive the huge drop in demand spurred on by the economic crisis? But while their governments had thrown money around during the commodities boom, they were forced to cut spending, which made the downturn worse, just as wealthy countries were spending billions in a panic to stimulate their economies. As well as plunging oil prices, Ecuador was also hit by lower remittances sent home by Ecuadoreans working abroad, which accounted for about 7 percent of its national income. After having repeatedly threatened to stop making interest payments on its debt, Correa decided to finally bite the bullet in December 2008, the second time in a decade that Ecuador had defaulted on its foreign debt. Argentina nationalized its private pension funds, a way of getting more money to pay its debts. In Venezuela, the economy shrank in 2009 and 2010. Chávez took reserves from the central bank and stepped up nationalizations and expropriations, but he was still forced to cut public spending.

Of course, the global economic slump wasn't just a problem for the radical Left. It threw both market-friendly and market-skeptic governments off course. Across Latin America as a whole economic growth either stopped or went into reverse. The economic development of all Latin America's 570 million people was in doubt, but those in the poorest countries—countries such as Bolivia and Ecuador—looked likely to suffer the worst. The United Nations warned that poverty in the region could rise by 15 percent. The World Bank said that because of the recession, 6 million more Latin Americans would fall into poverty. The more conservatively run economies—Chile, Brazil, Colombia—at least had saved enough reserves to increase government spending to try to stimulate their economies, but even they could hardly avoid the global recession.

Latin America had lived through many economic crises before—income per person in the region fell on five separate occasions since 1980—but this crisis was not one of its own making. Despite the pain it caused, this fact provoked a combination of relief, schadenfreude, and a sort of perverse pride among the region's leaders. "This crisis was caused by the irrational behavior of white people with blue eyes, who before the crisis appeared to know everything and now demonstrate that they know nothing," President Lula said. "I do not know any black or indigenous bankers so I can only say [it is wrong] that this part of mankind which is victimized more than any other should pay for the crisis."

What's more, unlike previous crises, Latin America didn't perform particularly worse than anywhere else. Spanish companies invested in Latin America found that it was a much stronger area of growth than their domestic market. By 2009, the notion of decoupling started to make a comeback, as people speculated that growth in developing world regions such as South America, rather than the United States, might be able to pull the world economy out of recession.

Most of the best-placed countries in the region were those with open economies and floating exchange rates—such as Brazil, Chile, Colombia, and Peru. But one of the most surprising economic performers was Evo Morales's Bolivia, largely removed from the global economy but heavily tied to Brazil through its natural gas exports. The revenues from nationalization had given Morales much stronger public finances, and he aided the stability by fixing the currency against the US dollar. Higher public spending in Bolivia was also a stimulus package that worked, getting money into the hands of the poorest and neediest who were eager to spend it. The relative political stability of Morales's rule also helped.

The region's worst performers were either those whose economies were in lockstep with the United States—such as Mexico and some in Central America—or those that were overdependent on commodity prices. Many free-market economists predicted that the downturn would at last call an end to the lavish spending in Venezuela, Ecuador, and Argentina. Many hoped that would topple their leaders in favor of more pragmatically minded presidents. Venezuela was mired in stagflation—a shrinking economy coupled with high inflation—that lasted through 2009 and 2010.

By the middle of 2009, things had eased a bit. Mainly that was thanks to the recovery of oil prices back up to more than $70 a barrel—not quite the windfall of previous years but enough to ensure that there were more dollars flowing into countries like Ecuador and Venezuela, although not enough to cope with the massive demands on the public purse that the radical Left had pledged.

Looking beyond Chávez

Another phenomenon was helping the region, too. While the arguments continued over economic decoupling, a kind of political decoupling threw these countries a lifeline. Where once the United States had held a dominant influence over South America, China, the world's newly emerging superpower, was keen to use the opportunity of America's hyperopia and economic weakness to extend its influence in Washington's backyard.

Venezuela, which needed cash more than most, was a target for China to extend its commercial interests in the region. The China Development Bank put $8 billion into a fund to help Chinese companies invest in the country. In 2009, Chinese companies pledged to invest $16 billion in Venezuela's oil fields. The following year, Beijing agreed to lend Caracas $20 billion for oil development. China became the biggest foreign investor in Ecuador, undeterred by Correa's decision in 2008 to default on the country's foreign debt. In 2010, China pumped $5 billion into the country, with Beijing lending Quito $1 billion and the Export-Import Bank of China investing $1.7 billion in an Ecuadorean hydroelectric plant.

These investments may not have been enough in themselves to save the economies of Venezuela and Ecuador, but they could at least help delay any comeuppance while their leaders prayed for commodity prices to recover. China may have generally been politically agnostic when it came to foreign relations, but the country's financial support certainly played a hand in keeping Chávez and Correa in power, and helped to reassure other foreign investors. Chinese investment in Venezuela, coupled with a pledge by Russian oil companies to invest $20 billion in the country, helped attract back investment from private energy companies: in 2010, ENI of Italy agreed to invest $17 billion in joint ventures with Venezuela, while consortia led by Chevron, the US oil group, and Repsol of Spain were given minority stakes in two $15 billion oil projects.

Beijing took advantage of the financial crisis and Washington's hyperopia to press its advantage elsewhere in the region. China became the biggest foreign investor in Brazil. Chinese companies paid $5 billion to build a steel plant in Rio state and $3 billion to invest in offshore oil fields. Its state grid bought seven Brazilian power companies for $1.7 billion. Chinese companies purchased a majority stake in YPF, Argentina's biggest oil company, as well as taking control of several other oil ventures. The China Development Bank invested $10 billion in Argentina's rail system. Chinese mining companies invested more than $1 billion in Peru and announced plans to invest another $4.5 billion in the country.

A shift was slowly occurring: in the early part of the decade, China had exclusively traded with Latin America by sucking up oil and metals and sending back cheap manufactured goods, but now it was starting to invest large sums of money in infrastructure projects as well. Beijing detected that the region was growing, and that as well as ensuring reliable supplies of raw materials, Latin America also presented an attractive long-term investment opportunity based on the region's own economic prospects—not just as a producer but as a consumer also.

Chinese investment—and indeed the process of globalization itself, so demonized by the radical Left—had, it seemed, bought Hugo Chávez and Rafael Correa more time in power. It had also served to underline the importance of Latin America to the world economy. Chávez may have been an unsavory figure to many, but he was still sitting on 100 billion barrels of oil—the largest reserves outside the Middle East, according to research by BP. In the second half of 2009, oil prices began a steady recovery and seemed on course for a long-term up cycle, making energy companies look harder at oil opportunities they might have spurned at the height of the financial crisis. In spite of its mismanagement, PDVSA, Venezuela's state oil company, defied skeptics and made a profit of $8 billion in 2009—at least according to the government's own figures.

Nevertheless, it would take a severe change of course for Chávez to turn Venezuela around. His country's economy shrank for two consecutive years while those of his neighbors surged forward. Inflation stood at about 25 percent, among the highest rates in the world. His popularity was at its lowest point since 2003. His own party was in danger of splintering as moderates jumped ship.

In early 2010, Chávez was forced to devalue the bolívar, the national currency. If oil exports (paid for in dollars) translated into more bolívars at home, he reasoned, that meant he had more money to spend on the sorts of projects that had made him popular. When stores responded by raising prices, Chávez accused them of profiteering, threatened to put troops on to the streets to stop such behavior, and shut down dozens of them.

He tightened foreign exchange controls to prevent capital from leaving the country and halt currency speculation. Instead, it meant companies could no longer import as they could not pay their bills in US dollars. One of Venezuela's biggest mobile phone companies said its customers couldn't use their phones abroad because it didn't have enough foreign currency to pay international operators. With nothing to do with their local currency but spend it, local subsidiaries of foreign companies started buying property. While that fueled inflation even further at the top end of the real estate market, the government had run out of money to pay for some public housing projects for the poor. By the end of 2010, left with few options, the government devalued the currency again.

The Venezuelan president seemed to have hit a new low. The economy was collapsing around him. His inability to deliver to his core supporters was becoming more evident by the day. Crime was soaring. Chávez's defenders around the world at least clung to the idea that his repeated election victories showed he remained popular, but now he had lost even that. Having lost control of Congress, he had started to trample more brazenly over his country's democratic institutions. On top of that, he was diagnosed with cancer. Chávez was a master of survival and a redoubtable campaigner. Few would discount him. But it seemed more than ever before that his future as president was in doubt. Were they privately celebrating in Washington? Was that not what they had long wanted?

In the days after the new representatives were sworn in following the 2010 elections, there were frequent standoffs between Chávez's supporters and his opponents. The opposition said it had no choice but to take to the streets, since the president had stripped Congress of its power. While opposition deputies demanded they be allowed their democratic right to represent those who had voted for them, the Chavistas stood firm in their defense of the president. With more fervor than ever, they chanted repeatedly, *"Ooh, ah, Chávez no se va."* A few months earlier, Chávez had called on tens of thousands of members of a militia he had organized to defend his revolution with their lives if necessary. As his more moderate supporters drifted away, the rump that was left was militant, devout, and fiercely loyal. His supporters would shout and scrawl on walls the slogan of the Cuban revolution—SOCIALISM OR DEATH. You couldn't help but wonder how this could be resolved peacefully. If the president lost the 2012 election, would Chávez and those who had benefited from his years in power accept the result? Or would something more sinister ensue? Might the real conundrum facing the United States no longer be how to tackle Chávez's Venezuela, but what might happen to the country after he was gone?

12

A Different Vision

In May 2010, Henrique Capriles Radonski, the governor of the
Venezuelan state of Miranda and a leading opponent of Hugo Chávez,
visited Chicago to address the Chicago Council on Global Affairs, a
think tank. The event took place in a smart downtown hotel, the sort
of place that oozes tradition and elegance. When it came to the Q&A,
the first question was fittingly traditional.

"What can our US State Department do to help?" asked an elderly
gentleman sitting in the front row with an earnest expression on his face.

Capriles's response was clear: "Venezuela's problems will be solved
by Venezuelans."

The audience in Chicago gave Capriles a big round of applause. In
an age of imperial overreach, his answer satisfied both their desire for
the United States to avoid further international entanglements that
damaged its reputation in the world and their wish to avoid repeating
Washington's long history of military misadventures in Latin America.

After all, most of the problems of Latin America were not the fault
of the United States. Although many in the region and the Left internationally had historically sought to blame Washington for their ills, it
simply wasn't true. The United States wasn't directly responsible for the
region's endemic corruption, for inequality and poverty, for the ineffec-
tiveness of democracy, for racism and the political marginalization of
certain groups, for populism, nationalism, or xenophobia. As Capriles

had said, these were Latin American problems and they needed to be solved by Latin Americans.

The last thing Latin America needs is yet another US-devised plan for the region, a hemispheric vision concocted in Washington and then delivered to the people—much as Moses brought down the Ten Commandments from Mount Sinai. Latin America had been the subject of the Monroe Doctrine in 1823, the Big Sister policy in the 1880s, the Roosevelt Corollary to the Monroe Doctrine in 1904, FDR's Good Neighbor policy in 1933, the Cold War military interventions from the 1950s, JFK's Alliance for Progress in 1961, Jimmy Carter's New Deal for Latin America in 1977, the Washington Consensus in the 1980s and 1990s, Bill Clinton's Partnership for Prosperity in 1994, and Hillary Clinton's Community of the Americas in 2009. Not one of them bore much fruit.

Clearly, Latin America is not in need of another grand plan dreamed up in Washington.

That doesn't mean that Washington shouldn't try to come up with a coherent, consistent approach to dealing with Latin American countries. Allowing Latin Americans to solve their own problems may entail dispensing with the traditional instinct of sending in the Marines at the first hint of trouble, but it should not imply that the region can simply be left to its own devices while the United States works on solving its own problems. Simply letting Latin Americans get on with it should not be the watchword for US policy toward the region.

The War on Drugs

One of the areas most in urgent need of reform is the thirty-year-old war on drugs. It has failed to reduce the flow of cocaine into the United States or raise its price to prohibitive levels. It has been responsible for the deaths of untold thousands of people in South America. In Mexico, it has sparked the violence that led to the deaths of more than thirty thousand people in drug-cartel warfare since 2006. It has continued to define US–Latin American relations in a militarized way. In the Andes, it has fueled anti-Americanism and given birth to the political career of Evo Morales.

Countries such as Bolivia and Venezuela have declared their unwillingness to cooperate with Washington on the issue any longer, using the war on drugs to bait the United States further. Even friendly countries such as Peru have effectively given up the struggle in many coca-growing regions.

Like oil or gas or metals, coca is another natural resource that South American countries increasingly want to control for themselves. Washington's involvement in the issue is not helping—in fact, it seems to be making things a lot worse in many ways. In that sense, the war on drugs resembles some of the economic policies that the United States has attempted to foist on Latin America.

The most obvious and simple answer would be for the United States to declare the war on drugs over and decriminalize cocaine—a move that would completely undermine the trade in one fell swoop. Conversely, it could ramp up the war on drugs, executing something similar to the surge strategy in Iraq and Afghanistan. Neither option is palatable. Although attitudes in the United States are changing on drugs such as marijuana, legalizing the international narcotics trade would be politically unfeasible and might actually increase drug use across the Americas. On the other hand, intensifying the campaign would be expensive and uncertain and would alienate Latin America even more.

If you have visited the South American highlands, you will no doubt have been offered coca tea. The leaves, steeped in hot water, are a traditional way to relieve aches, pains, and hunger pangs. Drinking the tea did not turn you into a drug addict. But currently it is illegal to export coca tea, even though to accumulate enough coca teabags to make cocaine would be so expensive and time-consuming that buying cocaine on the street would be cheaper and easier. On the one hand, the United States tells farmers in the Andes to engage in legitimate commerce. On the other, it criminalizes a plant that has long been grown in the region. This is absurd. Bolivian and Peruvian farmers should be allowed to grow coca for use in tea bags sold in the United States, Europe, and anywhere else. That might not end the international drug trade, but it would give farmers a route out of what is now a criminal activity and would earn the United States some goodwill in the Andes. Evo Morales has long been an advocate of distinguishing between the legitimate commercialization of coca and the cocaine industry.

The United States could also do more to address the issue at home. Latin Americans have long complained that the war on drugs focused exclusively on the supply side without putting similar effort into tackling the demand for narcotics in the United States. That this is a commonly expressed point doesn't make it any less valid. By showing it is serious about addressing the appetite for drugs back at home, Washington could not only put a dent in demand, but it would also earn brownie points in Latin America.

The Cuba Embargo

Another policy area crying out for change is the fifty-year-old Cuban trade embargo. If ever there were a policy that symbolizes US arrogance, that fuels the charge of imperialism, that reeks of hypocrisy, and that embarrasses even Washington's friends, this is it. That it has failed is patently obvious, since Cuba is still run by the Castro regime. It is hard to imagine it will spur the people to rise up now, spontaneously, after decades.

In its earliest days, the embargo helped push Cuba into the arms of the Soviet Union, which had been a tentative, wait-and-see ally until the United States' hostility toward Communist Cuba turned the Soviets into enthusiastic sponsors. The embargo gave Castro's regime the perfect argument for its own legitimation by portraying Cuba as the victim of US hostility. It elevated Fidel Castro's status within Latin America and further embittered Washington's relations with Latin America and the Caribbean. Meanwhile, Cubans still suffer low standards of living and shortages of virtually everything, thanks to the half-century-old embargo. The sheer meanness of the policy was on display in 2008, when two powerful hurricanes battered Cuba, causing $5 billion worth of damage. George W. Bush's administration offered the island $5 million in relief aid, but Raúl Castro, the Cuban president, turned down the offer, demanding instead that the United States lift the embargo so Havana could buy reconstruction materials. The US aid never made it through.

No doubt Cuba is a dictatorship and hardly anyone would argue that political life should continue there as it has done. But the United States does not have a policy of refusing to trade with dictatorships. It trades happily enough with China and Saudi Arabia (and Libya, up until Gadhafi turned on his own people in 2011). The embargo is a relic of the early Cold War and has no place in a world where Cuba is clearly not a security threat to the United States.

Washington could end trade sanctions without giving its blessing to the regime. The European Union, for example, has normal economic ties with Cuba, but is critical of its human rights record. Supporters of the embargo always argue that the dictatorship is always about to crumble, that to lift it would only prop up Castro. In fact, as pretty much everyone recognizes except the United States, the embargo actually serves to bolster the Castro regime by stoking nationalism in Cuba.

There is nothing radical about wanting to end the embargo. It is opposed by politicians such as Richard Lugar, the Republican senator from Indiana, by US corporations and business groups, not to mention respectable market-friendly publications such as the *Economist* and the *Financial Times*, which are rarely mistaken for leftist propaganda.

Like the drug issue, the embargo is politically sensitive in the United States, where it has traditionally been staunchly supported by the Cuban American community. But the policy serves no strategic purpose, and the United States should not jeopardize its relations with Latin America because of a small constituency in Florida and an even smaller group of conservatives across the country who are deeply interested in the issue. In any case, the generation that lost businesses and property in the Cuban revolution is gradually being replaced by those who have grown up in the United States. Attitudes are beginning to shift, with many Cuban Americans now saying they consider the embargo to be ineffective and counterproductive and that they would welcome more open relations with Cuba. As Cuba inches toward a more open economy and perhaps ultimately a more open society, Washington could have an important role to play in reconciling the island with its exiled community in Florida.

The Obama administration has seemed to recognize that the embargo is outdated and has relaxed travel, trade, and remittance provisions within the existing legislation. However, these have only started to reverse tighter restrictions that George W. Bush had put in place a few years earlier, and essentially leave the embargo intact. It remains illegal for non–Cuban Americans to visit the island, although they can legally visit Myanmar or Syria. By following the relaxing of restrictions to their logical conclusion and ending the embargo, Washington would remove one of the main arsenals of the radical anti-American Left and would improve relations more generally with Latin Americans.

Immigration

Whatever their views on the issue, Americans tend to agree that current US immigration policy isn't working. Within the United States, there is little genuine dialogue on the issue and the arguments on both sides are so well worn that they are hardly worth recounting here. Suffice it to say that not only would it be impossible to stop people illegally entering the United States and working without documentation, but such immigration is actually a sign of US economic strength. When the number of people entering illegally drops—as it did in response to the 2007–2009 financial crisis—the United States needs to think about why they no longer find America an attractive destination.

Immigration is seen almost exclusively as a domestic policy issue, but it is one with profound foreign policy implications. Most of the 12 million or so undocumented immigrants living in the United States come from Latin America and are thought of as expatriates by their native countries—that is, as people who may not have left permanently. Demonizing them while refusing to offer them a legitimate path to staying in the country permanently drives a wedge between the United States and Mexico, its closest ally in Latin America, and alienates countries across the region.

Back at home, US immigration policy is an open sore for Latinos—US citizens and undocumented workers alike. Barack Obama promised to make comprehensive immigration reform a top priority of his presidency. To date, he has not only failed to overhaul the system, but his administration has not even brought forward a plan for immigration reform. In late 2010, the US Senate defeated the DREAM Act, which would have given citizenship to tens of thousands of college students or soldiers in the US military who were brought to the country as infants by undocumented immigrants.

Between Domestic and Foreign Policy

All these issues—drugs, the Cuba embargo, immigration—are neither purely domestic nor purely foreign policy issues. In a sense, that is part of the problem. While they are maintained in large measure to pander to domestic constituencies, they create collateral damage in Latin America and animosity toward the United States. Perhaps thinking of them as foreign policy issues would force Washington to take them more seriously and consider their consequences more sensitively. In any case, tackling these policy failures would be beneficial both to the United States and to Latin America. It would set the stage for a new relationship between the Americas.

I can imagine the response to all this of the man who posed the State Department question to Henrique Capriles Radonski, who said Venezuela must solve Venezuela's problems: That's all well and good, but what are we actually going to do about Chávez? And for that matter, what are we going to do about Evo Morales, Rafael Correa, Ollanta Humala, and radical left-wing anti-American nationalism in general in Latin America?

Through its long relationship with Latin America, the United States became used to the idea that "doing" in Latin America meant smuggling arms to sympathetic guerrilla groups, pumping money into military aid to friendly regimes, using commerce as a political weapon, propaganda, black ops, and the like. This is the sort of thinking that produced leaders such as Castro and Chávez and helps keep them in power.

The United States needs to think anew about what "doing" means when it comes to Latin America. If it tackled the sources of grievance outlined above, the United States would be doing a great deal by "undoing" some of the most harmful policies of the past.

Tomorrow's Commodities

The Salar de Uyuni may be the most otherworldly place on the planet.

The terrain is vast and pure white, with no animals or vegetation to speak of. It is perfectly flat—so flat that it is used to calibrate altimeters for Earth observation satellites. The clear skies are reflected perfectly in the water that sits on the surface. The sun bounces fiercely. The air is thin at twelve thousand feet above sea level.

The Salar is the largest salt flat in the world, occupying more than four thousand square miles in the highlands of southern Bolivia. It is a remarkable resource, one of the country's top tourist destinations. But it has recently been found to be an even more important kind of resource. As I tramped over salt, squinting in the snowlike glare and straining to hear the salt-muffled noise of my own footsteps, I had no idea I was walking directly above a potential windfall for the Bolivian state. Beneath the Salar is lithium—a lot of lithium, as it turns out, perhaps as much as 70 percent of the world's entire supply. Lithium is a mineral that is expected to grow in importance—you need it to make batteries for electric cars. There is some irony to the fact that this reserve was found in Bolivia. For some years, Chávez's opponents in the United States had urged the country to reduce its use of oil, so as to weaken America's dependence on Venezuela and thereby undermine his threats to divert energy exports elsewhere. But the vast lithium reserves in Bolivia raise the prospect that in their pursuit of alternative technology, carmakers may be swapping their dependence on one resource-rich country run by a radical left-wing anti-American leader for another.

The Salar de Uyuni demonstrates that, at least in the medium term, South America is likely to remain a continent that produces raw materials largely for markets elsewhere. In recent years, both Brazil and Colombia have discovered large oil deposits that will make their economies more dependent on exporting commodities. As China, India, and Russia—and a host of smaller developing countries—continue their economic ascent, resource-rich Latin America looks set to play a greater role in the global economy. For the rising global powers, the region offers both a long-term source of raw materials and an opportunity to take advantage of Washington's hyperopia by building political alliances in the United States' backyard.

The United States should avoid being drawn into a battle for influence in Latin America. On the other hand, Washington would do well to think more strategically about its relations with the region.

Too often—as with the war on drugs, the Cuba embargo, and immigration—US policy reflects emotions rather than considered thought.
Too often it seems fixated on personalities rather than broader regional
objectives. It sends inconsistent, mixed messages that are hard to
interpret.

A prime example is trade policy—the United States' main tool
for dealing with Latin America. The United States has permanent
agreements in place with Mexico (through NAFTA, the 1994 North
American Free Trade Agreement) and Central America (through
DR-CAFTA, the 2004 Dominican Republic–Central America Free
Trade Agreement). Yet its South American trade policy is a mess. For
instance, the United States has a preferential trade agreement with
Peru but took five years to ratify an agreement with Colombia that
was first struck in 2006 and only approved in 2011. (Another agreement with Panama had been lingering unratified in Washington since
2007.)

By late 2010, there were signs that the United States' close relationship with Colombia might be straining because of Washington's
inability to ratify the pact. Juan Manuel Santos, the country's new
center-right president, showed signs of distancing himself from
his predecessor's closeness with the United States and of moving
closer to neighboring Venezuela—one of Colombia's biggest trade
partners. Santos met regularly with Chávez, whom he called his
"new best friend," and both vowed to improve the ties between
their countries. The two leaders collaborated on bringing a final
resolution to the leadership crisis in Honduras. While waiting
for the United States, Colombia had fallen behind other South
American countries in developing ties with Asian countries. In
late 2010, it signaled that it would join the Asia-Pacific Economic
Cooperation organization and would pursue bilateral trade deals
with South Korea, Japan, and Singapore. And in February 2011, the
United States ended a twenty-year-old low-tariff arrangement with
Ecuador and Colombia—hardly a reward for Bogotá's lonely alliance
with Washington.

On the other side, Bolivia had been excluded from the Andean
trade preferences in 2008 on the basis that it was no longer
cooperating in the war on drugs. So even as Washington appeared

to be losing influence with Colombia because it could not follow
through on its trade commitments, the United States willingly for-
feited the only tool it had to use as an incentive to secure La Paz's
cooperation.

Having said all that, trade is likely to be one important area that
the United States could use to rebuild ties with the region. But
given the level of hostility to Washington's motives on the issue—
indicated by the death of the US-sponsored Free Trade Area of
the Americas—the United States will struggle to establish a new
relationship with Latin America based on trade alone. Moreover, in
practice, "free trade" agreements—such as NAFTA, DR-CAFTA,
and bilateral agreements with Peru and Chile—are not free.
Instead, they give preferential treatment to certain imports while
leaving other tariffs in place. Florida's farmers, for example, managed to have sugar excluded from the DR-CAFTA. These backroom
arrangements mean that such deals are often highly contentious
and politicized. US elections frequently see candidates vowing to
reform NAFTA, as Barack Obama promised to do during his 2008
campaign.

If the United States were able to build up some goodwill in Latin
America, however, in time, countries in the region could eventually
come to see that trade with the United States is critical to their economic well-being. In spite of the oil relationship between the United
States and Venezuela, much of US–Latin American trade is in value-
added or specialized products rather than raw materials. By contrast,
the surge in trade with Asia has made Latin America more focused
than ever on exporting basic commodities. Latin America is now
experiencing a phenomenon that recalls the dependency theory popular in the 1960s and 1970s: exporting primary products and natural
resources to Asia, helping the economies of China and India boom,
in return for manufactured goods that undermine its own industrial
base. Raw materials account for more than 80 percent of the economies of Venezuela, Bolivia, Ecuador, and Chile, according to the UN
Development Program, with Peru and Argentina not far behind. South
American countries worry they are stuck in a natural resources rut
and cannot diversify their economies. This trend and the concerns it
provokes could open an opportunity for the United States to promote

itself quietly in the region as a trading partner that is interested in a trade relationship based on more complex goods, helping the region to industrialize and develop.

As its response to the 2009 coup in Honduras showed, outside of trade or the war on drugs, the United States has appeared uncreative and hesitant. It has few positive initiatives that would enable a multipronged approach (of which trade would be merely one prong) to rebuilding its influence in the region. Had it had such a strategy in place, the United States might have been able to strengthen ties with Colombia in ways other than depending on the whims and petty political considerations of Capitol Hill.

Reforming or scrapping the war on drugs, the Cuba embargo, and immigration policy would help soften or remove the most counterproductive aspects of US policy toward Latin America. But what could Washington do to regain the initiative and rebuild trust and influence in the region? Again, this entails a different way of thinking about what to "do" with Chávez and his allies. Rather than allowing the radical Left to set the agenda and then either lashing out or suffering in silence, the United States needs to change the conversation to one of substance—by focusing on addressing the region's main problems.

Democracy, Policing, and Education

One of the region's central weaknesses is the fragility of democratic institutions and the pervasiveness of corruption. First, the United States should reiterate its commitment to democracy and the democratic transfer of power in every single instance. In the case of Venezuela in 2002, the United States ended up approving a coup. In the case of Honduras in 2009, it failed to overturn the results of a coup. Washington should spell out clearly that it will always oppose coups against democratically elected regimes. Second, the United States—and not just Washington—has much to offer in terms of democratic education. Government in the United States may not work perfectly, as the brinkmanship in 2011 over raising the debt ceiling demonstrated, but it is much more robust than that

in many Latin American countries. Just as the United States offered
help in establishing the institutions of democracy in the countries
of the former Soviet Union, it could do much to advise on institution and capacity building—not to force a blueprint on the region
in some grand plan but instead to offer help to those across the
political spectrum in building solid, robust, and durable national and
regional governments, bureaucracies, and political parties. A new
policy could also extend political education to the electorate, for
example, explaining how a person might win elected office should
he or she wish to do so. Such initiatives should be carried out in
cooperation with the government of the day, whatever its complex-
ion. The ability of the United States to work with administrations
that have spoken out against its views would do much to enhance its
reputation in the region.

A second area for cooperation could be in energy security in which the
United States could benefit from working toward a longer-term strategy
for fulfilling energy demand across the Americas using the natural
resources available in both North and Latin America. If the United States
is currently dependent on Latin American energy exports, it would do
well to try to forge agreements to ensure that the security of supply is
assured in the future.

A third initiative the United States could pursue could be in
policing and security. Latin America has the highest homicide rate of
any region in the world, and crime is now the top issue of concern
to Latin Americans. The United States and its big cities have much to
offer in terms of their experience in turning crime-ridden areas into
safe neighborhoods. Helping Latin American countries deal with
crime would not only do much to boost the United States' image in
the region, but it would also benefit the United States. The drug
violence in Mexico in recent years has shown that security and
policing are international issues. The gangs that terrorize the streets
of many Central American countries have counterparts in the United
States. South American countries are as eager as the United States to
clamp down on human trafficking. These could be fruitful areas for
collaboration as part of a wider initiative of cooperation across the
Americas, and, to be fair, the Obama administration has shown an
urgency on this issue that previous US governments lacked.

Security cooperation is also important because there are signs that international terrorist groups may have found a haven in Latin America. Chávez has been accused of aiding the Colombian FARC, the Basque separatist group ETA, as well as Hamas, Hezbollah, and Islamic Jihad. While these claims are contentious, US officials have also long been concerned about the "tri-border" area where Argentina, Brazil, and Paraguay meet. The United States suspects that Hezbollah may have a base in the area and is concerned that Chinese criminal organizations may also be active there. Iran's greater involvement in the region is also a worrying development. The United States' inattentiveness has not helped alleviate these concerns, which require its security establishment to pay attention to Latin America and to think strategically about how best to tackle the problems in cooperation with local authorities.

A fourth area where the United States could initiate a new kind of foreign policy toward Latin America would be in education. As the economies of the region develop, there is ever more demand for education. But much of what is offered in the region is woefully substandard. The United States, by contrast, has the finest educational establishments in the world. It could do a great deal to promote quality education in the region and could step up and expand programs to educate gifted young people and emerging leaders in North America. In the Andes, the United States has a perfect opportunity to focus on improving educational opportunities for indigenous people. Only about one in five indigenous people in Latin America completes secondary education, according to the UN Economic Commission for Latin America, much lower than other social groups. There are efforts to address this disparity, but they are not well funded or part of a comprehensive plan to raise educational standards across the region. In terms of bringing young leaders to North America, the United States could benefit from a "grand gesture," such as transforming the notorious School of the Americas—the institute that trained future dictators across Latin America—into a nonmilitary establishment to educate community leaders, young journalists, lawyers, and others who might help to build up their countries upon return. There would be tremendous power in such a move.

Initiatives such as these need not replace US trade efforts, but they are as worthy policy areas for it to dedicate its attention. However much they are able to expand trade and investment with Latin America, the likes of China, India, and Russia are hardly well placed to help the region develop its democracy, policing, and education systems.

In spite of everything that has happened in recent years, the United States is still the region's most natural "big power" ally. And in spite of Washington's hyperopia, Latin America still represents the United States' best chance to regain influence in a multipolar world. The United States and Latin America belong together.

The Meaning of America

The word "America" has quite distinct meanings in English and Spanish.

In English, we use "America" to mean only the United States. In Spanish, *América* means the entire Americas, from Canada down to Chile and Argentina. If the United States is to overcome its hyperopia and rebuild a new role for itself in the globalized world, its policy toward Latin America in future would do well to reflect the Spanish notion of *América*—that the Western Hemisphere is naturally one region, with a common future.

The challenge for the United States in the coming decades will be to adjust to the rise of China, India, Russia, Brazil, and other emerging powers. In part, this is a challenge of domestic policy—how to cope with the effects of no longer being the world's biggest manufacturer, how to serve the new markets most effectively, how to reform immigration so as to attract the best and brightest from around the world, how to remain competitive, and so on. In part, it is a foreign policy challenge—how to play a more subtle international game than that required of a sole superpower, how to build alliances and lead with others, rather than alone. Both challenges are significant, but it is the change in foreign policy that will perhaps require the biggest shift in mind-set. As Fareed Zakaria frames it in *The Post-American World*, "Can Washington truly embrace a world with a diversity of voices and viewpoints? Can it thrive in a world it cannot dominate?"

Zakaria is surely right to conclude that the United States is up to the challenge, and yet it requires more clear thinking and practical, strategic policymaking than Washington has yet demonstrated. The task is most urgent. The worst thing to happen to the United States would be for it to wake up and realize that the opportunity to reposition itself to take full advantage of the post-American world had already passed. It is high time for the United States to embark on the process of carving out its new role.

Latin America must play a central part in that new role—simply because if the United States has no influence in the Americas, then it cannot hope to have much influence elsewhere. Reengaging with Latin America is not only a critical element of the United States' ability to build itself a role in the post-American world. It is also a test of its willingness to cooperate with those who express ideas it does not necessarily agree with. If it is able to do so, the challenge of Castro, Chávez, Morales, Correa, Humala, and any other leader who thumbs his or her nose at Washington would be much diminished. To be sure, the Obama administration has signaled a willingness both to work more through international alliances and to strengthen ties with Latin America. But much remains to be done in fleshing out these policies and making them a permanent aspect of Washington's worldview.

The United States has all too often behaved as though Chávez et al. were the be-all and end-all of the problem. It has given the impression that if only the leader were removed, everything would be fine. Lest we forget, this "decapitation" strategy guided US thinking when it attacked Saddam Hussein's Iraq. A further danger of this approach is that if Chávez were to fall from power, Latin America might drop even lower down the agenda in Washington. The radical Left came to power because of a range of Latin American problems—poverty and inequality, corruption and lack of governance, racism and marginalization. They reflected powerful socioeconomic forces shaping the region—globalization, urbanization, the rise of street protest. In a longer-term, strategic sense, these are the issues that have to be addressed, rather than focusing on the day-to-day foreign policy Ping-Pong of how to score one better than an antagonistic leader.

Washington may wonder if reengagement is really necessary or if it can just depend on benign neglect. After all, there are signs that the moment of resource nationalism has passed. Latin America's economies look to be on a path of steady growth, and there is an emerging middle class that should temper radicalism and populism. The influence of the radical Left has waned considerably since they were first elected. Chávez, whose battle with cancer in 2011 underlined both his physical and political weakness, may win reelection in 2012, but he is surely closer to the end of his time in power than its beginning. Morales, Correa, and Humala are unlikely to be in power for as long as him, and without his leadership they would be less of an influence in the region. Besides, Morales and Correa have both seen their popularity drop as they struggle with the thorny problem of governing and battle a growing army of domestic critics. Moreover, the shift to the left was occurring in other countries. In 2010, for example, Sebastián Piñera, a right-wing businessman, took power in Chile. In Brazil, Dilma Rousseff had more centrist instincts than Lula, her predecessor, even though they were from the same political party.

If the United States were to undo its policies on drugs, Cuba, and immigration and then effectively withdraw from the region, Latin America might well turn out all right in the long run. There might be more upsets and bursts of populism and economic nationalism along the way, but the region's biggest countries—Mexico and Brazil—are already two of the world's most important economies and look set to continue to grow for the time being. Increased involvement from China, India, and Russia could also have a stabilizing effect on the region, since those countries need stability to protect their long-term investments and trade ties.

But benign neglect would not help the United States find a new international role. Since Washington already has some influence in Latin America, albeit less than it has had historically, benign neglect would entail Washington losing some of its global power by letting the region slip away to the hands of China, India, Russia, Iran, and any other country that appreciates the opportunity.

The cry for the United States to engage with Latin America is by now familiar and repetitive. But it has always been made on the premise that the region was in desperate need of being rescued by the United States—that its political, economic, and social well-being depended on Washington "rediscovering" its neighbors to the south. Latin America was Sleeping Beauty, the United States the prince who could raise the sleeper from slumber—if only it could be bothered to cut through the weeds and kiss the region back to life. But with the United States in relative economic decline, it is Washington that needs international partners and allies. And, just as the United States recognized in 1994, when it signed NAFTA, that it needed to tie its economy to the neighboring economies of Canada and Mexico, there is no more natural partner for it than Latin America.

As Chávez's reaction to the Honduras coup showed, for all the anti-US sentiment expressed in Latin America, the region is crying out for Washington to reengage and provide leadership—not domination, but leadership in cooperation with other regional leaders.

An American G4

The Americas have their own natural "G4"—Canada, the United States, Mexico, and Brazil. The United States could work to establish that group (perhaps including Argentina and making it a G5) as a force in global politics and economics. Working in tandem with such countries might help improve the United States' reputation both in Latin America and around the world. The United States should at all times seek equality within this group between the four. It must not try to set the agenda, though it should help shape it, and it should use its international clout to help deliver the group's message. It should champion Brazil and Mexico in international institutions such as the United Nations. For example, the United States should be promoting Brazil as a permanent member of the UN Security Council as much as India, which it put forward for such a position in November 2010. In that same month, the United Kingdom proposed giving Brazil a permanent Security Council seat as part of London's strategy to step up its engagement with the region. In a visit to Brazil in 2011, however, Obama declined to back Brazil for a Security Council seat.

If there were any broad plan for the region, it should come from this G4 of the Americas, which could jointly set regional targets for poverty reduction, human rights, education, and infrastructure. It could establish best practices for democratic institutions, judiciaries, and the governance of civil society.

Washington should play a long-term diplomatic game, on occasion letting others win in order to build trust and goodwill. The United States has become too used to either getting its own way or refusing to play the game. Building long-term alliances will require it at times to bow to the will of others, to submit itself to rules that may result in it losing some arguments along the way. It must cede some power in order to gain more clout internationally as the senior member of a bigger strategic alliance.

That diplomatic behavior should also shape US relations with the rest of Latin America and the Caribbean. In terms of relations within the Americas, Washington should pursue a multilateral approach with a new commitment to work within groups such as the Organization of American States. It should not seek to play friends against enemies. It should accept the legitimacy of policies with which it does not agree. This last point is of the utmost importance. Latin Americans do not demand agreement, but they tend to insist on the rights of national sovereignty. The United States will have to accept that Latin American countries may prefer a larger role for state-owned enterprise and have the right to set their own terms for foreign investors. In short, US reengagement with the region would work best if Washington were more of a team player, seen to be trying for the best for the Americas as a whole and not merely serving its own interests or those of small constituencies back home.

To recognize that the United States is part of *América* is to acknowledge that Latin America and North America are already fast becoming a single entity. Latinos are the fastest-growing group in the United States, an ethnicity that is playing an ever more important role in US society, economics, and politics. By 2003, they had become the United States' largest minority group, according to the Census Bureau, surpassing African Americans. By 2010, they represented about 15 percent of the US population. By 2050, they are forecast to make up one-quarter of the population. In that sense, the United States increasingly resembles a Latin American country. While the rest of the world is learning English, the United States is increasingly speaking Spanish. At the same time, far more Latin Americans want to learn English—American English, that is—than any other language. Spanish-language soap operas made in Caracas and Mexico City are watched across the United States, while Andrés Oppenheimer, one of the Spanish language's most widely read political pundits, comments on Latin America from Miami.

Many US corporations have long recognized the opportunities the region presents, and as Latin America continues to grow faster than their home markets, they are dependent on it for an increasing portion of their revenues. US companies have not always found it easy doing business in China, a country with different attitudes to intellectual property and ownership than multinationals were normally used to dealing with, for example. By contrast, Latin America is culturally similar to the United States. The United States and Latin America share many more of the same values than the other emerging regions of the world. Both continents have struggled to win independence from colonial rule. In an era when US efforts to foist democracy on Iraq and Afghanistan have had limited success and in which hopes for a democratic tide in China have been dashed, Latin America has emerged as the most democratic of emerging regions. Both the United States and Latin America are also more religious than the region that colonized them, with Latin American–style Catholicism playing an increasingly prominent role in the United States and evangelical Christianity rising in the South.

For US politicians, reengaging with Latin America would pay political dividends at home. Latinos—a swing voting group that will increasingly determine the results of US national elections—would be sure to support such an initiative to bring the Americas closer together, and would reward any administration that could do so.

Part of the change of mind-set in Washington would be to change the idea that relations with the rest of the Americas are purely a matter of foreign policy. Thinking of *América* rather than America would require the United States to formulate a vision of its own role within the Americas, rather than outside it. As with drugs, Cuba, and immigration, US policies toward Latin America tend to blur the line between domestic policy and foreign policy. That is entirely natural, and Washington should recognize that and account for it. Latin America is not just a State Department issue.

The United States is likely to be under financial strain for years to come, and its strategy for the future will have to take account of its reduced ability to pay for many more expensive military adventures. The beauty of reengaging with the Americas is that it is more a question of good policy and diplomacy than of spending money. Throughout its history, the United States has demonstrated a remarkable ability to adapt to circumstances, to build international alliances, and to lead. The United States is resilient. It is innovative. At its heart, it is more practical than ideological. The global political order is changing, and the United States needs a concrete strategy to address that change. Whatever the details, it is clear that will involve developing partnerships with those countries whose economies are growing and whose global influence is growing. The best place to start would be near to home, with a new, practical, strategic reengagement with the rest of the Americas.

Washington needs urgently to correct its inattentiveness toward its southern neighbors. It is not yet too late. The standing of the United States in the world may depend on it.

ACKNOWLEDGMENTS

This book sprang out of hundreds of conversations with all sorts of people, each of whom helped me build an understanding of the Andes. But as with any correspondent posting, I returned again and again to a small group of individuals whose insights were always fascinating and perceptive. Chief among them were Carlos Toranzo, Roberto Laserna, Jim Shultz, Felix Muruchi, Luis Hernandez, Walter Spurrier, Wilfredo Ardito, Luis Benavente, and David Greenlee. They were all exceptionally generous with their time.

I was also privileged to work alongside a group of outstanding foreign correspondents, who welcomed me warmly into their cadre and were always willing to share information and coach me on the byzantine bureaucracies of South America. This merry band included Lucien Chauvin, Paola Ugaz, Barbara Fraser, Robin Emmott, Jude Webber, Sally Bowen, Hannah Hennessy, Dan Collyns, Daniel Schweimler, Juan Forero, and the late and much-missed Mary Powers.

Working as a foreign correspondent for the *Financial Times* is the best job in journalism. Lionel Barber took a gamble on me by sending me to fill the exotic-sounding post of Andes correspondent. Richard Lapper was a much-valued mentor and an unflagging champion of the far-flung reporter.

I joined a great team of *FT* correspondents in the region, which at the time included Adam Thomson, Benedict Mander, Jonathan

259

Wheatley, and Andy Webb-Vidal. They were always happy to collaborate and covered my behind on more than one occasion.

My editors in London and New York were models of grace and good humor. Jeff Pruzan did his best to interrupt an occasional long lunch with news of the latest coup. Pat Ferguson, Naomi Mapstone, David Fickling, Rosie Blau, Rose Jacobs, and Lorien Kite deftly handled copy that invariably arrived late and overlength. I am most grateful to all.

Zoë Pagnamenta, my agent, and Eric Nelson, my editor at John Wiley & Sons, demonstrated extraordinary patience and faith in me, for which many thanks.

The *FT*, *New Statesman*, and JTA were good enough to give me permission to use passages in this book based on reporting that they originally published.

David Weitzman, Jeff Pruzan, and Michael Shifter all kindly made the time to read (and reread) the entire manuscript and make helpful and thought-provoking comments. Joel Segel read portions of various drafts and offered devastating but much-valued criticism.

My parents and parents-in-law have always been hugely encouraging and knew when not to ask, "How's the book coming along?" My daughters, Orlie and Tess, didn't help at all in writing, but they are a true delight.

And then there is my wife, Lorna. Not only is she the woman of my dreams, she's also a person of saintly virtue who agreed to move with me to Peru, a country in a continent that neither of us had ever visited. She never tires of encouraging, challenging, and supporting me. She has a wonderful sense of humor, proved by the fact that she laughs at my jokes. Thanks, Tato, for putting up with me. This book—and my life—are dedicated to you.

SELECT BIBLIOGRAPHY

Bowen, Sally, and Jane Holligan. *The Imperfect Spy: The Many Lives of Vladimiro Montesinos*. Lima: PEISA, 2003.

Bremmer, Ian. *The End of the Free Market: Who Wins the War Between States and Corporations?* New York: Portfolio, 2010.

Chapman, Peter. *Bananas: How the United Fruit Company Shaped the World*. Edinburgh: Canongate, 2009.

Crabtree, John. *Patterns of Protest: Politics and Social Movements in Bolivia*. Latin American Bureau, 2005.

Fernández-Armesto, Felipe. *The Americas: The History of a Hemisphere*. London: Phoenix, 2004.

Galeano, Eduardo. "Open Veins of Latin America: Five Centuries of the Pillage of a Continent." *Monthly Review Press*, 1997.

Galen Carpenter, Ted. *Bad Neighbor Policy: Washington's Futile War on Drugs in Latin America*. New York: Palgrave Macmillan, 2003.

Hemming, John. *The Conquest of the Incas*. Boston: Mariner Books, 2003.

Mendoza, Plinio Apuleyo, Carlos Alberto Montaner, and Alvaro Vargas Llosa. *Guide to the Perfect Latin American Idiot*. Boulder, CO: Madison Books, 2001.

Oppenheimer, Andrés. *Saving the Americas: The Dangerous Decline of Latin America and What the U.S. Must Do*. New York: Random House Mondadori, 2007.

Rachman, Gideon. *Zero-Sum Future: American Power in an Age of Anxiety*. New York: Simon & Schuster, 2011.

Reid, Michael. *Forgotten Continent: The Battle for Latin America's Soul*. New Haven, CT: Yale University Press, 2008.

Shifter, Michael. *Hugo Chávez: A Test for US Policy*. Special Report of the Inter-American Dialogue, Washington, D.C., March 2007.

Sweig, Julia. *Friendly Fire: Losing Friends and Making Enemies in the Anti-American Century*. New York: PublicAffairs, 2007.

Williamson, Edwin. *The Penguin History of Latin America*. New York: Penguin, 2010.

Zakaria, Fareed. *The Post-American World*. New York: W. W. Norton, 2009.

Referred to in Chapter 8

"Piracy on the Streets of Peru," Daniel Schweimler, *From Our Own Correspondent*, August 12, 2006. Transcript available at http://news.bbc.co.uk/1/hi/programmes/from_our_own_correspondent/4783041.stm.

INDEX